TRANSFORMATIONAL LEADERSHIP

Second Edition

TRANSFORMATIONAL LEADERSHIP

Second Edition

Bernard M. Bass
Center for Leadership Studies
Binghamton University

Ronald E. Riggio
Kravis Leadership Institute
Claremont McKenna College

LEA LAWRENCE ERLBAUM ASSOCIATES, PUBLISHERS
2006   Mahwah, New Jersey   London

Cover design by Kathryn Houghtaling Lacey

Library of Congress Cataloging-in-Publication Data

Bass, Bernard M.
  Transformational leadership / Bernard M. Bass, Ronald E. Riggio — 2nd ed.
    p.   cm.
  Includes bibliographical references and index.
    ISBN 0–8058–4761–8 (cloth : alk. paper) — ISBN 0–8058–4762–6 (pbk. : alk. paper)
    1. Leadership. 2. Organizational change. I. Riggio, Ronald E. II. Title.
HD57.7.B373 2005
658.4'092—dc22   2005040138

Contents

Foreword

More than a decade ago in a small conference room at the University of Maryland, we sat with a group of leadership scholars and thrashed out that recurring and problematic question, "Was Hitler a transforming leader?" Mark Moore, one of our colleagues in the Kellogg Leadership Studies Project, had asked, "Can a person be a transformational leader without charisma and virtue? Can the effects of transformational leadership be achieved without charisma and virtue in a leader?"

"The Hitler Problem," as we called it back then, was an emblematic question that had routinely arisen in every leadership studies class for the last decade. Whether we spoke of Burns's conception of large scale change or Bass's contingency-based approach, Hitler (and those of his ilk) indeed displayed many of the leadership qualities in question. As Dick Couto was to later write, "Bass initially considered transformation to be any fundamental social change without regard to moral values. Transformational leaders, like Hitler, Jim Jones, and David Koresh, may be 'immoral, brutal, and extremely costly in life, liberty, property, and the pursuit of happiness to [their] victims,'" but they met his definition of transforming change. Burns was less certain, but he did admit to Hitler's invigoration and realignment of his followers, surely a large-scale effort. It was a thorny question.

As our meeting progressed, Burns and Bass parsed the distinctions, dipping into history, philosophy, and real life. Burns first sketched out Gunnar Myrdal's discussion of cumulative causation from *An American Dilemma*, arguing that it can serve as a basis for understanding real, intended social change. To bring the debate down to earth, Bernie suggested using Franklin D. Roosevelt's presidential leadership as a lens to examine Myrdal's premises, and the two older scholars who had lived through the Roosevelt presidency and its effects captivated the attention of the younger scholars until early evening. On Day 2, we turned to Bass, who sketched out his recent empirical work on the topic. As the hours stretched on, the rest of the small group—Dick Couto, Georgia Sorenson, Jane Howell, Larraine Matusak, Bruce Avolio, and Gill Hickman—sat back and watched Burns and Bass reason and cajole each other.

After 3 days of intense debate, Burns, the scholar, took a bold stand: From his perspective, the term "leadership" should be reserved for the forces of good, and other terms like "tyrant," "despot," and so forth should serve as descriptors for other normative behaviors. Bass, the master researcher, took perhaps an even bolder approach as he began to mentally scan his prodigious research output of many decades and to challenge his own basic assumptions. In the end, Bass crafted the concept of "pseudotransformational" (which later informed his thinking on authentic vs. inauthentic transformational leadership), and thus both Burns and Bass came to agreement on this long-standing conundrum: Hitler was not a transformational leader.

That small group, so many years ago, revealed the essential Bernie Bass. Brilliant, unrelenting, but profoundly intellectually honest, Bernie is the very model of an intellectual—kindly toward other scholars, inclusive of younger colleagues, modest about his own achievements, and consistently raising basic questions than can help guide and challenge other scholars.

His legacy is an international tidal wave of researchers and scholars exploring transformational leadership. Bernie authored 18 books and conducted research studies, edited books, and wrote articles (including many with younger authors) that number in the hundreds. Those of us who care about leadership owe a tremendous debt to his scholarship and to his leadership. The study of leadership has many mothers, but it was Bernie Bass who became its driving force.

We are delighted to have this new edition of *Transformational Leadership* and to find the markedly thoughtful influence of leadership scholar and social psychologist Ron Riggio. This volume brings in substantial new findings, consolidates and conceptualizes previous work and brings the work of leadership to life with real leaders in real-life situations. If we were to be involved in the next edition, we would insist that one more example be included in the book's stable of outstanding transformational leaders: Bernard Bass.

James MacGregor Burns
James MacGregor Burns Academy of Leadership
University of Maryland

Georgia Sorenson
James MacGregor Burns Academy of Leadership
University of Maryland

Preface to the Second Edition

Transformational leadership has rapidly become the approach of choice for much of the research and application of leadership theory. In many ways, transformational leadership has captured the imagination of scholars, of noted practitioners, and of students of leadership. Research on transformational leadership and related charismatic approaches has grown exponentially—so much so that a new edition of this book, originally published in 1998, was necessary.

Why such interest in transformational leadership? Perhaps it is because transformational leadership, with its emphasis on intrinsic motivation and on the positive development of followers, represents a more appealing view of leadership compared to the seemingly "cold," social exchange process of transactional leadership. Perhaps it is because transformational leadership provides a better fit for leading today's complex work groups and organizations, where followers not only seek an inspirational leader to help guide them through an uncertain environment but where followers also want to be challenged and to feel empowered, if they are to be loyal, high performers.

More than a quarter century has passed since the publication of James MacGregor Burns's seminal *Leadership*, which introduced the concept of transforming leadership. Inspired by this, and by Robert House's 1976 theory of charismatic leadership, Bass and his colleagues developed the model of transformational leadership and the means to measure it. This evolved into looking at the full range of leadership, from passive, laissez-faire leadership to levels of transactional leadership and finally to transformational leadership. Passive leadership is least effective and satisfying. Leaders may use all of these approaches, but they may use more of one approach than others. Better leaders are transformational more frequently; less adequate leaders are passive or concentrate more on corrective actions.

More than 20 years of research and development by Bass and colleagues is reviewed in this book, along with research by hundreds of scholars from around the globe. Although the early research draws heavily on leadership research in the military, later research on transformational leadership explored business leadership and leadership in governmental institutions, in education, in health care settings, and in the nonprofit sector. Whereas much of the early research was conducted in the United States, later studies of transformational leadership have been conducted in numerous settings around the world. Moreover, there is great generality to transformational leadership. It has proven an effective form of leadership in a variety of settings in many countries. Of course, there are moderators and contingencies influencing the effectiveness of transformational leadership, and these are reviewed in this book.

This revised book is intended for both scholars and serious students of leadership. It is a comprehensive review of theorizing and empirical research on transformational leadership that can serve as a reference and starting point for additional research on the theory. In addition, we have tried to make the book reader friendly, with many current and historical examples. It could be used as a supplementary textbook in an intense course on leadership or as a primary textbook in a course or seminar focusing on transformational leadership—particularly if accompanied by *Developing Potential Across a Full Range of Leadership: Cases on Transactional and Transformational Leadership* (Avolio & Bass, 2002).

This new edition has been greatly expanded, with more than double the number of references in the previous edition. Many new, updated examples of leadership have been included to help illustrate concepts as well as show the broad range of transformational leadership in a variety of settings. New chapters have been added focusing specifically on the measurement of effectiveness of transformational leadership. Greatly expanded is the discussion of both predictors and effects of transformational leadership. Importantly, there is much more emphasis on authentic versus inauthentic transformational leadership. Finally, suggestions are made for guiding the future of research and for applications of transformational leadership.

It is important to recognize colleagues from the Center for Leadership Studies who collaborated in much of the early research on transformational leadership and the full range of leadership model. In particular, the enormous contributions of Bruce Avolio must be recognized, as well as those of Fran Yammarino, David Waldman, and Leanne Atwater. Thanks also to students in the Center for Leadership Studies and many other students and scholars around the world who chose to carry out their studies about transformational leadership. A special thanks to Joanne Lee for her contributions to this revised edition, to Susan Murphy for her suggestions, and especially to Sandy Counts at the Kravis Leadership Institute, who helped in preparing the manuscript and took care of a thousand details. We are indebted to Anne Duffy at Lawrence Erlbaum Associates for her editorial work and her encouragement. Finally, to Ruth Bass and Heidi Riggio who contributed in substantive ways to the book and to our lives.

Bernard M. Bass
Center for Leadership Studies
Binghamton University

Ronald E. Riggio
Kravis Leadership Institute
Claremont McKenna College

1

Introduction

There has been an explosion of interest in leadership. Each day stories appear in the newspapers discussing instances of successful leadership, as well as significant failures of leadership. The stories usually concern world class and national politicians and statesmen, chief executive officers (CEO) of business and industry, directors of government and health care agencies, or generals and admirals. Sometimes the stories are of high-level leaders who are often in the spotlight.

Carly Fiorina was the CEO of Hewlett Packard (HP) from 1999 until ousted in early 2005. As one of only a handful of women CEOs of Fortune 100 companies, she was often in the news, but no more so than when she led HP through the choppy waters of its merger with Compaq. Through a contentious fight to win over the support of HP's board of directors, Fiorina kept her eyes on the vision of transforming HP into a "full service" technology company to rival IBM (Lashinsky, 2002). To make this a reality, Fiorina had to first persuade board members and inspire rank and file employees to buy in to her vision:

> Indeed, the day after the merger, she and Michael Capellas, the CEO of Compaq—now the No. 2 at HP—spent two hours simply marching through the one-mile-plus walkway that connects Compaq's 17-building corporate headquarters in Houston, meeting and greeting as many people as they could. "She was like this massive figure," recalls HP employee Antonio Humphreys, who worked for Compaq before the merger. "She took pictures and put on hats. The fact that she was willing to do that for the common folk—that earned her a lot of points." (Lashinsky, 2002, p. 94)

CEO Fiorina immediately focused on implementing the vision by empowering subordinates and providing an example of the hard work needed to transform an organization, its culture, and its trajectory.

The key to success, particularly in the fast-paced, high-tech sector in which HP resides, is to challenge followers to perform beyond normal expectations, to stimulate them to be creative and innovative, and to develop their collective leadership capacity. Unfortunately, the story for CEO Fiorina has an unhappy ending. As HP's earnings and stock price continued to sink, an impatient board removed her in 2005, even though many analysts believe the jury is still out on whether the merger will eventually prove to have been the correct strategy. Some analysts believe that both HP and Compaq are better off together than they would have been separately. Regardless of outcomes, most agree that Carly Fiorina typifies a high-profile CEO leader who catches the interest and imagination of the business community and the general public.

But sometimes the story is about an ordinary citizen who shows the persistent leadership to organize what is needed to get the job done. This was the case in an incident that occurred a few years ago in South Korea.

By midnight of September 18, 1996, a North Korean submarine found itself stranded in low water off the east coast of South Korea near Kangnung. It was carrying at least 20 armed North Korean infiltrators and crew. Many South Korean outposts were in place to deal with such intrusions. South Korean troops, posted on the coast nearby, were shown on television, patrolling mountain paths and manning roadblocks. Nonetheless, the discovery of the intrusion was due to the leadership of a taxi driver:

> The driver, Lee Jin Gyu, [said] that he saw a group of men by the road, looking very out of place, when he drove by with a passenger. . . . He dropped off the passenger and returned to the spot and saw the submarine. . . . He then went to a police station, and he and a policeman together called an army outpost to report the discovery. [But] the army outpost refused to help because it said it was not responsible for the area where the submarine was spotted. Mr. Lee . . . and the policemen then went to an army barracks, roused the sleeping soldiers, and led them to the site. (Kristof, 1996, pp. A1, A11)

Thus, leadership is not just the province of people at the top. Leadership can occur at all levels and by any individual. In fact, we see that it is important for leaders to develop leadership in those below them. This notion is at the heart of the paradigm of transformational leadership. The principles derived from this theory are fundamental to effective leadership and are widely applicable to many segments of life, ranging from work to family to sport and classroom and, importantly, to issues of social change.

THE TRANSFORMATIONAL MODEL
OF LEADERSHIP

A new paradigm of leadership has captured widespread attention. James MacGregor Burns (1978) conceptualized leadership as either transactional or transformational. Transactional leaders are those who lead through social exchange. As Burns (1978) notes, politicians, for example, lead by "exchanging one thing for another: jobs for votes, or subsidies for campaign contributions" (p. 4). In the same way, transactional business leaders offer financial rewards for productivity or deny rewards for lack of productivity. Transformational leaders, on the other hand, are those who stimulate and inspire followers to both achieve extraordinary outcomes and, in the process, develop their own leadership capacity. Transformational leaders help followers grow and develop into leaders by responding to individual followers' needs by empowering them and by aligning the objectives and goals of the individual followers, the leader, the group, and the larger organization. More evidence has accumulated to demonstrate that transformational leadership can move followers to exceed expected performance, as well as lead to high levels of follower satisfaction and commitment to the group and organization (Bass, 1985, 1998a).

Although early research demonstrated that transformational leadership was a particularly powerful source in military settings (e.g., Bass, 1985; Boyd, 1988; Curphy, 1992; Longshore, 1988; O'Keefe, 1989; Yammarino & Bass, 1990a), more recent research has accumulated that demonstrates that transformational leadership is important in every sector and in every setting (Avolio & Yammarino, 2002). We soon review the components of transformational leadership, examine transactional leadership, and present the Full Range of Leadership model, which incorporates all of these aspects of leadership. But first, we provide a brief discussion of the roots of transformational leadership.

Historical Background
of Transformational Leadership

Historians, political scientists, and sociologists have long recognized leadership that went beyond the notion of a social exchange between leader and followers. Weber's (1924/1947) examination of charisma epitomized such study. However, both psychology and economics supported contingent reinforcement—offering a reward or compensation for a desired behavior—as the underlying concept for the study of leadership. Leadership was seen primarily as an exchange relationship (e.g., Homans, 1950). Research exemplified by Podsakoff and Schriescheim (1985), as well as much of the research with the Full Range of Leadership (FRL) model (Avolio & Bass, 1991) to be described subsequently, indicated that contingent reward is reasonably effective under most circumstances. In addition, active management-by-exception (corrective leadership for failure of a follower to comply) is more varied in effects, and passive management-by-exception ("if it ain't broke, don't fix it") is contraindicated as an effective act of leadership, for, as Levinson (1980) suggested, if you limit leadership of a follower to rewards with carrots for compliance or punishment with a stick for failure to comply with agreed-on work to be done by the follower, the follower will continue to feel like a jackass. Leadership must also address the follower's sense of self-worth to engage the follower in true commitment and involvement in the effort at hand. This is what transformational leadership adds to the transactional exchange.

Transformational leaders motivate others to do more than they originally intended and often even more than they thought possible. They set more challenging expectations and typically achieve higher performances. Transformational leaders also tend to have more committed and satisfied followers. Moreover, transformational leaders empower followers and pay attention to their individual needs and personal development, helping followers to develop their own leadership potential.

Transformational leadership is in some ways an expansion of transactional leadership. Transactional leadership emphasizes the transaction or exchange that takes place among leaders, colleagues, and followers. This exchange is based on the leader discussing with others what is required and specifying the conditions and rewards these others will receive if they fulfill those requirements. Transformational leadership, however, raises leadership to the next level. Transformational leadership involves inspiring followers to commit to a shared vision and goals for an organization or unit, challenging them to be innovative problem solvers, and developing followers' leadership capacity via coaching, mentoring, and provision of both challenge and support.

Early social science perspectives on leadership focused on the dichotomy of directive (task-oriented) versus participative (people-oriented) leadership. As we soon show, transformational leadership can be either directive or participative and is not an either–or proposition.

Transformational leadership has much in common with charismatic leadership, but charisma is only part of transformational leadership. The Weberian notion of charismatic leadership was, in fact, fairly limited. More modern conceptions of charismatic leadership take a much broader perspective (e.g., Conger & Kanungo, 1998; House & Shamir, 1993), however, and have much in common with transformational leadership.

A critical concern for theories of both transformational and charismatic leadership involves what many refer to as the dark side of charisma—those charismatic leaders who use their abilities to inspire and lead followers to destructive, selfish, and even evil ends. Most often coming to mind are international leaders who wreaked havoc, death, and destruction on thousands and even millions—Adolf Hitler, Pol Pot, Josef Stalin, Osama Bin Laden. But these leaders are those who can be called pseudotransformational. They exhibit many elements of transformational leadership (the charismatic elements particularly) but have personal, exploitative, and self-aggrandizing motives. Thus, we speak at length near the end of this chapter about the notions of authenticity and authentic transformational leaders.

Components of Transformational Leadership

Transformational leaders do more with colleagues and followers than set up simple exchanges or agreements. They behave in ways to achieve superior results by employing one or more of the four core components of transformational leadership described later.

To some extent, the components of transformational leadership have evolved as refinements have been made in both the conceptualization and measurement of transformational leadership. Conceptually, leadership is charismatic, and followers seek to identify with the leader and emulate him or her. The leadership inspires followers with challenge and persuasion, providing both meaning and understanding. The leadership is intellectually stimulating, expanding the followers' use of their abilities. Finally, the leadership is individually considerate, providing the follower with support, mentoring, and coaching. Each of these components can be measured with the Multifactor Leadership Questionnaire (MLQ). Factor analytic studies from Bass (1985) to Howell and Avolio (1993), and Bycio, Hackett, and Allen (1995) to

Avolio, Bass, and Jung (1997) have identified the components of transformational leadership. The MLQ, its psychometric properties, and these factor analytic studies are discussed fully in chapter 2.

Descriptions of the components of transformational leadership are presented in the following sections.

Idealized Influence (II). Transformational leaders behave in ways that allow them to serve as role models for their followers. The leaders are admired, respected, and trusted. Followers identify with the leaders and want to emulate them; leaders are endowed by their followers as having extraordinary capabilities, persistence, and determination. Thus, there are two aspects to idealized influence: the leader's behaviors and the elements that are attributed to the leader by followers and other associates. These two aspects, measured by separate subfactors of the MLQ, represent the interactional nature of idealized influence—it is both embodied in the leader's behavior and in attributions that are made concerning the leader by followers. A sample item from the MLQ that represents idealized influence behavior is "The leader emphasizes the importance of having a collective sense of mission." A sample item from the idealized influence attributed factor is "The leader reassures others that obstacles will be overcome."

In addition, leaders who have a great deal of idealized influence are willing to take risks and are consistent rather than arbitrary. They can be counted on to do the right thing, demonstrating high standards of ethical and moral conduct.

Inspirational Motivation (IM). Transformational leaders behave in ways that motivate and inspire those around them by providing meaning and challenge to their followers' work. Team spirit is aroused. Enthusiasm and optimism are displayed. Leaders get followers involved in envisioning attractive future states; they create clearly communicated expectations that followers want to meet and also demonstrate commitment to goals and the shared vision. A sample MLQ item for IM is "The leader articulates a compelling vision of the future."

Idealized influence leadership and inspirational motivation usually form a combined single factor of charismatic-inspirational leadership. The charismatic-inspirational factor is similar to the behaviors described in charismatic leadership theory (Bass & Avolio, 1993a; House, 1977).

Intellectual Stimulation (IS). Transformational leaders stimulate their followers' efforts to be innovative and creative by questioning assumptions, reframing problems, and approaching old situations in new ways. Creativity is encouraged. There is no public criticism of individual members' mistakes. New ideas and creative problem solutions are solicited from followers, who are included in the process of addressing problems and finding solutions. Followers are encouraged to try new approaches, and their ideas are not criticized because they differ from the leaders' ideas. A sample item from the MLQ that represents intellectual stimulation is "The leader gets others to look at problems from many different angles."

Individualized Consideration (IC). Transformational leaders pay special attention to each individual follower's needs for achievement and growth by acting as a coach or mentor. Followers and colleagues are developed to successively higher levels of potential. Individualized consideration is practiced when new learning opportunities are created along with a supportive climate. Individual differences in terms of needs and desires are recognized. The leader's behavior demonstrates acceptance of individual differences (e.g., some employees receive more encouragement, some more autonomy, others firmer standards, and still others more task structure). A two-way exchange in communication is encouraged, and "management by walking around" workspaces is practiced. Interactions with followers are personalized (e.g., the leader remembers previous conversations, is aware of individual concerns, and sees the individual as a whole person rather than as just an employee). The individually considerate leader listens effectively. The leader delegates tasks as a means of developing followers. Delegated tasks are monitored to see if the followers need additional direction or support and to assess progress; ideally, followers do not feel they are being checked on. A sample MLQ item from the individualized consideration scale is "The leader spends time teaching and coaching."

The Full Range of Leadership Model

In addition to the four components of transformational leadership, the Full Range of Leadership model also includes several components of transactional leadership behavior, along with laissez-faire (or nonleadership) behavior.

Transactional leadership occurs when the leader rewards or disciplines the follower, depending on the adequacy of the follower's performance. Transactional leadership depends on contingent reinforcement, either positive contingent reward (CR) or the more negative active or passive forms of management-by-exception (MBE-A or MBE-P).

Contingent Reward (CR). This constructive transaction has been found to be reasonably effective in motivating others to achieve higher levels of development and performance, although not as much as any of the transformational components. Contingent reward leadership involves the leader assigning or obtaining follower agreement on what needs to be done with promised or actual rewards offered in exchange for satisfactorily carrying out the assignment. A sample contingent reward item is "The leader makes clear what one can expect to receive when performance goals are achieved." Contingent reward is transactional when the reward is a material one, such as a bonus. Contingent reward can be transformational, however, when the reward is psychological, such as praise (Antonakis, Avolio, & Sivasubramaniam, 2003).

Management-by-Exception (MBE). This corrective transaction tends to be more ineffective than contingent reward or the components of transformational leadership. The corrective transaction may be active (MBE-A) or passive (MBE-P). In active MBE, the leader arranges to actively monitor deviances from standards, mistakes, and errors in the follower's assignments and to take corrective action as necessary. MBE-P implies waiting passively for deviances, mistakes, and errors to occur and then taking corrective action. Active MBE may be required and effective in some situations, such as when safety is paramount in importance. Leaders sometimes must practice passive MBE when required to supervise a large number of subordinates who report directly to the leaders. Sample MLQ items for management-by-exception are "The leader directs attention toward failures to meet standards" (active) and "The leader takes no action until complaints are received" (passive).

Laissez-Faire Leadership (LF). As mentioned, laissez-faire leadership is the avoidance or absence of leadership and is, by definition, most inactive, as well as most ineffective according to almost all research on the style. As opposed to transactional leadership, laissez-

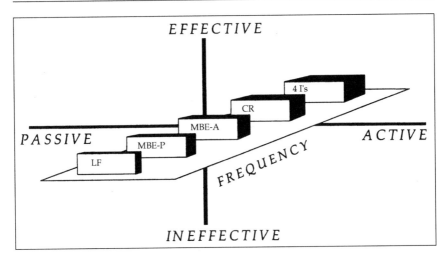

FIG. 1.1.   The model of the Full Range of Leadership: Suboptimal profile.

faire represents a nontransaction. Necessary decisions are not made. Actions are delayed. Responsibilities of leadership are ignored. Authority remains unused. A sample laissez-faire item is "The leader avoids getting involved when important issues arise."

Fundamental to the FRL model is that every leader displays each style to some amount. An optimal profile is shown in Fig. 1.1. The third dimension of this model (depth) represents how frequently a leader displays a particular style of leadership. The horizontal active dimension is by self-evident definition; the vertical effectiveness dimension is based on empirical findings.

In Fig. 1.1, the person with an optimal profile infrequently displays (LF) leadership. This individual displays successively higher frequencies of the transactional leadership styles of MBE-P, MBE-A, and CR and displays the transformational components most frequently. In contrast, as shown in Fig. 1.2, the poorly performing leader tends toward inactivity and ineffectiveness, exhibiting LF most frequently and the transformational components least frequently.

The Effectiveness of Transformational Leadership

There is a large and growing body of evidence that supports the effectiveness of transformational leadership over transactional leadership and the other components in the Full Range of Leadership model.

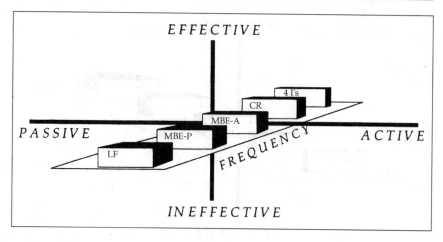

FIG. 1.2.   The model of the Full Range of Leadership: Optimal profile.

Chapters 2, 3, and 4 review the research evidence that supports this claim, beginning with meta-analytic findings (chap. 2); continue with a focus on how transformational leadership leads to more committed, loyal, and satisfied followers (one version of effectiveness; chap. 3); and goes on to explain how transformational leadership relates to performance (another way to operationalize effectiveness; chap. 4). In fact, the results suggest a hierarchy, with the four Is—the components of transformational leadership—at the top, followed by contingent reward, then active and passive management-by-exception, respectively; with laissez-faire leadership at the bottom as a style generally proving to be ineffective.

Clearly, there is nothing wrong with transactional leadership. It can, in most instances, be quite effective. Likewise, active, and even passive, management-by-exception can work depending on the circumstances. However, Bass (1985) proposed an augmentation relationship between transformational and transactional leadership. It was suggested that transformational leadership augments transactional in predicting effects on follower satisfaction and performance. Specifically, in statistical terms, transformational leadership should and does account for unique variance in ratings of performance (or other outcomes) over and above that accounted for by active transactional leadership.

Waldman, Bass, and Yammarino (1990) reported evidence for the augmentation effect among various samples of industrial managers and military officers, and Elenkov (2002) found it with Russian managers. The augmentation effect was also obtained by Seltzer and Bass

(1990) for a sample of 300 part-time MBA students, each describing their superiors at their full-time working settings. For another sample of 130 MBAs, who each asked three of their followers to complete MLQs about them, the augmentation effect held when one follower's leadership ratings and a second follower's outcomes were correlated. The same augmentation effect occurred when initiation and consideration, as measured by the Leader Behavior Description Questionnaire (LBDQ), were substituted as the measure of transactional leadership. These results demonstrate a fundamental point emphasized in the Bass (1985) theory of leadership: Transactional leadership, particularly contingent reward, provides a broad basis for effective leadership, but a greater amount of effort, effectiveness, and satisfaction is possible from transactional leadership if augmented by transformational leadership. Finally, as reported earlier by Avolio and Howell (1992), transformational leadership also augments transactional in predicting levels of innovation, risk taking, and creativity.

Transformational Leadership: Directive or Participative?

Critics perceive transformational leadership as elitist and antidemocratic. Indeed, particularly when dealing with charisma, Weber (1947) and his successors emphasized the extent that the charismatic leader directed dependent followers out of crises with radical solutions to deal with their problems; inspirational leaders were seen to be highly directive in their means and methods. The intellectually stimulating leader challenged his followers, and the individually considerate leader could rise above the demands for equality from his followers to treat them differently according to their different needs for growth. At the same time, however, such transformational leaders could share the building of visions and ideas that could be a democratic and collective enterprise. They could encourage follower participation in the change processes involved. In the same way, transactional leadership can be either directive or participative.

Table 1.1 illustrates formulaic statements illustrating that transformational and transactional leadership can be either directive or participative, authoritarian or democratic. This theory has been found useful and essential in convincing trainees that transformational leadership is not a veiled attempt at resurrecting participative leadership. It can be participative as well as more directive in orientation (Avolio & Bass, 1991).

TABLE 1.1

Descriptions of Participative Versus Directive Leadership
and the Components of the Full Range of Leadership Model

	Participative	*Directive*
Laissez-faire	"Whatever you think is the correct choice is okay with me."	"If my followers need answers to questions, let them find the answers themselves."
Management-by-exception	"Let's develop the rules together that we will use to identify mistakes."	"These are the rules, and this is how you have violated them."
Contingent reward	"Let's agree on what has to be done and how you will be rewarded if you achieve the objectives."	"If you achieve the objectives I've set, I will recognize your accomplishment with the following reward . . ."
Individualized consideration	"What can we do as a group to give each other the necessary support to develop our capabilities?"	"I will provide the support you need in your efforts to develop yourself in the job."
Intellectual stimulation	"Can we try to look at our assumptions as a ground without being critical of each other's ideas until all assumptions have been listed?"	"You must reexamine the assumption that a cold fusion engine is a physical impossibility. Revisit this problem and question your assumption."
Inspirational motivation	"Let's work together to merge our aspirations and goals for the good of our group."	"You need to say to yourself that every day you are getting better. You must look at your progression and continue to build upon it over time."
Idealized influence	"We can be a winning team because of our faith in each other. I need your support to achieve our mission."	"*Alea icta ist* (i.e., "I've made the decision to cross the Rubicon, so there's no going back"). You must trust me and my direction to achieve what we have set out to do."

Note. From *The Full Range of Leadership Development: Basic and Advanced Manuals* (pp. 5.5–5.6), by B. J. Avolio and B. M. Bass, 1991, Binghamton, NY: Bass, Avolio, and Associates. Copyright 1991 by Bass, Avolio, and Associates. Reprinted with permission.

Authentic Versus Inauthentic (Pseudotransformational) Transformational Leadership

A crucial element for James MacGregor Burns's conception of transformational leadership was his firm belief that to be transforming leaders had to be morally uplifting. Bass (1985) originally expected the dynamics of transformational leadership to be the same whether beneficial or harmful to others. As noted earlier, this notion of morally "good" and "evil" leaders has also been a dilemma for charismatic leadership theories.

Charismatic leadership has been differentiated as socialized or personalized. Socialized charismatic leadership is based on egalitarian behavior, serves collective interests, and develops and empowers others. Socialized leaders tend to be altruistic and to use legitimate established channels of authority (House & Howell, 1992; McClelland, 1975). Personalized charismatic leadership is based on personal dominance and authoritarian behavior, is self-aggrandizing, serves the self-interest, and is exploitative of others (McClelland, 1975). Personalized leaders rely heavily on manipulation, threat, and punishment and show disregard for the established institutional procedures and for the rights and feelings of others. They are impulsively aggressive, narcissistic, and impetuous (House & Howell, 1992; Popper, 2002). For Howell and Avolio (1993) authentic charismatic/transformational leaders must be socialized leaders.

This notion of personalized versus socialized leaders can apply to both charismatic and noncharismatic leaders. The defining issue is whether the leader works primarily toward personal gains as opposed to focusing also on the outcomes for followers (i.e., costs and benefits for self vs. costs and benefits for others; Bass & Steidlmeier, 1999). For example, Tyco's CEO, Dennis Kozlowski, who was prosecuted for raiding his company of $600 million to support his lavish lifestyle, represents the extreme of a personalized leader. However, a socialized leader can both achieve personal gains as well as enrich followers. An example is Bill Gates, whose Microsoft Corporation is regularly considered one of the best companies to work for and a company that made many of its employees into millionaires via generous stock options. It is important to note that for most leaders it is not clear-cut. Being personalized or socialized is usually a matter of degree, being more or less selfish or selfless in one's actions (Bass, 1998b).

Originally, the dynamics of transformational leadership were expected to be the same, whether beneficial or harmful to followers (Bass, 1985), although Burns (1978) believed that to be transforming, leaders had to be morally uplifting. Since those early writings, Bass (1998b) has come to agree with Burns. Personalized transformational leaders are pseudotransformational, or inauthentic transformational leaders. They may exhibit many transforming displays but cater, in the long run, to their own self-interests. Self-concerned, self-aggrandizing, exploitative, and power oriented, pseudotransformational leaders believe in distorted utilitarian and warped moral principles. This is in contrast to the authentic transformational leaders, who transcend their own self-interests for one of two reasons: utilitarian or moral. If utilitarian, their objective is to benefit their group or its individual members, their organization, or society, as well as themselves, and to meet the challenges of the task or mission. If a matter of moral principles, the objective is to do the right thing, to do what fits principles of morality, responsibility, sense of discipline, and respect for authority, customs, rules, and traditions of a society. There is belief in the social responsibility of the leader and the organization. Thomas Paine's writings illustrated the authentic transforming leader in his appeals to reason in "Common Sense" and "Age of Reason," his appeals to principle in "Rights of Man," and his often quoted need for transcendence: "These are the times that try men's souls."

Each of the components of transformational leadership (as well as the elements of transactional leadership) can be scrutinized to determine whether they indicate authentic or inauthentic leadership. For example, the transformational components of idealized influence and inspirational motivation can be used authentically to create follower commitment and motivation to a noble cause that benefits all, or they can be used to manipulate followers and produce an unhealthy dependence on the leader. Table 1.2 displays some of the moral elements associated with components of transformational and transactional leadership to demonstrate how these can lead to authentic or inauthentic transformational leadership.

The element of transformational leadership that usually best distinguishes authentic from inauthentic leaders is individualized consideration. The authentic transformational leader is truly concerned with the desires and needs of followers and cares about their individual development. Followers are treated as ends not just means (Bass & Steidlmeier, 1999).

In recent years, scholars have begun to examine the relationship between transformational leadership and ethical leadership behavior or perceptions of leader authenticity. For example, one study examined the relationship between transformational leadership and the perceived integrity of New Zealand managers, as rated by subordinates, peers, and superiors (Parry & Proctor-Thompson, 2002). The results showed that transformational leaders were rated as having more integrity and being more effective than were nontransformational leaders. An interesting study of marketing managers from multinational companies in India presented these leaders with vignettes depicting certain unethical business situations (e.g., bribery, endangerment of the physical environment, personal gain, displays of favoritism) and asked the leaders how they might act in these situations. Transformational leaders, particularly those high on inspirational motivation and intellectual stimulation, were more likely to behave ethically in the tempting scenarios (Banerji & Krishnan, 2000).

In an important study, Turner, Barling, Epitropaki, Butcher, and Milner (2002) found that managers/leaders from a Canadian university

TABLE 1.2
Moral Elements of Transformational and Transactional Leadership

Leadership Dynamic	Transactional Leadership Ethical Concern
Task	Whether what is being done (the end) and the means employed to do it are morally legitimate
Reward system	Whether sanctions or incentives impair effective freedom and respect conscience
Intentions	Truth telling
Trust	Promise keeping
Consequences	Egoism versus altruism—whether the legitimate moral standing and interests of all those affected are respected
Due process	Impartial process of settling conflicts and claims
	Transformational Leadership
Idealized influence	Whether "puffery" and egoism on part of the leader predominate and whether the leader is manipulative or not
Inspirational motivation	Whether providing for true empowerment and self-actualization of followers or not
Intellectual stimulation	Whether the leader's program is open to dynamic transcendence and spirituality or is closed propaganda and a "line" to follow
Individualized consideration	Whether followers are treated as ends or means, whether their unique dignity and interests are respected or not

Note. From "Ethics, Character, and Authentic Transformational Leadership Behavior," by B. M. Bass and P. Steidlmeier, 1999, *Leadership Quarterly, 10*(2), p. 185. Copyright by Elsevier. Reprinted with permission.

and a British telecommunications company who had higher levels of moral reasoning, as assessed by a self-report, pencil-and-paper measure, were rated by their subordinates as being more transformational. Finally, Brown and Trevino (2003) found that employees of transformational leaders engaged in less employee deviant behavior than followers of leaders who were well liked but not transformational.

Clearly, and as Burns (1978) emphasized, the morality of transformational leadership is critical. Throughout our discussion of transformational leadership, we assume for the most part that we are speaking of authentic transformational leadership. Yet it is clear that much work needs to be done to better understand the dynamics of authentic leadership, in general, and authentic transformational leadership in particular.

THE UNIVERSALITY
OF TRANSFORMATIONAL LEADERSHIP

Bass (1997) argued that transactional and transformational leadership can be found in all parts of the globe and in all forms of organizations. Indeed, research on transformational leadership, including the use of the MLQ, has taken place in every continent and in nearly every industrialized nation. Research from the Global Leadership and Organizational Behavior Effectiveness (GLOBE) research program supports earlier notions that elements of charismatic-transformational leadership are valued leader qualities in all countries and cultures (Den Hartog, House, Hanges, Ruiz-Quintanilla, & Dorfman, 1999; Dorfman, Hanges, & Brodbeck, 2004).

Research evidence from around the world suggests that transformational leadership typically provides a positive augmentation in leader performance beyond the effects of transactional leadership. Furthermore, transformational leadership should be a more effective form of leadership globally because the transformational leader is consistent with people's prototypes of an ideal leader (Bass, 1997). Of course, there are cultural contingencies, as well as organizational factors, that can affect the impact of transformational leadership in particular instances. However, authentic transformational leadership has an impact in all cultures and organizations because transformational leaders have goals that transcend their own self-interests and work toward the common good of the followers (Burns, 1978).

BOOK OVERVIEW

This book reviews theory and research on transformational leadership. It examines transformational leadership in the broader context of the FRL model. The FRL model includes transformational leadership and its components as the most effective, or optimal, level of leadership, with transactional leadership (based on rewards and disciplinary actions) as the "mid" level, and laissez-faire leadership anchoring the ineffective, or suboptimal, level. The previous edition sought to answer key questions about transformational (and transactional) leadership to help guide future leadership research and application. These key questions provided the structure to the first edition. This edition follows a similar structure but includes some new chapters and a great deal of new research, the bulk of which was conducted after the prior edition's publication date of 1998.

Chapter 2 looks at the structure and measurement of transformational leadership and the FRL model. Much of this chapter involves a discussion of the MLQ, but discussion of other methods of measuring transformational leadership is also presented.

Chapter 3 examines the contribution of transformational leadership to follower commitment, involvement, loyalty, and satisfaction. The dynamics involved explain why transformational leadership contributes positively to followers' feelings about the leader and the organization.

Chapter 4 reviews research on how transformational leadership relates to performance. Performance is broadly defined to include follower, group, and organizational performance (measured both subjectively and objectively), as well as measures of creativity.

Chapter 5 details how transformational leadership helps followers to cope with stress in crises, emergencies, and various other stressful conditions, such as panic and disasters.

Chapter 6 reviews how contingencies affect the emergence and effectiveness of transformational leadership. Some variation is expected and obtained in transformational leadership as a function of the stability or turbulence of the environment, differences in the larger culture, the mechanistic or organic character of the organization, the sector, and the characteristics of the group.

Chapter 7 considers how organizational cultures can be described in terms of their transformational and transactional qualities. Transformational cultures are more adaptive. Also explored is how transformational leadership is influenced by the larger culture of the nation, territory, or region.

Chapter 8 reviews the large and growing literature on transformational leadership and gender. Women leaders tend to be somewhat more transformational and effective; men manage more by exception. Explanations are offered for these findings.

Chapter 9 explores the implications of transformational leadership on the organization's image, policies, and strategic planning. Also examined is its impact on recruitment, selection, promotion, personnel development, and management education.

Chapter 10 addresses the issues of the development of transformational leaders as assessed from biodata, as modified through counseling and feedback, and as generated from formal training programs based on the FRL model. Evaluations of successful training efforts are provided.

Chapter 11 reviews research exploring the correlates and predictors of transformational leadership, including research on how personality and multiple dimensions of intelligence predict transformational leadership. In addition, the interaction of traits and situations in the prediction of transformational leadership behavior is discusssed.

Chapter 12 relates what is known about how status, rank, or means of acquisition of a leadership position relates to transformational leader behavior. The public, private, and service organizational sectors are examined.

Chapter 13 discusses the role of empowerment in transformational leadership and contrasts this with laissez-faire leadership. The importance of empowerment is discussed, along with ways leaders effectively empower followers.

Chapter 14 considers whether or not there could be valid substitutes for transformational leadership, proposes some possibilities, and explores the role of transformational leadership in shared and team models of groups and organizations.

Chapter 15 concludes with suggestions for future research in transformational leadership. Despite the large amount of research on transformational leadership that has been conducted in the past decade, there are still many gaps in our knowledge.

2

The Measurement of Transformational Leadership

Although the concept of transformational leadership struck a sympathetic chord with those generally interested in leadership topics, as evidenced by the popularity of Burns's (1978) book, the surge of research on transformational leadership is due in large part to the development of measurement tools to assess the construct. The most widely accepted instrument to measure transformational leadership is the Multifactor Leadership Questionnaire (MLQ; Bass & Avolio, 2000), which actually assesses the Full Range of Leadership (FRL) model, including laissez-faire leadership; the components of transactional leadership, namely, management by exception (both active and passive forms); and contingent reward, as well as the components of transformational leadership. Although much of the research on transformational leadership uses the MLQ, it is important to note that other measures of transformational leadership exist, and these are reviewed later in this chapter.

DEVELOPMENT OF THE MLQ

Burns's (1978) concept of the transforming leader, along with the responses of 70 senior executives who reported that they had experiences with transformational leaders, were used to elicit accounts of leaders who fit the description. These were converted to 142 behavioral statements. Eleven judges were presented with detailed definitions of transactional and transformational leadership, and these judges agreed that 73 of the 142 statements reflected either transformational or transactional leader behaviors.

The 73 items representing transactional and transformational behaviors were presented to 176 high-ranking U.S. military officials, who rated how well each item pertained to their immediate superiors. Initial factor analyses of these data, along with subsequent factor analyses (Bycio et al., 1995; Howell & Avolio, 1993), suggested several factors. Three factors were extracted from the transactional leadership items and four factors from the transformational items.

It was originally believed that there were three components to transformational leadership: charismatic-inspirational, intellectually stimulating, and individually considerate. However, later factor analyses suggested that the charisma factor, what has been subsequently termed Idealized Influence, was separate from the inspiration factor (Inspirational Motivation). More recent research on the factor structure of the MLQ is discussed later in this chapter.

The transactional items formed factors of contingent reward, management-by-exception, and laissez-faire leadership behaviors. Subsequent factor analyses supported splitting management-by-exception into passive and active factors (Hater & Bass, 1988). Combined, these transactional and transformational leadership factors formed the early FRL model.

There are two forms of the MLQ. The first is the Leader Form that asks the leader to rate the frequency of his or her own leader behavior. Research has shown that self-ratings of one's own leader behavior are prone to bias. Therefore, the more important version of the MLQ is the Rater Form. The MLQ Rater Form requires associates of leaders (usually supervisees or direct reports) to rate the frequency of their leader's transactional and transformational leadership behavior using 5-point ratings scales, with anchors ranging from 0 = *Not at all* to 4 = *Frequently, if not always*. The Rater Form is most commonly used in research to measure transformational and transactional leadership. Sample items from the MLQ are presented in Table 2.1.

Revisions to the MLQ

As noted, the original MLQ consisted of 73 items, measuring five factors. Responding to criticisms about the incorporation of items that did not focus directly on leader behaviors (Hunt, 1991; Yukl, 1998) and concerns about the factor structure and subscales, the MLQ was

TABLE 2.1
Sample Items From the MLQ (5X)

Factor	Sample Item
Idealized Influence (Attributed Charisma)	My leader instills pride in me for being associated with him or her.
Idealized Influence (Behaviors)	My leader specifies the importance of having a strong sense of purpose.
Inspirational Motivation	My leader articulates a compelling vision of the future.
Intellectual Stimulation	My leader seeks differing perspectives when solving problems.
Individualized Consideration	My leader spends time teaching and coaching
Contingent Reward	My leader makes clear what one can expect to receive when performance goals are achieved.
Management-by-Exception (Active)	My leader focuses attention on irregularities, mistakes, exceptions, and deviations from standards.
Management-by-Exception (Passive)	My leader shows that he or she is a firm believer in "If it ain't broke, don't fix it."
Laissez-Faire	My leader delays responding to urgent requests.

substantially revised. The first published version of the MLQ (Bass & Avolio, 1990c) contained 67 items measuring the FRL Model (with 37 of these items assessing transformational leadership). Also included were nine items measuring outcomes, including ratings of the leader's effectiveness, satisfaction with the leader, and the extent to which followers exert extra effort as a result of the leader's performance.

The current, revised form of the MLQ (5X) (Bass & Avolio, 1997) is substantially refined and contains 36 standardized items, 4 items assessing each of the nine leadership dimensions associated with the FRL model (see Table 2.1), and the additional 9 outcome items mentioned previously. In addition to this version of the MLQ, there is a longer form (63 items) used for providing feedback in leadership development programs (see chap. 10).

Psychometric Properties of the MLQ

Several different approaches have been used to confirm the reliability and validity of the MLQ. A first question is the integrity of the MLQ scales themselves. Do the MLQ scales have good internal consistency?

In other words, is there evidence that the items within each of the MLQ scales hang together and seem to be measuring the same construct? The MLQ scales have demonstrated good to excellent internal consistency, with alpha coefficients above the .80 level for all MLQ scales, using the most recent version of the MLQ across a large sample. Some of the earlier MLQ scales (particularly the active management-by-exception scale) had lower levels of internal consistency, but they were still adequate given the small number of items per scale. The MLQ has been completed by more than 15,000 respondents and translated into many languages, ranging from German and French to Japanese and Hebrew.

Rate-Rerate Consistency. A second question concerns the consistency of MLQ assessments. If we know a leader's MLQ profile, can we predict the leader's profile at a later date? The evidence is supportive. When 6 months intervene between the first and second assessments of the MLQ by self and subordinates, Pile (1988) found that the first set of results predicted the second set with correlations obtained as shown in Table 2.2. Subsequent test-retest reliability coefficents have been even higher (Bass & Avolio, 1997).

Subordinate–Superior Agreement. If supervisors complete the MLQ on a target leader, does it agree with the ratings of that target

TABLE 2.2
MLQ Rate–Rerate Correlations

MLQ Scale	Rate-Rerate Leader Self-Ratings (N = 33)	Rate-Rerate Follower Ratings (N = 193)
Transformational		
Idealized Influence (Charismatic Behavior)	.60	.79
Inspirational Motivation	.45	.66
Intellectual Stimulation	.61	.66
Individualized Consideration	.70	.77
Transactional		
Contingent Reward	.44	.52
Management-by-Exception	.74	.61
Laissez-Faire	.73	.82

Note. From *Visionary Leadership: Creating a Generative Internal Map,* by S. Pile, 1988, unpublished master's thesis, Pepperdine University, Los Angeles. Copyright 1988 by Pile. Reprinted with permission.

leader's subordinates? There is evidence of general agreement, but such different perspectives also present unique pictures of the focal, target leader. For example, Atwater and Yammarino (1993) found that of the 107 midshipmen at the U.S. Naval Academy, subordinates and superiors of the focal midshipmen correlated .35 and .34, respectively, for composite measures of transformational and transactional leadership. Considering that subordinates saw their focal leaders in a quite different relationship than did the superiors of the focal leaders, the correlations of .35 and .34 indicated that considerable variance in the MLQ was attributable to consistent individual differences in the focal midshipmen.

Peer Ratings Based on Performance in Small Groups. Participants in the FRL development program, which is described briefly in chapter 10, used a list of 21 items to assess the components of the MLQ model displayed by their peers in the training program. The mean correlation between the sets, each of three items, dealing with the seven components of the model of transactional and transformational leadership, correlated .35 on the average with the same components of the MLQ as obtained from the participants' subordinates back on the job prior to beginning the basic program.

There are also some data to suggest that peers and observers of small group discussions may be able to predict with some validity the transformational and transactional behavior of examinees placed in a leaderless group-testing situation because, as Bass (1954) concluded, performance in a leaderless group discussion (LGD) correlates significantly with the examinees' subsequent leadership potential, status, esteem, and merit. The rationale for such positive correlations was that the LGD requires examinees to be cooperative and competitive, often at the same time, mirroring an important challenge leaders face in everyday circumstances (Handy, 1994).

Evidence of Construct Validity of the MLQ. As mentioned, the MLQ, in its various forms, has been subjected to extensive factor analyses to examine both the model of transformational leadership, the larger FRL theory (FRLT), as well as the question of whether the MLQ adequately measures these constructs. For example, a number of researchers have been unable to replicate the nine-factor FRLT (e.g., Bycio et al., 1995; Den Hartog, Van Muijen, & Koopman, 1997; Tejeda, Scandura, & Pillai, 2001), although they did find evidence of many of the hypothesized MLQ dimensions. Typically, these researchers found fewer than the proposed nine factors, suggesting that factors could be combined or collapsed. However, recent research (Antonakis et al., 2003) suggested that the inconsistent findings of some of these researchers occurred because they used very heterogeneous samples of leaders from different cultures, organizational types, and organizational levels (e.g., combining front-line and upper level managers).

Although there is some evidence of inconsistency in the MLQ's factor structure, we think it is important to distinguish the theorized subcomponents of transformational leadership and the FRL model for conceptual clarity and for leadership development purposes. Transformational leadership is clearly multidimensional, and there is support for the structure represented by the MLQ (e.g., Antonakis et al., 2003). It is important to also note that a recent alternative model for the elements of transformational leadership has been proposed, but it too is multidimensional, consisting of five components (Rafferty & Griffin, 2004).

Interdependence of the Components

Although each of the components of the FRL model is conceptually distinct, there are consistent correlations among them. For instance, charisma (idealized influence) and inspirational leadership are highly correlated, but followers may want to emulate the charismatic leader and not necessarily the inspirational leader. Nevertheless, the same persons who are charismatic, in general, are likely to be inspirational. To a lesser extent, all the components of transformational leadership are likely to correlate with each other and with contingent reward. In the same way, passive management-by-exception (MBE-P) is likely to correlate with laissez-faire leadership, but the leader who frequently displays MBE-P corrects followers; the laissez-faire leader does not.

A confirmatory factor analysis was completed for 14 samples involving 3,786 MLQ descriptions of leaders from a variety of organizations and agencies that suggested that the factor model that best fit the data was one combining the charisma-inspirational leadership components into one factor and also combining the passive management-by-exception and laissez-faire components into one factor. Yet all the remaining components of the FRL model could stand alone as separate factors (Avolio, Bass, & Jung, 1997, 1999). As mentioned, however, the more recent investigation by Antonakis et al. (2002) provided evidence to support the full nine-factor structure represented by the FRL model. Moreover, we maintain that conceptually, and for leadership development purposes, it may be helpful to use the full nine factors.

In much of the research on transformational leadership, the components are combined. For example, the Idealized Influence and Inspirational Motivation MLQ subscales are frequently combined to create a composite index of inspirational charisma or charisma, or all four components are summed to create a total score on transformational leadership. This is acceptable given the intercorrelations among the MLQ transformational leadership scales. Although researchers may want to make general statements about transformational leadership using the summed score, it is often important to understand how the individual elements fare. However, because the transactional factors tend to be more independent of each other, combining them into a single composite score is a questionable practice.

Correlations With Independent Criteria

Transformational leadership as measured by subordinates' ratings was shown in early research to correlate more highly than transactional leadership with various independent criteria. For example, 25 project champions based on interviews in 28 different organizations were shown to display more transformational behaviors than 25 matched nonchampions (Howell & Higgins, 1990). Transformational scores were also higher among innovative school principals, U.S. Marine Corps commanders of more highly effective helicopter squadrons (Salter, 1989), Methodist ministers with greater Sunday church attendance and membership growth (Onnen, 1987), presidents of MBA teams completing complex simulations with greater financial success (Avolio, Waldman, & Einstein, 1988), middle business managers with future financial success of their business units (Howell & Avolio, 1993), middle managers with better management committee evaluations (Hater & Bass, 1988), and junior naval officers with recommendations for early promotion and better fitness reports (Yammarino & Bass, 1990a).

Although numerous individual studies, such as those mentioned earlier, demonstrated relationships between transformational leadership and various indexes of leadership effectiveness, the most convincing evidence for the predictive validity of transformational leadership comes from meta-analyses.

Meta-Analyses. The hierarchy of correlations in individual studies that is found in the correlation of the MLQ components with effectiveness is usually charisma-inspiration, intellectual stimulation,
and individualized consideration > contingent reward > active managing-by-exception > passive managing-by-exception > laissez-faire
leadership. Three early meta-analyses were completed that support
the model: Lowe, Kroeck, and Sivasubramaniam (1996) completed a
meta-analysis of data for 2,873 to 4,242 respondents in public agencies and the private sector and showed that the correlation between
each component of the MLQ generally was consistent with the model.
Thus, as Table 2.3 shows, the mean corrected correlations with effectiveness for the public (including military) and private sectors were,
respectively, charisma-inspiration, .74, .69; intellectual stimulation, .65,
.56; individualized consideration, .63, .62; contingent reward, .41, .41;
and managing-by-exception, .10, −.02.

Gasper (1992) completed another meta-analysis of demonstrated
transformational and transactional leadership. He pooled the transformational components in one composite and the transactional in a
separate composite. For 20 studies, the mean corrected transformational leadership correlated respectively, .76, .71, and .88 with effectiveness, satisfaction, and extra effort perceived by the followers. The
corresponding corrected correlations with transactional leadership
were .27, .22, and .32. Patterson, Fuller, Kester, and Stringer (1995) cor-
roborated the findings of these last two meta-analyses for the effects
of transformational and transactional leadership on selected follower
compliance outcomes.

TABLE 2.3
Correlations With Effectiveness
in Public and Private Organizations

Leadership	Sector	
	Public	Private
Transformational		
Charisma-inspiration	.74	.69
Intellectual stimulation	.65	.56
Individual consideration	.63	.62
Transactional		
Contingent reward	.41	.41
Managing-by-exception	.10	−.02

In summary, there is substantial evidence that transformational leadership, particularly as measured by the MLQ, correlates significantly with measures of leadership effectiveness. Moreover, there is value added from transformational leadership over and above the positive effects of transactional leadership. Yet the relationship between transformational leadership and leadership outcomes is complex. We explore the results of the research summarized by these meta-analyses more fully in chapters 3 and 4, where we individually examine the influence of transformational leadership on performance and on other follower outcomes (e.g., follower commitment, follower satisfaction). In subsequent chapters, we further explore the complex nature of the transformational leadership–outcomes relationship looking at various mediators and moderators.

OTHER MEASURES
OF TRANSFORMATIONAL
LEADERSHIP

The MLQ has been both a boon and a bane to research on transformational leadership. The popularity of the MLQ among researchers has helped lead to a near explosion of research on transformational leadership, and this work has advanced our knowledge of transformational leadership greatly. Its computerized data collection, scoring, feedback, and norms make it readily available not only for research purposes but also for training and development (www.mindgarden .com). However, the ready availability of the MLQ, coupled with a bit of a bandwagon effect, may have somewhat stifled the development of other measures of transformational leadership leading to an over-reliance on pencil-and-paper report methodology. Yet there are other methods for assessing transformational leadership, some of which were used in developing both the MLQ and refining transformational leadership theory.

Diaries

Virginia Military Academy (VMI) cadets reported in unstructured logs or diaries the leadership behavior they observed during a given set of days. It was found that these logs could be reliably scored in terms of all of the various components of the FRL model. These diary reports could then be linked to independently obtained questionnaire measures (Atwater, Avolio, & Bass, 1991).

Interviews

Interviews with executives about the leadership they saw produced numerous other behavioral examples of transformational leadership and were helpful in both constructing the MLQ and in better understanding transformational leadership. Charismatic leadership was attributed to the interviewees' bosses for setting examples, showing determination, displaying extraordinary talents, taking risks, creating a sense of empowerment in subordinates, showing dedication to the cause, creating a sense of a joint mission, dealing with crises using radical solutions, and engendering faith in the subordinates for their leadership.

Inspirational leadership included providing meaning and challenge, painting an optimistic future, molding expectations, creating self-fulfilling prophesies, and thinking ahead. Intellectual stimulation was judged present when superiors questioned assumptions, encouraged subordinates to employ intuition, entertained ideas that seemed unusual, created imaginative visions, asked subordinates to rework the same problems they thought they had solved, and saw unusual patterns. Individualized consideration was apparent to interviewees when their bosses answered them with minimum delay, showed they were concerned for their subordinates' well-being, assigned tasks based on subordinate needs and abilities, encouraged two-way exchanges of ideas, were available when needed, encouraged self-development, practiced walk-around management, and effectively mentored, counseled, and coached.

When peers of VMI military cadet leaders were asked what characterized the important traits of a good leader, they tended to describe traits of inspiration, intellectual stimulation, and individualized consideration, such as self-confidence, persuasiveness, concern for the well-being of others, and the ability to articulate one's ideas and thoughts as well as providing models to be emulated by others, holding high expectations for themselves and others, keeping others well informed, and maintaining high motivation in themselves (Atwater et al., 1994).

In a similar vein, the Full Range of Leadership Development Program (Avolio & Bass, 1991) begins with participants describing their implicit theories of leadership as evidenced by ideal leaders they have known. Invariably, for well over 2,000 trainees, the characteristics of the ideal leader included the components of transformational leadership and contingent reward.

Observational Methods

To date, there have been very few attempts to assess transformational leadership via systematic, objective, third-party (i.e., nonfollowers) observations. One exception is a study by Ployhart, Lim, and Chan (2001) that rated the transformational leadership behaviors of Singaporean military recruits during a leadership assessment center at the beginning of their basic training. Some of the transformational leadership behaviors observed and rated included leading by example, inspiring others, maintaining trusting and cordial relationships with peers, and demonstrating initiative and courage. These behaviors were mapped onto the components of the transformational leadership model.

Clearly, the development of systematic observational coding schemes for transformational leadership could be an important advancement in measurement. Researchers would then have a more objective indicator of a leader's transformational leadership behaviors that does not rely on followers' ratings, which can be affected somewhat by the group's level of performance.

Alternative Pencil-and-Paper Measures

There are a number of measures that have been developed to assess transformational leadership besides the MLQ (Goodstein & Lanyon, 1999, provide a nice review). The most widely used of these is the Transformational Leadership Behavior Inventory (TLI) developed by Podsakoff, MacKenzie, Moorman, and Fetter (1990). This instrument measures four key dimensions of transformational leadership. The first dimension captures the core transformational leadership behavior, which includes developing and articulating a vision, providing a positive role model, and motivating employees to look beyond their self-interest for the good of the group. The remaining three dimensions measure the leader's individualized consideration, intellectual stimulation, and high expectations for performance. The TLI has been used in various forms in research by Podsakoff and his colleagues and by others.

Warner Burke (1994) used his Leadership Assessment Inventory (LAI) to measure transformational and transactional leadership for some time. Unfortunately, this instrument is now difficult to obtain and rarely used in research.

The Transformational Leadership Questionnaire (TLQ) is a relatively new instrument that measures nine factors associated with transformational leaders and is specifically designed for use in public sector organizations in the United Kingdom (Alban-Metcalfe & Alimo-Metcalfe, 2000; Alimo-Metcalfe & Alban-Metcalfe, 2001). The TLQ has eight scales, labeled Genuine Concern for Others; Decisiveness, Determination, Self-Confidence; Integrity, Trustworthy, Honest and Open; Empowers, Develops Potential; Inspirational Networker and Promoter; Accessible, Approachable; Clarifies Boundaries, Involves Others in Decisions; Encourages Critical and Strategic Thinking. Like the MLQ, the TLQ is completed by the manager's direct reports. Initial validation studies for the TLQ have been completed. As can be seen, there is conceptual similarity between the TLQ and MLQ.

Carless, Wearing, and Mann (2000) developed a short measure of transformational leadership, the Global Transformational Leadership scale (GTL). This seven-item scale assesses a single, global construct of transformational leadership.

Another new alternative measure of transformational leadership was developed by Rafferty and Griffin (2004), based on leadership measures created by House (1998) and Podsakoff et al. (1990). This 15-item rating scale measures the transformational leader's vision, inspirational communication, intellectual stimulation, supportive leadership, and personal recognition. The authors claim that these components provide a better factor structure than the MLQ.

Behling and McFillen (1996) created two measures, the Follower Belief Questionnaire and the Attributes of Leader Behavior Questionnaire that are follower reports of their leader's transformational/charismatic leadership. Subscales include inspiration, awe, empowerment, displays empathy, dramatizes mission, projects self-assurance, enhances image, assures followers of competence, and provides opportunities to experience success. It is easy to see how these dimensions map onto the components of transformational leadership. This measure has not been widely used in research.

In addition to measures of transformational leadership, some researchers have been interested primarily in the charisma elements of transformational leadership (and many scholars have used the terms "charismatic" and "transformational" interchangeably). In assessing charisma, a variety of instruments have been used. Most popular among these is the Conger-Kanungo scale (CK-scale; Conger & Kanungo, 1988), which measures transformational characteristics such as vision and articulation, environmental sensitivity, unconventional behavior, sensitivity to member needs, taking personal risks, and not maintaining the status quo.

A number of other leadership measures assess dimensions related to transformational leadership, although they have not been labeled explicitly as such. One such measure that is widely used in leadership development programs is Kouzes and Posner's (1988) Leadership Practices Inventory (LPI). Given the popularity of the Kouzes and Posner model in leadership development programs, this measure is widely used in practice but more rarely used in published empirical research. Sashkin (1996) created a measure, the Leadership Behavior Questionnaire (LBQ), which measures visionary leadership and is different from, but tangentially related to, transformational leadership.

CONCLUSIONS

The measurement of transformational leadership has been dominated by the MLQ, although there have been alternative measures developed to assess both transformational and charismatic leadership. As research on transformational leadership continues, it will be advantageous to use multiple methods for assessing the construct.

3

Commitment, Loyalty, and Satisfaction of Followers of Transformational Leaders

Employees may feel strong commitment to their organizations and jobs for many different reasons. They may like the type of work they do, and the pay and benefits may be better than what they can get elsewhere. They may find the work and people interesting. Recognition or career advancement may be anticipated. Likewise, volunteers supporting a grassroots movement may have a similarly strong commitment for numerous reasons. They may feel that what they are doing is giving them the opportunity to make a contribution to others as well as to themselves. The commitment of volunteers in a charitable organization may be sustained by the gratitude from the recipients of services and the positive feelings of helping others. Another important factor that helps build commitment and loyalty to an organization is leadership—leadership that is inspirational, stimulating, and considerate of followers' needs.

In this chapter, we examine the contribution of transformational leadership to commitment and its concomitants of involvement, loyalty, and satisfaction. We also consider the mechanisms underlying the process. Although transformational leadership clearly affects the performance of work groups and organizations (the topic of the next chapter), the strongest effects of transformational leadership seem to be on followers' attitudes and their commitment to the leader and the organization. Moreover, it may be that it is the extraordinary commitment of followers of transformational leaders that underlies the exceptional performance of many groups led by transformational leaders.

In a doctoral study, Pitman (1993) showed how much the commitment of 245 white-collar workers in six organizations correlated with various measures of transformational leadership among their supervisors. The Multifactor Leadership Questionnaire (MLQ) scales of Charisma (Idealized Influence) and Inspirational Motivation correlated .40 with commitment to stay with the organization and .24 with commitment to organizational values. The Conger–Kanungo (CK) scales (Conger & Kanungo, 1988) that measured such transformational attributes as vision, articulation, sensitivity, unconventional behavior, personal risk taking, and lack of maintenance of the status quo correlated .38 with commitment to stay and commitment to values. The correlation of commitment was .23 with endorsement of organizational values.

In a study of 261 middle managers in a number of public sector banks in India, managers' scores on transformational leadership accounted for significant amounts of variance in bank workers' commitment to their organizations (Rai & Sinha, 2000). Moreover, this strong follower commitment seemed to translate into better financial performance for bank branches. Similar results were found when looking at 70 university department chairs. Transformational department chairs had more committed and satisfied departmental members (Brown & Moshavi, 2002). In another study, transformational leaders of production teams in a metal processing plant demonstrated stronger commitment to engaging in safe work practices and had a stronger overall safety climate than groups led by non-transformational leaders (Zohar, 2002).

When commitment to unionism and willingness to vote to support the union were strong, actual participation in union activities remained low. Nonetheless, when there was a lot of contact with shop stewards by rank-and-file employees, participation in union activities increased if the stewards exhibited transformational leadership as measured by 15 transformational leadership items assessing charisma, inspirational motivation, intellectual stimulation, and individualized consideration:

> Most striking . . . is the pervasive effect exerted by perception of the stewards' (transformational) leadership styles. Members' perceptions of shop stewards' leadership styles predicted members' loyalty, sense of responsibility and actual participation in union activities. (Kelloway & Barling, 1993, p. 263)

Fullagar, McCoy, and Shull (1992) noted that the loyalty toward their union of 70 electrical apprentices was related to the transformational characteristics of the socializing agents.

A study involving 846 teachers and principals of 89 secondary schools in Singapore likewise demonstrated that commitment to the organization and related organizational citizenship behavior and job satisfaction were significantly greater when the principals were described by the teachers as more transformational on the scales of the MLQ (Koh, 1990; Koh, Steers, & Terborg, 1995). Commitment may also be a matter of attachment to supervisor and work group or attachment to senior management and the organization, or both (Becker & Billings, 1993). Niehoff, Enz, and Grover (1990) surveyed 862 insurance company employees in various positions at the home office and in the field. Commitment to the organization was positively affected by the extent to which top management inspired a shared vision ($r = .58$), encouraged innovativeness ($r = .69$), and supported employees' efforts ($r = .32$). Commitment and job satisfaction correlated .75.

Intentions to quit, job satisfaction, and organizational citizenship behaviors likewise depend on commitment. Transformational leadership by the immediate superior can enhance local, departmental commitment and help in commitment to the organization, but transformational leadership at the top of the organization is likely to be needed for commitment to extend to the organization as a whole.

DYNAMICS OF LEADERSHIP AND COMMITMENT

The commitment and loyalty of members of organizations are multifaceted. There is commitment to the larger organization, to the work group or team, and to the leader. There is commitment to the task and to one's personal career. There can also be a moral commitment to one's own beliefs and values, to the values of others in the organization, and to the values of the organization as a whole. Leaders in organizations can play an important part in affecting organizational members' levels of commitment by fostering followers' commitment to the team, to the leader, and to the organization. The effective leader is able to align these facets of commitment to show how the goals and values of the follower, the group, the leader, and the organization are in basic agreement. Kark and Shamir (2002; Kark, Shamir, & Chen, 2003) argue that transformational leaders influence both followers' identification with and commitment to the leader and also positively influence followers' social identification with the group or organization. A good example of the role of transformational leadership in building commitment and motivation is the military.

Gal (1987) argued that commitment is a central concept in military motivation in contrast to the military's earlier emphasis on compliance through obedience. The will to fight may be lacking without commitment. The commitment to the point of death creates the unlimited liability clause of the members of the military (Hackett, 1979, p. 101). And for such commitment, Gal (1985) argued strongly that transformational leadership is needed at all levels:

> Commitment is the backbone of the military profession. For most military professionals, belonging to the armed forces is not merely a question of a place to work, a job, or an occupation. It is a way of life and frequently a lifetime commitment. . . .
>
> Commitment can be a very powerful motivation, more so than a paycheck, especially when military activities involve high risk, extreme demands, and severe stress. Obedience and compliance with orders and commands becomes the key to organizational functioning. Obedience and commitment can be considered as the two modes of military compliance. . . .
>
> Obedience is initiated by fear and punishment during the early phases of socialization into military life (highly transactional; coupled with increasing substitutions of rewards of recognition, badges, promotion, etc.). It is enhanced by threat and sanction and instilled through endless drills and orders. Obedience is gradually replaced by internalized patterns of behavior that become autonomous. . . . Even when the legitimacy of an organizational goal is questionable, if behavior is motivated by obedience, well-indoctrinated soldiers will continue to comply even though orders are debatable. Military obedience succeeds in shielding soldiers from conflicts emerging from concerns about the legitimacy of missions. Thus, fear and external power predominantly generate military discipline and its obedient behavior . . . obedience is essential for good performance, efficiency, and mission completion as well; without it, the whole military structure would collapse.
>
> However, obedience can be a double-edged sword, especially when it becomes blind . . . under certain circumstances most individuals can be pushed to the point of fully obedient behavior despite their doubts or distress . . . acting in obedience to a perceived legitimized authority, individuals can lose all sense of responsibility for their most destructive acts. (pp. 553–554)

There are three facets of commitment within the military: organization, career, and moral commitment to what one believes in and for which one will sacrifice (Sarkesian, 1981). These three facets need to be in alignment for military professionals to be in harmony with their organization. For those in a command position, there is commitment to one's personnel, one's unit, and one's task. Commitment, according to Gal (1985), is derived from one's own internalized sense of duty, responsibility, and conviction. Orders do not come from a single external source as in the case of obedience but reflect the interaction of beliefs, values, and conscience.

Aligning the different facets of commitment is not limited to military leadership. In an era of organizational downsizing, coupled with workers who put the care and enhancement of their own careers above loyalty to an employer, in a time where many believe the traditional employer–employee "contract" has been irrevocably broken, aligning the facets of commitment is critical. Thus, an important aspect of transformational leadership is developing, maintaining, and enhancing this alignment. Flowing from this alignment are societal and organizational goals complementing the professionals' values and norms, making them willing to devote themselves, or even sacrifice themselves, to attain the goals. Transformational leaders' commitment additionally includes the feelings of responsibility for personnel and task; this responsibility derives from the leader's own conscience and internalized values.

Impact of Transformational Leadership on Commitment

Each of the components of transformational leadership can help build follower commitment in different ways. Idealized influence— wanting to emulate the leader or identify with the leader emotionally—leads to identification with the goals, interests, and values of the leader. A leader who is a role model for followers, and one who behaves consistently with the values she or he espouses, can more easily build commitment to a group's or an organization's values, goals, or standards of behavior. Simons (1999) refers to the degree of congruency between the values or actions espoused by leaders and the actual adherence to them (i.e., whether the leader "walks the talk") as behavioral integrity.

Leaders use inspirational motivation to build emotional commitment to a mission or goal. Physical and emotional excitation is aroused in the process. Values, beliefs, and responsibilities are all encouraged by the transformational leader. The inspirational leader works to move followers to consider the moral values involved in their duties as members of their unit, organization, and profession. For example, Cromwell's New Model Army became invincible as its soldiers saw themselves fighting for the cause of Puritanism, righteousness, and freedom from royal arbitrariness. Similarly, Islamic leaders call followers to arms by declaring a religious holy war, or *jihad*.

The transformational leader, whether a manager supervising a sales team or a commanding general leading an army, further increases commitment by employing intellectual stimulation. The education, concerns, and experiences of the follower are enlisted in a joint effort to deal with problems in a creative way. For example, renowned 3M chief executive officer (CEO) William McKnight encouraged engineers to spend up to 15% of their time pursuing whatever projects they liked, leading to the development of breakthrough products such as Scotch tape and Post-it Notes. Unusual approaches emerge, such as when a U.S. Army noncommissioned officer in World War II reframed a problem when challenged, figured out how to quickly convert tanks into bulldozers to cut through the Normandy hedgerows, and was empowered to do so. Pride in the actions of all those involved as well as joint success in overcoming obstacles are combined. Commitments are reinforced.

Individualized consideration at all levels also enhances commitment. Followers feel their personal career needs are being met. Additionally, the coaching and mentoring provided them by their leader provides them with a sense of increased competence to carry out orders. Indirect evidence of the importance to military commitment of perceiving fulfillment of training goals was provided by Tannenbaum, Mathieu, Salas, and Cannon-Bowers (1991). For 666 military trainees in socialization training, their posttraining organizational commitment was related to training fulfillment as well as to their levels of motivation and self-efficacy.

Whereas commitment itself has many facets (e.g., career, ideological, organizational), a number of scholars have suggested that commitment to the organization takes different forms. Allen and Mayer (1990) distinguish affective commitment, the employee's emotional attachment to the organization, from continuance commitment, which deals with the anticipated costs of leaving the organization, and normative commitment, the employee's sense of obligation to stay (with the latter somewhat related to the notion of the implied psychological contract between employer and employee). Penley and Gould (1988) refer to moral commitment (similar to affective commitment) and calculative commmitment (associated with both the costs and benefits of leaving vs. staying). As one can imagine, transformational leadership should have its strongest influence on affective (or moral) commitment, with the other forms of commitment (continuance, normative, calculative) being more influenced by transactional leader behaviors. In a study of nurses, transformational leadership components were indeed strongly correlated (rs in the .40 range) with affective commitment but less strongly correlated with normative commitment (Bycio et al., 1995). Contrary to expectations, contingent reward was not correlated with continuance commitment. In another study of U.S. Army leaders, both transactional and transformational leadership were correlated with both affective/moral commitment and commitment to stay, but transformational leadership augmented the effects of transactional leadership on affective commitment (Kane & Tremble, 2000).

Although it is clear that transformational leadership helps build strong follower commitment, the process of building follower commitment and inspiring followers is quite complex. The role of charisma in understanding this process is important.

A Charismatic–Inspirational Approach

For organizational life in general, Shamir, House, and Arthur (1993) explained the dynamic mechanisms involved in transformational leadership, particularly charismatic leadership as defined in House (1977), which includes the components of idealized influence, inspirational leadership, and intellectual stimulation. Humans are practical and goal-oriented, seeking rewards and avoiding punishments. But we also express feelings, aesthetic values, and self-concepts to recognize and affirm our attitudes, beliefs, and values. We are motivated to maintain and enhance our self-esteem and sense of competence to cope with our environment. Meaning is provided in the continuity of past, present, and future and the match between our behavior and our self-concept. Our self-concept is a composite of our identities as members of a nationality, social group, and sex, some of which are more important to us than others. Faith, as well as rational calculation, motivates us. Given this appreciation of human nature, it becomes possible to understand the different effects of transformational and transactional leaders on commitment.

By emphasizing the symbolic and expressive aspects of task–goal efforts and the important values involved, the transformational leader makes a moral statement. In contrast, the transactional leader stresses benefits to satisfy the self-interests of the follower. Under the transformational leader, participation in the efforts becomes an expression of membership and identity with a social collective. The salience of that identity is increased in the follower's self-concept, enhancing commitment.

The followers' self-esteem is reinforced by the transformational leader through expressions of confidence in the followers. High expectations are set by the transformational leader, which induce greater commitment to the effort. The Pygmalion effect—holding and subtly communicating high performance expectations for followers—has been demonstrated to positively influence followers' performance in organizations (Kierein & Gold, 2000; McNatt, 2000). This Pygmalion effect is presumably effective because it raises a particular form of self-esteem, or self-efficacy, in followers, instilling in them the idea that they can indeed perform up to high expectations and assuring them that the leader will help ensure that they have the means to do it (Eden & Sulimani, 2002).

By articulating a vision or a mission, the transformational leader increases the intrinsic value of goal accomplishment. Going beyond a transactional leader's specification and clarification of goals, the transformational leader presents the values in the goals. Accomplishment of the goals becomes more meaningful and consistent with the self-concepts of the followers. Emphasized also by the transformational leader is the importance of the goal as a basis for group identity, further connecting self-identity with group identity.

Intuitive elements in human aspirations that go beyond rational calculations are dwelt over by the transformational leader. If charismatic, they personify these as desires going beyond understanding and larger than life. An irrational bond is created between the leaders and the followers, providing the followers with a way of transcending the reasonable.

Charismatic and inspirational leaders instill faith in a better future for the followers in terms of their self-expression, self-evaluation, and self-consistency. Followers attribute their own extra effort to internal self-related causes rather than to extrinsic rewards, further adding to the followers' commitment to the cause, and to vague and distant goals. Faith in a better future is an intrinsically satisfying condition in itself.

Authentic Transformational Leadership and Follower Commitment

The concepts of authentic and inauthentic (pseudotransformational) leaders were introduced in chapter 1. Authentic transformational leaders are socialized. Commitment, involvement, and loyalty from followers derives from the truly transformational leader's referent power and esteem. At the other extreme are coercive, pseudotransformational leaders who are personalized in outlook. They use their power to reward and punish in arbitrary ways to dominate their followers. They tend to be authoritarian in attitude, self-aggrandizing, and exploitive of their followers. Manipulation, threats, and promises are used to induce compliance. Punishments may be capricious and noncontingent. They can be pseudotransformational in that followers fear loss of support from the powerful figures. Such tyrants are narcissistic, impetuous, and impulsively aggressive. They bring about obedience and compliance in followers, but it is less likely to be internalized. Commitment is public but not private. Commitment, involvement, and loyalty derive from dependence on the leader, resulting from fear of punishment or loss of the leader's affection.

The infamous Reverend Jim Jones, leader of the People's Temple, whose members engaged in a mass suicide, typified this extreme sort of inauthentic leadership. Jones would use his "divine powers" to both diagnose and cure his followers' supposed life-threatening diseases to make them feel indebted and increase commitment. He regularly used public punishment and threat to subjugate followers and provided and withheld affection and support to gain commitment (Mills, 1979).

Authentic transformational leaders such as Mahatma Gandhi or Martin Luther King, Jr., appealed ideologically to a better future for their followers without harming others. They talked about universal brotherhood. Such leaders looked to developing their followers and stimulated them intellectually. They were authentic—true to themselves and true to others. In contrast, personalized, pseudotransformational tyrants demand domination over others at the others' expense. Of Kelman's (1958) three different influence processes—compliance, identification, and internalization—socialized leaders try to achieve internalization. Convergence of values between leaders and followers is stressed. Personalized tyrants emphasize compliance (transactional) and identification (pseudotransformational). They demand unquestioning obedience. Pseudotransformational, personalized leaders bring about change by articulating goals that are ethnocentric or xenophobic (or both) deriving from the leaders' personality needs and motives. Followers achieve influence through personal identification with the leaders, dependence on the leaders for approval, and the need for followers to devote themselves to the leaders' interests.

In contrast to the commitment of followers that can be achieved by the socially oriented transformational leader, commitment under personalized pseudotransformational leaders is likely to be ephemeral for most followers, lasting only as long as the leader can continue to induce fear and promise in the followers either directly or as a consequence of conditioning. Furthermore, when commitment is a consequence of the power of a coercive leader, it may generate hostility, withdrawal, and overreaction (Bass, 1960).

In achieving internalization and commitment in followers, authentic, socialized transformational leaders foster changes in their individual self-concepts and in followers' collective sense of self-worth. There is evidence that transformational leaders' combination of charisma and individualized consideration makes followers' self-concept more readily accessible (Paul, Costley, Howell, Dorfman, & Trafimow, 2001). The followers' self-concept becomes closer to that of the leader. There is a greater sense of a collective identity and collective efficacy. Self-worth is enhanced. There is a drive to maintain consistency between followers' actions and their self-concepts. They are more committed to their roles. The meanings of their actions, roles, and identities come closer together. Self-efficacy and collective efficacy are enhanced (Shamir et al., 1993).

TRANSFORMATIONAL LEADERSHIP AND FOLLOWER SATISFACTION

Transformational leaders have more satisfied followers than nontransformational leaders. This is a strong and consistent finding. Two meta-analyses (Dumdum, Lowe, & Avolio, 2002; Lowe et al., 1996) show very high average correlations (ranging from .51 to .81) between all of the components of transformational leadership and measures of follower satisfaction. In comparison, mean correlations of contingent

TABLE 3.1
Relationship of MLQ Scales With Satisfaction

MLQ Scale	Number of r coefficients	Mean Raw r
Transformational	19	.35
Idealized Influence (Charismatic Behavior)	20	.54
Inspirational Motivation	24	.62
Intellectual Stimulation	26	.58
Individualized Consideration	26	.64
Transactional	5	.17
Contingent Reward	30	.60
Management-by-Exception	5	-.31
Management-by-Exception (Active)	19	-.07
Management-by-Exception (Passive)	18	-.35
Laissez-Faire	19	-.41

Note. Adapted from "A Meta-Analysis of Transformational and Transactional Leadership Correlates of Effectiveness and Satisfaction: An Update and Extension," by U. R. Dumdum, K. B Lowe, and B. J. Avolio, 2002, *Transformational and Charismatic Leadership: The Road Ahead*, pp. 35–66. Copyright 2002 by JAI/Elsevier. Adpated with permission.

reward and satisfaction are somewhat lower (rs = .34 to .60), and follower satisfaction tends to be negatively correlated with management-by-exception and laissez-faire leadership (see Table 3.1).

Another meta-analysis (DeGroot, Kiker, & Cross, 2000) looked only at charisma and follower commitment and satisfaction, although in many cases the measure of charisma was derived from the MLQ. They found that charisma correlated with follower commitment at r = .43 and with follower satisfaction at r = .77; these are results consistent with the other meta-analyses.

To some extent, the exceptionally high correlations between the components of transformational leadership and satisfaction are to be expected. Most often, followers provide both the ratings of the leader's possession of transformational leadership dimensions (i.e., using the MLQ) and the ratings of either their own job satisfaction or, more directly, their satisfaction with the leader. As expected, correlations for the MLQ dimensions are higher for followers' satisfaction with the leader than for followers' own job satisfaction (Dumdum et al., 2002).

Yet the correlations between having a transformational leader and being satisfied with one's job are still substantial. It is important to note that there is both a form of shared method variance in followers rating their leader in terms of transformational characteristics and then sometimes rating this same leader using the MLQ outcome scales. In addition, there may be a bleeding of these constructs into one another (i.e., more satisfied workers may simply feel more positive about their leaders). Despite these limitations, the connection between transformational leadership and follower satisfaction is likely substantial, as it should be. Leaders who are inspirational and show commitment to a cause or organization, who challenge their followers to think and provide input, and who show genuine concern for them (or, for that matter, leaders who contingently reward followers) should have more satisfied followers. The critical question is, does this then lead to other outcomes, such as better attendance at work, longer tenure with the organization, and better unit performance? There is some limited evidence of these connections. For example, Martin and Epitropaki (2001) found that followers of transformational leadership demonstrated greater commitment to their organizations as evidenced by their lowered intentions to turnover. Vandenberghe, Stordeur, and D'hoore (2002) also found that nurses following transformational leaders had lower turnover intentions. The impact of transformational leadership on performance is explored in the next chapter, but first we must set the stage by showing how increased follower commitment and satisfaction might affect factors connected to individual, group, and organizational performance.

The Role of Trust

Transformational leaders gain follower trust by maintaining their integrity and dedication, by being fair in their treatment of followers, and by demonstrating their faith in followers by empowering them. It has been suggested that one way that charismatic and transformational leaders can demonstrate their dedication and build follower trust is through self-sacrificial behaviors (Conger & Kanungo, 1998; House & Shamir, 1993). Leaders can self-sacrifice by taking on a proportionately larger workload, by foregoing the trappings of power (e.g., Gandhi's peasant lifestyle), or by postponing rewards, such as Chrysler's Lee Iacocca and Apple's Steve Jobs deciding to work for $1 a year (Choi & Mai-Dalton, 1999).

Podsakoff et al. (1990) explored the role that follower satisfaction with the leader and trust of the leader played in mediating the influence of transformational leadership on organizational citizenship behaviors (defined as followers engaging in helping behavior, expressing loyalty to the company, being conscientious, and treating others fairly; Organ, 1988). The results indicated that followers of transformational leaders were indeed better organizational citizens but that this effect was mediated by trust in and satisfaction with the leader. Pillai, Schriesheim, and Williams (1999) hypothesized that the transformational leader–follower commitment connection was mediated by both trust in the leader and perceptions of leader fairness. In a test of this model, they found partial support with both perceived leader fairness and followers' trust in the leader partly mediating the relationship between transformational leadership and organizational citizenship behaviors (but not job satisfaction and organizational commitment). Deluga (1995) also found a connection between trust in a leader and engagement in organizational citizenship behaviors. Taking these findings one step futher, one study found a connection between employees' engagement in organizational citizenship behaviors and actual employee turnover (Chen, Hui, & Sego, 1998). As has already been established, transformational leaders tend to enhance employees' organizational citizenship behaviors.

As more organizations make use of virtual work teams where members are connected electronically rather than face to face, the issue of leader trust becomes even more important. Avolio, Kahai, and Dodge (2000) assert that transformational leaders are better able to establish follower trust in e-teams than nontransformational leaders. Research by Hoyt and Blascovich (2003) provides evidence of this, finding that group members in virtual teams had greater trust in transformational leaders, which led to greater satisfaction with the leader and more work group cohesiveness.

The Role of Empowerment and Efficacy

Follower satisfaction and commitment can be the result of transformational leaders empowering followers. For example, in a study of nurses, follower empowerment mediated the relationship between transformational leadership and job satisfaction (Fuller, Morrison, Jones, Bridger, & Brown, 1999).

It can be argued that transformational leaders empower followers to perform their jobs autonomously and creatively and that this empowerment leads followers to feel more efficacious. This in turn leads to both greater follower commitment and to better group performance. Jung and Sosik (2002) found just this in a study of groups of Korean workers. Transformational leaders empowered followers whose collective sense of efficacy increased and had a positive impact on performance. Another study of banking leaders in China and India found that followers' sense of collective efficacy mediated the relationship between transformational leadership and organizational commitment (Walumbwa, Wang, Lawler, & Shi, 2004).

The Role of Emotions

Dasborough and Ashkanasy (2002) assert that leadership is intrinsically an emotional process, in which leaders display emotions to evoke emotional reactions in followers. This should be particularly true for transformational and charismatic leaders, who use inspirational motivation to encourage followers. Leaders presumably can affect the overall affective climate of a group and levels of job satisfaction. In a meta-analysis, Connolly and Viswesvaran (2000) demonstrated a connection between positive affective states and job satisfaction.

McColl-Kennedy and Anderson (2002) found that transformational leaders have a positive impact on followers' sense of optimism, which facilitates group performance. In addition, transformational leadership helped followers overcome the negative affect associated with instances of frustration. In all likelihood, good leadership helps buffer the negative affect generated when a group encounters a roadblock to successful performance (Pirola-Merlo, Hartel, Mann, & Hirst, 2002).

Transference.   Kets de Vries (1994) likened a leader to a psychiatric social worker, who can become a container for the emotions of the followers. The empathy of the individually considerate leader can cause this to happen in the leader–follower relationship. As a consequence, some psychodynamic transference may result, which in turn promotes the followers' attachment to the individually considerate leader and the leader's organizational interests. This issue is discussed in psychodynamic perspectives on the charismatic leader (e.g., Schiffer, 1973).

Perceived Leader Competence.   The charismatic component of transformational leadership involves a variety of dynamics; one that enhances the commitment of followers to charismatic leaders is the followers' perception of the competence of the leader. In turn, the leader "creates the impression of competence and success" (House, 1977). So obedience and allegiance to the transformational leader are seen by followers as ways to ensure their own competence. Leaders "communicate high expectations of, and confidence in followers" (House, 1977), generating the Pygmalion effect (Eden & Ravid, 1982). Followers are moved to fulfill the leader's prophecies of confidence in them. The followers accept the leader's goals and believe they can contribute to reaching the goals; their motivation to achieve the goals is aroused.

Disinhibition. Disinhibition in the followers may occur when they endow the leader with charisma and become emotionally aroused. In their excitation by the leader, their judgments may be restricted and their inhibition reduced (Schiffer, 1973). "The sense of reality of the charismatic leaders and their followers are inordinately affected by psychodynamic mechanisms such as projection, repression, and disassociation" (Bass, 1985, p. 56). The charismatic leader may become a catalyst for rationalization by the followers as they develop shared norms and fantasies about the leader and what the leader can accomplish for them (Hummel, 1973). Charismatic leadership is most likely to emerge when followers are under stress or in a state of crises. The charismatic leader has the temerity to propose radical solutions to deal with the stress or crises, which further enhances his or her esteem in the eyes of the followers (Weber, 1924/1947). The more general effects of transformational leadership on stress and crisis conditions are the subject of chapter 5.

CONCLUSIONS

It is clear that transformational leaders are able to build strong follower commitment and loyalty. Building on follower trust and promoting follower self-esteem and self-efficacy create more satisfied followers, generally, and followers who are more satisfied with the quality of their leadership than the followers of nontransformational leaders.

4

Transformational Leadership and Performance

In *Leadership and Performance Beyond Expectations,* Bass (1985) addresses the question of why some leaders elicit competent performance from their followers, whereas other leaders inspire extraordinary effort and outcomes. Of course, the answer is that transformational leadership makes the difference. However, there are many ways to think about leadership and performance.

One approach to the study of performance is to focus on what leaders themselves do. What behaviors do they engage in, and are they the "right" kinds of behaviors to effectively lead? In a very simple sense, does a leader look and act like a leader? When it comes to decision making, do leaders make the correct decisions or do they make the morally right decisions?

Another way to conceptualize leader performance is to focus on the outcomes of the leader's followers, group, team, unit, or organization. In evaluating this type of leader performance, two general strategies are typically used. The first relies on subjective perceptions of the leader's performance from subordinates, superiors, or occasionally peers or other parties. The other type of effectiveness measures are more objective indicators of follower or unit performance, such as measures of productivity, goal attainment, sales figures, or unit financial performance.

THE EFFECTIVENESS
OF TRANSFORMATIONAL LEADERS

In the past 20 years, many studies have examined transformational leadership and performance in a wide variety of settings. For example, transformational leadership has been shown to relate positively to performance in U.S. and North American companies (e.g., LeBrasseur, Whissell, & Ojha, 2002; Seltzer & Bass, 1990), in Russian companies (Elenkov, 2002), and in companies in Korea (Jung & Sosik, 2002) and New Zealand (Singer, 1985). It is important in military (e.g., Bass, Avolio, Jung, & Berson, 2003; Masi & Cooke, 2000), private sector (e.g., Hater & Bass, 1988; Yammarino & Dubinsky, 1994), governmental (e.g. Wofford, Whittington, & Goodwin, 2001), educational (Harvey, Royal, & Stout, 2003; Tucker, Bass, & Daniel, 1990) and nonprofit organizations (e.g., Egri & Herman, 2000; Riggio, Bass, & Orr, 2004). Transformational leadership is related to the effectiveness of groups of salespersons (e.g., Jolson, Dubinsky, Yammarino, & Comer, 1993; MacKenzie, Podsakoff, & Rich, 2001), health care workers (Gellis, 2001; Bycio et al., 1995), high school principals (Hoover, Petrosko, & Schulz, 1991; Kirby, Paradise, & King, 1992), and even athletes (Charbonneau, Barling, & Kelloway, 2001) and prison workers (Walters, 1998).

As was the case with the relationship between transformational leadership and follower satisfaction, leader scores on the transformational leadership scales of the Multifactor Leadership Questionnaire (MLQ) substantially correlated with measures of leader effectiveness (mean rs equal to or greater than .60 from one meta-analysis [Lowe et al., 1996] and equal to or greater than .46 from the other meta-analysis [Dumdum et al., 2002]). In both cases, contingent reward also strongly correlated with leader effectiveness, although not as great in magnitude as the transformational components, whereas the other leadership styles in the Full Range of Leadership (FRL) model (e.g., management-by-exception) did not correlate or were negatively correlated with leader effectiveness.

As might be expected, the relationships between transformational leadership components and subjective measures of leader effectiveness are much stronger (rs in the .50–.70 range) than the relationships between transformational leadership and objective measures (rs ranging from .17 to .30; see Tables 4.1a & 4.1b). (These are mean raw correlation coefficients that have not been corrected for attenua-

TABLE 4.1a
Relationship of MLQ Scales With Effectiveness

MLQ Scale	Number of r coefficients	Mean Raw r
Transformational	45	.43
Idealized Influence (Charismatic Behavior)	43	.52
Inspirational Motivation	70	.46
Intellectual Stimulation	76	.47
Individualized Consideration	82	.47
Transactional	18	.15
Contingent Reward	80	.45
Management-by-Exception	8	−.23
Management-by-Exception (Active)	65	.06
Management-by-Exception (Passive)	44	−.28
Laissez-Faire	70	−.29

Note. Adapted from "A Meta-Analysis of Transformational and Transactional Leadership Correlates of Effectiveness and Satisfaction: An Update and Extension," by U. R. Dumdum, K. B Lowe, and B. J. Avolio, 2002, *Transformational and Charismatic Leadership: The Road Ahead*, pp. 35–66. Copyright 2002 by JAI/Elsevier. Adapted with permission.

TABLE 4.1b
Relationship of MLQ Scales With Effectiveness

MLQ Scale	Subjective Measures		Objective Measures	
	Number of r coefficients	Mean Raw r	Number of r coefficients	Mean Raw r
Transformational				
Charisma	32	.71	15	.30
Intellectual Stimulation	31	.58	14	.22
Individualized Consideration	29	.59	12	.24
Transactional				
Contingent Reward	28	.46	15	.07
Management-by-Exception	29	.07	12	−.03

Note. Adapted from "Effectiveness Correlates of Transformational Leadership: A Meta-Analytic Review of the MLQ Literature," by K. B. Lowe, K. G. Kroek, N. Sivasubramaniam, 1996, *Leadership Quarterly, 7*(3), pp. 385–425. Copyright 1996 by JAI/Elsevier. Adapted with permission.

tion, so the actual effect sizes may be larger than what the coefficients suggest.)

A more recent meta-analysis by Judge and Piccolo (2004) found similar results as previous meta-analyses, with both transformational leadership and contingent reward having strong positive relationships to follower job satisfaction, satisfaction with the leader, and follower motivation (corrected correlations ranging from .53 to .71) but weaker relationships with group or organizational performance (.26 for transformational leadership; .16 for contingent reward). As expected, relationships between management-by-exception and laissez-faire leadership and follower satisfaction and performance ranged from slightly positive to negative. Importantly, and consistent with previous results, transformational leadership had an augmentation effect when controlling for the effects of transactional leadership.

In summary, it appears that transformational leadership positively affects performance, regardless of whether performance is conceptualized as what others in the unit or organization (i.e., subordinates, superiors) perceive as performance or whether performance relates to more objective, bottom-line sorts of variables. The critical element is to understand the process of how transformational leaders affect follower and unit performance.

The Dynamics of Performance Beyond Expectations

Shamir et al.'s (1993) formal theory, presented earlier, explained how and why charismatic-transformational leadership moves followers to exceed expectations in performance. In short, transformational leaders enhance the self-concepts of followers and encourage followers' personal and collective identification with both the leader's and the organization's goals and objectives. This is further enhanced by the follower becoming engaged in the challenges of the mission as set forth by the transformational leader, the identification of the follower's self with the successful leader and team effort, the exciting experience of unexpected discoveries, and a sense of empowerment by way of association with a successful leader. The resulting performance is beyond what would be motivated by other forms of leadership, such as purely transactional behavior. Broken down, this theory suggests several mediators affecting the relationship between transformational leadership and exceptional performance. First, transformational leaders enhance the self-concept and sense of self-efficacy of followers. Self-efficacy has been shown to consistently enhance both individual and group performance (Bandura, 1997; Stajkovic & Luthans, 1998). Second, identification with the leader, both individually and collectively, and identification with the group or unit are important. Third, shared or aligned goals and values are key to motivating follower performance. Finally, the transformational leader empowers followers to perform beyond expectations. We consider each of the first three mediators of the transformational leadership–performance relationship briefly here and focus on the role of empowerment and transformational leadership in chapter 13.

In a very interesting study, Kahai and colleagues (Kahai, Sosik, & Avolio, 2003) demonstrated that groups of students engaged in a collective task engaged in social loafing (a "counterproductive" behavior) when working under transactional leaders. However, transformational leadership seemed to reduce the incidence of social loafing. It may very well be the case that transformational leadership not only increases the performance of individuals and groups but also may work to lessen the impact of counterproductive work behaviors, presumably because transformational leaders are able to get followers committed to collective goals, rather than just to their own personal goals.

Self-Concept/Self-Efficacy. House (1977) first suggested that charismatic-transformational leaders communicated both their confidence in followers and the expectations that they could perform at high levels. Kirkpatrick and Locke (1996) found that followers' self-efficacy (along with performance goals) mediated the relationship between charismatic leadership and performance. The enhancement of followers' self-concepts and increases in their sense of self-efficacy likely occur partly through the leader's direct influence on followers and partly through a sense of collective efficacy among members of the group, team, or unit. Bandura (1997) characterizes collective self-efficacy as "a group's shared belief in its conjoint capabilities to organize and execute the courses of action required to produce given levels of attainment" (p. 477). A recent study found that a leader's self-efficacy predicted followers' collective sense of self-efficacy, which in turn predicted the group's task performance (Hoyt, Murphy, Halverson, & Watson, 2003). In another study, transformational leadership had a positive impact on the sense of work group potency (i.e., collective efficacy), which in turn had positive effects on group performance (Sosik, Avolio, Kahai, & Jung, 1998).

In a similar vein, transformational leaders' ability to influence followers' collective sense of optimism and buffer the experience of frustration has a positive impact on group performance (McColl-Kennedy & Anderson, 2002). Chemers and his associates (Chemers, 1997, 2002; Chemers, Watson, & May, 2000; Watson, Chemers & Preiser, 2001) also emphasize the role that optimism and a collective sense of efficacy play in leadership and group effectiveness.

In an interesting longitudinal study of leaders in a teaching hospital, it was found that transformational leadership led to higher morale in work teams, which in turn led to greater work group innovation that directly benefited patients (Wilson-Evered, Hartel, & Neale, 2001). The authors believe that increased self-confidence/efficacy among the followers was the primary reason for the high morale and subsequent innovative behaviors.

Identification With the Leader.   Leaders who are, or who appear to be, competent engender follower identification with the leader. In addition, confidence and trust in a leader also strengthen the followers' identification with the leader. This identification with a competent, trustworthy leader may be an important determinant of follower commitment to performance goals and outcomes. Moreover, transformational leaders who are entrepreneurial and champions for the group or organization may help spur positive entrepreneurial activities in followers (Elkins & Keller, 2003; Howell & Higgins, 1990).

Aligned Goals and Values.   In a study of workers in a disaster relief organization, transformational leadership as measured by the MLQ was related to the alignment of leader and follower values (Krishnan, 2002). Another study of hospital chief executive officers (CEOs) suggested that the transformational leader's ability to align the conflicting goals of quality patient care and cost cutting are critical elements for successful team performance (LeBrasseur et al., 2002). Sparks and Schenck (2001) argued that transformational leaders are able to encourage followers' belief in the higher purposes of the work, which builds follower commitment, effort, and performance.

Studies by Barling, Loughlin, and Kelloway (2002) illustrated how transformational leaders can use value alignment to influence group performance. Using leaders and workers in the fast food industry, this research demonstrated that transformational leaders are able to raise the safety consciousness of followers, which in turn leads to an increased safety climate and reduced incidence of accidents and injuries. Barling et al. discussed how the components of transformational leadership come into play in the area of safety: Managers use idealized influence to model safety-conscious behavior, make inspirational appeals to achieve safety records, and use intellectual stimulation to encourage innovative safety strategies. In addition, these transformational leaders demonstrate individualized consideration by showing an active concern for followers' physical safety and health.

We have already seen that transformational leadership is related to follower commitment and job satisfaction and that it is partially mediated by leader fairness and trust in the leader. As Shamir et al. (1993) suggest, shared goals or values should also be important in fostering commitment, which should in turn positively affect performance. In a straightforward experiment designed to test this hypothesis, Jung and Avolio (2000) had groups of students work on a brainstorming task. Groups were assigned a confederate leader, who was either trained to display a transformational or a transactional leadership style. Measures of trust in the leader, leader–follower value congruence, and followers' satisfaction with the leader were collected. Objective measures of quantity and quality of task output were also obtained. The results clearly supported the positive relationships between transformational leadership and trust and value congruence. However, trust and value congruence only partially mediated the relationship between transformational leadership and performance, suggesting that other mediators exist.

Hoyt and Blascovich (2003) found that transactional leaders elicited greater quantitative performance, whereas transformational leaders elicited greater qualitative performance. They suggest that trust mediated the relationship between transformational leadership and quality of work.

Transformational Leadership and Creativity

Rather than focusing on performance only in quantitative terms, transformational leadership should also have a positive impact on the quality of follower and group performance. Transformational leaders should be better equipped to motivate followers to be more creative in their efforts and products via inspirational motivation (Sosik, Kahai, & Avolio, 1998, 1999). Similarly, the transformational component of intellectual stimulation should encourage followers to greater innovation and creativity. Indeed, Mumford and colleagues (Mumford, Connelly, & Gaddis, 2003; Mumford, Scott, Gaddis, & Strange, 2002) suggest that in today's creative work groups leaders are more likely to be involved in stimulating followers' creativity and evaluating their creative products, rather than being the source of the group's innovation. Sosik (1997) found that computer-mediated groups with transformational leaders generated more original solutions, more supportive remarks, and greater solution clarification and asked more questions about solutions than did groups with transactional leaders. Moreover, groups with transformational leaders reported higher levels of perceived performance, extra effort, and satisfaction. Jung (2001) found that transformational leaders promote higher levels of creativity, as measured by the divergent thinking of group members, than did transactional leaders.

Research by Jung, Chow, and Wu (2003) suggests how transformational leadership might affect creativity. First, transformational leaders increase followers' intrinsic motivation (as opposed to the transactional leaders' emphasis on extrinsic motivation), which stimulates creativity (see also Shin & Zhou, 2003). Second, the intellectually stimulating transformational leader encourages followers to think "outside of the box" (see also Elkins & Keller, 2003). Their results show that transformational leaders primarily encourage follower creativity and innovation by providing a climate that supports followers' innovative efforts.

Other Effects on Performance of Transformational Leadership

In later chapters, we detail how transformational leadership contributes to coping with stress and crisis conditions, how transformational leaders help initiate and implement change processes, and how transformational leaders develop the leadership capacity of followers. Here, however, we briefly review these elements of leader performance.

Transformational Leadership and Coping With Stress/Crisis. Paradoxically, highly committed employees, for instance, those who take their work home with them at night and are highly ego involved in their work, may experience more stress than those who are indifferent to their work. Nonetheless, transformational leaders both enhance follower commitment and, at the same time, serve to reduce employees' feelings of stress. Thus, another indicator of the effectiveness of transformational leadership involves reducing feelings of stress as well as providing the tools to help followers cope with stress and crisis. Indeed, as we show in the next chapter, transactional leadership increases feelings of stress, whereas transformational leadership decreases such feelings.

Transformational Leadership and Implementing Change. Transformational leadership, particularly its charismatic elements, has been associated with producing change in groups and organizations. Indeed, the notion of change was central to Weber's (1947) notion of charisma, and to Burns's (1978) concept of the transforming leader. Unfortunately, there has been relatively little research directly examining how transformational leadership affects change in organizations. However, a recent study by Waldman, Javidan, and Varella (2004) found that CEO charisma and intellectual stimulation as measured by the MLQ were related to strategic organizational change and to company performance. We explore how transformational leadership affects an organization in chapters 7 and 9.

Transformational Leadership and Developing Leaders. A core element of transformational leadership is the development of followers to enhance their capabilities and their capacity to lead. Sosik and colleagues note the similarities between transformational leadership and effective mentoring (Sosik & Godshalk, 2000; Sosik, Godshalk, & Yammarino, 2004):

> [B]oth mentors and transformational leaders act as role models who encourage learning and development, and work to develop others' self-confidence, personal identity, and well-being. Thus, transformational leaders likely serve as mentors, and mentors likely exhibit various degrees of transformational leadership behavior. (Sosik et al., 2004, p. 245)

Therefore, a major determinant of the effective performance of transformational leaders may be the extent to which the leaders are able to have a positive influence on followers' development—an outcome that is often ignored in evaluating leader effectiveness. Sosik and Godshalk (2000) found that transformational leaders were more likely than nontransformational leaders to provide good mentoring (e.g., providing career development advice, providing networking opportunities) to proteges. Levy, Cober, and Miller (2002) found that followers of transformational leaders were more likely than followers of transactional leaders to seek feedback that would help in their development. In addition, transformational leadership tended to have a stress-buffering effect on followers such that proteges of transformational leaders reported less job-related stress. We explore more fully the relationship between transformational leadership and stress and crisis in the next chapter.

CONCLUSIONS

A common criticism (and misconception) of transformational leadership is that it is all smoke and mirrors—a feel-good type of leadership that leads to happy followers but does not affect group performance. However, it is clear that transformational leadership does indeed affect group performance, regardless of whether performance is measured subjectively or by more objective means. Moreover, transformational leadership does lead to performance beyond expectations in relation to transactional leadership. What is often overlooked is how transformational leaders help develop followers to be better contributors to the group effort—more creative, more resistant to stress, more flexible and open to change, and more likely to one day become transformational leaders themselves.

5

Stress and Transformational Leadership

The terrorist attack of September 11, 2001, on the World Trade Center was one of the greatest modern crises to strike any U.S. city. It offered the opportunity for leaders to demonstrate transformational leadership under a time of serious emergency and stress. A number of leaders played important parts in New York City's recovery. Mayor Rudy Giuliani was the most visible leader, and he displayed many transformational leadership qualities following the attacks (Giuliani & Kurson, 2002):

> New York City Mayor Rudolph Giuliani arrived at the World Trade Center within minutes of the first attack. . . . In the days and weeks that followed, he would conduct several press conferences in the vicinity of the destroyed towers, attend many funerals and memorial services, and maintain what seemed like a ubiquitous presence in the city. His visibility, combined with his decisiveness, candor, and compassion, lifted the spirits of all New Yorkers—indeed, of all Americans. (Argenti, 2002, p. 104)

Leaders can help their groups cope with stress in many ways. For instance, individuals, groups, or organizations may be paralyzed into inertia and disbelief when faced with a crisis in which they are seriously threatened. Such was the case on September 11, 2001. Transformational leaders can use idealized influence to portray a leader who is not panicking. A leader who is concerned but calm, who is decisive but not impulsive, and who is clearly in charge can inspire the confidence and trust of followers. Clearly in the aftermath of the World Trade Center disaster, Mayor Giuliani's calm, authoritative demeanor helped to calm a panicked and anxious citizenry.

Transformational leaders may also do better in a crisis because, unlike directive or transactional leaders who focus on short-term results and who may be prone to hasty, poorly thought-out decisions, transformational leaders are more likely to delay premature choices among options. Transformational leaders are also more likely to call for follower input in reconsidering proposals, stimulate followers to develop creative solutions to problems, and be more resistant to public pressure to "act now." In the immediate aftermath of the September 11, 2001, terrorist attacks, charismatic Southwest Airlines chief executive officer (CEO), Herb Kelleher, called together his decision-making team. Through extensive discussion, the team decided not to follow other airlines in cutting back personnel and services, instead taking a long-term strategy of continuing to offer reliable service, which paid off for the airline.

When action is called for, the transformational leader in a crisis can use inspirational appeals to arouse and motivate followers. World War II leaders Winston Churchill and Franklin Delano Roosevelt (FDR) used radio broadcasts to inspire their respective citizenry. FDR needed to motivate support for U.S. involvement in the war, and Churchill used inspirational appeals to bolster the flagging spirits of the British people during nightly enemy bombing raids.

When their followers are engaged in defensive avoidance, transformational leaders bring them back to reality. Panic can be reduced or avoided by inspirational leadership that points the way to safety. In general, groups with leaders, transactional or transformational, are likely to cope better with stress than those without such leadership. When groups and organizations are under stress, more directiveness from leaders is expected and desired. During times of social stress, inspirational leadership is expected to revise missions, define common objectives, restructure situations, and suggest solutions to deal with the sources of stress and conflict (Downton, 1973). Yet, as we discuss later, although such directive leadership is most expected, desired, and successful in influencing the course of events when stress is high, it may not always be effective in coping with the stress.

LEADERSHIP AND STRESS

Groups and organizations experience stress when confronted with threats to their steady states of well-being (Janis & Mann, 1977). In many instances, leadership makes the difference in coping with the stress. Decision making is likely to suffer unless effective leadership is provided that can help foster the quality of the decision. In the acute stress of emergencies and disasters, panic is prevented by leaders who encourage advanced preparation and well-trained, well-organized, credible systems. The 1993 terrorist bombing of the World Trade Center resulted in New York City's increased readiness and preparation for future attacks, which made the reaction to the 2001 attack more effective. In addition, in the aftermath of the World Trade Center attacks, Mayor Giuliani was constantly on television, flanked by the city's high-ranking police and fire officials to provide professional, credible updates regarding the current state of the crisis.

In situations of chronic stress, transformational and charismatic leadership helps followers deal with the stress and its effects. Chronic stress is better handled when leaders transform personal concerns into efforts to achieve group goals. Leadership that is charismatic and inspirational has been shown to reduce feelings of burnout and symptoms of stress in professionals (Seltzer, Numerof, & Bass, 1989).

Stressful environments contain much uncertainty, volatility, and turbulence. Business and start-up ventures, mergers, acquisitions and divestitures, economic downturns, new competitive challenges, erosion of market share, and rapid technology changes can all create stresses and dislocations. Combat often involves surprise, threat, and unforeseen contingencies. In government and nonprofit organizations, significant loss of funding can throw an organization into a state of crisis and turmoil. In addition, and as seen in recent years, ethical scandals can shake the very foundations of well-established entities.

Under crisis-ridden or uncertain conditions, transactional leaders, who are reactive and depend on old rules and regulations to maintain and control the system, are unlikely to help followers cope with the situation. More effective are transformational leaders, who are proactive, break with tradition, provide innovative solutions, and institutionalize new arrangements (Bass, 1990b).

Hasty Decision Making

When followers are under stress, speedy decisions are likely to be readily accepted (Janis, 1982). Followers exchange their desires for deliberation, participation, and time to reflect for the promise of speedy delivery from the distressing conditions. But speedy decisions do not necessarily provide the best solutions to the problems facing the followers. The speed of the decisions may result in inadequate solutions to the stressful circumstances. The decisions are likely to lack the inclusion of careful structuring and support. Generally, rapid decision making is sought in crisis and disasters and is effective if the decisions are not hastily made at the last minute but are based on advanced warning, preparation, and organization, along with commitment and support.

According to Fiedler's cognitive resources theory (Fiedler, 2002; Fiedler & Garcia, 1987), experienced leaders perform better under stress, presumably because they are better prepared, organized, and practiced at their craft. This is in contrast to more intelligent but less experienced leaders, who may waste time trying to analyze the situation and come up with the perfect solution (Zaccaro, 1995).

In emergencies when danger threatens, followers want to be told what to do—and in a hurry. They believe that they have no time to consider alternatives. Rapid, decisive leadership is demanded. Leaders who fail to make decisions quickly are judged as inadequate. Leaders speed up their decision making as a consequence of stress and crises. Failure to do so leads to their rejection as leaders. Acceptance of their rapid, arbitrary decisions without consultation, negotiation, or participation is also increased. A leader who can react quickly in emergencies is judged as better by followers than one who cannot (Korten, 1962). Taking prompt action in emergency situations differentiated those judged to be better military officers from those judged as worse in performance. Particularly at lower levels in the military organization, emphasized is the rapidity of response to orders from higher authority. This is despite that most units seldom operate under combat conditions (Stouffer, Suchman, DeVinney, Star, & Williams, 1949).

Where rapid decisions are called for, executives are likely to manage-by-exception. The more organizations wish to be prepared for emergency action, the more the executives are likely to stress a high degree of structure, attention to orders, and active management-by-exception by their supervisors. When 181 airmen gave their opinions about missile teams, rescue teams, scientific teams, or other small crews facing emergencies, the majority strongly agreed that they should respond to the orders of the commander with less question than under normal conditions. In an emergency, the commander was expected to "check more closely to see that everyone is carrying out his responsibility" (Torrance, 1957). Similarly, Mulder, deJong, Koppelaar, and

Verhage (1986) reported that Dutch naval officers were more favorably evaluated by their superiors and subordinates if they used their formal power when facing crisis situations. More direction was sought from the officers akin to contingent reinforcement using the power to reward and discipline.

But this kind of arbitrary decision making may prove costly. For example, in three research and development organizations, stress was caused by a reduction in available research funds. This resulted in strong internal pressures for controls on spending and top management control and direction. There was a reduction in individualized consideration reflected in reduced consultation with the researchers. Subsequently, researchers' satisfaction and identification with the organization declined (Hall & Mansfield, 1971).

To conclude, directive leadership is preferred and successful in influencing followers under stress. Hasty decision making is likely to be promoted, possibly providing instant or temporary relief, but may fail to deal with the root causes of the stress. Such leadership may be counterproductive in the long run.

Leaders as the Cause of Stress

Indeed, leadership may contribute to stress. Personalized, self-aggrandizing, charismatic leaders can cause more stress among their followers, for instance, when they excite a mob to take hasty actions. Pseudotransformational political leaders manufacture crises to enhance their own power, to divert public attention from real problems, and to gain public support for their own arbitrary actions. Thus, leadership may cause rather than ameliorate stressful conditions that result in emotionally driven actions by the followers and poorer long-term outcomes. And the leaders who emerge are likely to be different from those in unstressed situations.

Transactional leaders, particularly those who rely on management-by-exception, who emphasize reactive corrective actions, may actually increase stress in their followers; transformational leaders who emphasize charismatic, inspirational, and individualized consideration and proactive vigilant solutions are likely to reduce the feelings of stress in their followers. As noted in chapter 3, transformational leadership raises the self-esteem of followers. Transactional leadership that is coercive in its promises and threats does the opposite, lowering the self-esteem of followers who feel stressed, angry, subjugated, and victimized by the coercive leader. In support of this idea, Atwater, Camobreco, Dionne, Avolio, and Lau (1997) found that leader noncontingent punishment elicited negative emotional reactions from followers.

Seltzer et al. (1989) found that, when other factors were held constant, transactional leaders, those in particular who practiced management-by-exception, increased the felt stress and job burnout among their subordinates. In a series of experiments, Misumi (1985) showed that production-oriented leadership, with comments such as "work more quickly," "work accurately," "you could do more," and "hurry up, we haven't much time left," generated detectable physiological stress symptoms. Systolic and diastolic blood pressure increased in experimental subjects as compared to control subjects, as did galvanic skin responses. In similar experiments, production-oriented leadership caused feelings of hostility and anxiety about the experiments.

Abrasive leaders use their power to coerce their followers. This causes stress. For many subordinates, immediate supervisors may be the most stressful aspect of the work situation (e.g., Herzberg, 1966). Tyrannical bosses are frequently mentioned as a main source of stress on the job. This becomes most extreme when the transactional leader says, "Either you do as I say or else." Such leaders base the transaction or exchange on their power to coerce their followers (Bass, 1960). In addition, the leaders themselves may be personally more prone to stress. Sanders and Malkis (1982) found that Type A (stress-prone) personalities were nominated more often as leaders than Type Bs. However, the fewer Type Bs who were chosen as leaders tended to be more effective as individuals in the assigned task than were the Type A leaders.

Defensive Avoidance

As already noted, often it is the leaders themselves who contrive the threats, crises, and ambiguities that lead to stress. For millennia, pseudotransformational political leaders have used real or fictitious threats as the way to increase cohesion among their followers and to gain unquestioning support for themselves. Other nations or groups are characterized as "evil" or potential threats as a means to increase within-group cohesiveness (see Shaw, 1981). Often, such leaders arise in crises of national weakness, dislocation, and of institutional breakdown. Pseudotransformational leaders provide ready-made, immediate solutions that soothe, flatter, and exalt the public. Defensive avoidance is promoted. Blame is directed elsewhere. The same leaders also are transactional when they say, "If you follow me and do exactly what I say, you will escape harm from the forces that I've told you are threatening your well-being." The success of such leaders in being influential depends on how seemingly charismatic and inspirational they are, but they are unlikely to be effective in the long run in dealing with the true problems.

Even when pseudotransformational business and government leaders appear to consult and share decisions with subordinates in times of crises (Berkowitz, 1953), they may often do so because they seek support from their subordinates regarding the wisdom of the solutions the leaders have already chosen. These leaders may only appear to be sharing decision making, when in reality they are merely looking for affirmation for the decisions they have made without true consultation and input from followers. Even worse, these leaders may appear to share the decision in an effort to spread the blame from themselves to others should the decision go awry.

LEADERSHIP AND CRISES

Crises call for special leadership talents.

> "Crisis" refers to a situation facing an organization which requires that the organization, under time constraints, engage in new, untested, unlearned behaviors in order to obtain or maintain its desired goal states . . . a crisis requires uncertain action under time pressure. When uncertain action is required without time pressure, the situation may be viewed as a problem rather than a crisis. When required actions and outcomes are known but when time pressure exists, organizations engage standard, albeit critical, procedures or routines. (Krackhardt & Stern, 1988, p. 125)

In such organizational crises, Krackhardt and Stern emphasized the importance of adaptation and cooperation that subsequently require trust and friendly relationships. Such trust can be created by charismatic and inspirational leaders, and such relationships can be developed by individually considerate leaders. This suggests that the organization is in better shape to handle crises, uncertainty, and threats of required change if headed by transformational leaders.

THE DYNAMICS OF CHARISMA
AND CRISIS

Weber (1924/1947) noted that charismatic leaders are likely to emerge during times of instability, crisis, and turmoil. Such times increase the feelings among people of helplessness, agitation, anxiety, and frustration. They accept the directions of charismatic leaders who appear to be qualified to lead them out of their distress. This potential for reducing stress creates the "special emotional intensity of the charismatic response. . . . Followers respond to the charismatic leader with passionate loyalty because the salvation, or promise of it, that he appears to embody represents the fulfillment of urgently felt needs" (Tucker, 1970, p. 81).

Those under stress and seeking its relief readily respond zealously to leaders who strengthen their faith in that relief. By calling for a transcendental goal or innovative mission to relieve the stress, charismatic leaders induce renewal and mobilize collective efforts to face the stress or crisis. Radical changes and bold, unconventional actions are advocated, consistent with followers' own ideologies, values, and beliefs. Without such collective perception of crisis or stress, charismatic leadership is less likely to appear. In that case, there is no need for an exceptional leader with radical solutions. If charismatic leadership is attempted under such circumstances, the attempts are seen as unsettling and likely to disturb stability, continuity, and certainty (Conger & Kanungo, 1988; Howell, 1992).

Nonetheless, charismatic leadership does occur in the absence of crisis or distress (Conger & Kanungo, 1998). Personally seeking to shake up the status quo, charismatic leaders, particularly the pseudotransformational personalized ones, identify and exaggerate existing shortcomings in the situation and the grievances of followers. They create dissatisfaction with the status quo so that followers are motivated to accept the radical solutions that the charismatic leaders advocate to eliminate the distressful problems (Conger & Kanungo, 1988).

Some of the stress and sense of crisis of charismatic leaders, particularly those at the head of organizations, may be felt by themselves as they manufacture it for their followers. Other stresses may be felt by those at the top. There is the well-known experience of loneliness of command. Leaders may find themselves, when at the top, without the collegial supports to which they had been accustomed. Each of their moves carries a lot of responsibility and symbolic meaning. Their own dependency needs cannot be met. Yet they also are envied for their power and position, which can be a cause of anxiety for them. They fear losing their power and position because of envy, and a dysfunctional consequence is that they may fear being too innovative or too successful. A cause of both depression and possible adventurism for those who are at the top is the feeling that there is nothing else to strive for (Kets de Vries, 1994).

Janis and Mann (1977) argued that the completely rational approach to an authentic threat requires vigilant reponses—a full examination of objectives, of values, and of alternative course of action. Costs and risks of various alternatives should be weighed. And the final choice should be based on a cost–benefit analysis. Careful development, implementation, and contingency planning are also part of the vigilant response to threat. Yet such vigilance—thorough search, appraisal, and contingency planning—is short-circuited by the emotional arousal of the side-effects of the impending threat observed in the irrational reactions to crises. These defective reactions include the fixed adherence to the status quo, a too hasty change, defensive avoidance, or panic. Whether formal or informal, leadership makes a difference in whether followers act rationally or irrationally in coping with stress and crisis conditions.

Often in times of crisis, informal leadership is likely to emerge if the formal authorities and emergency services cannot deal with the crisis events (Mileti, Drabek, & Haas, 1975). The direct removal of the threats and obstacles that are the source of stress may be facilitated by supportive (individually considerate) informal leadership. On the other hand, pseudotransformational leaders whose goal is to use a crisis to seize greater power may increase the stress and increase anxieties. The authentic transformational leader seeks to reduce these anxieties by providing supportive, individually considerate leadership that results in an increasing sense of security.

TRANSFORMATIONAL LEADERSHIP AND COPING WITH STRESS AND CRISES

Dealing With Panic and Disasters

The most effective leaders in helping groups to escape from panic conditions begin with transformational support and encouragement, then concentrate on the transactional performance requirements (Misumi & Sako, 1982). A panic situation was simulated with 672 Japanese undergraduates in 6-person groups. Recorded were the students' aggressiveness, jamming up, and escapes. Aggression was lowest, and escaping occurred most often when leaders focused both on performance planning and on maintenance of relationships (the PM condition), rather than when they focused only on performance planning or maintenance of relationships or when they focused on neither (Misumi, 1985). When subjects dealing with a maze under fearful and unfearful conditions were compared (Kugihara & Misumi, 1984), again PM leadership generated the least fear, the largest amount of planning, and the least feelings of unreasonable pressure from the leader.

In an experimental study of the panic condition, when too many people try to escape through the same door, the stressed group preferred a strong, nonelected leader. Without the stress, a weaker elected leader was acceptable (Klein, 1976). Acceptance and election, which under conditions of low stress gave the accepted legitimate leader control of the group's fate, was replaced under high stress by the group turning to a less legitimate but stronger leader, seen to be endowed with more competence. Transactional structuring combined with transformational competence and consideration appear required for effective leadership under panic conditions. This is seen again when community disasters occur.

At the national, state, and community levels, effective leadership promotes the development of credible warning systems and preparations long before disasters actually strike. The absence of such effective leadership is marked by maladaptive defensiveness by the public and exacerbation of panic reactions (Harman, 1984). Needed at the organizational level are technical and behavioral preparations for crises. Management needs warning systems and crisis command centers for management-by-exception as well as for maintaining readiness, confidence, and support. Employees need training in safety, security, and detection along with emotional preparation for emergencies (Mitroff, Shrivastava, & Udwadia, 1987). Weinberg (1978) reviewed 30 cases of how groups dealt with earthquakes, blizzards, accidents, and hurricanes. Breakdown occurred when there was laissez-faire leadership. Effective leadership provided the needed vision and support of individualized consideration and the structure and preparations of transactional leadership.

The amelioration of much of the panic in the immediate aftermath of the September 11, 2001, terrorist attacks owed much to the advance emergency preparations and practice run-throughs that Mayor Giuliani's administration conducted in the preceding years. Also, Giuliani recognized that the public needed to be completely informed via television and radio that the government was in charge of the situation. Such structure and preparedness was previously seen in the readiness and the strong chain of command found in tests of the Lawrence–Douglas County, Kansas emergency preparedness system. The community was well prepared for disasters because resources were well organized and staff was highly trained (Watson, 1984). Similarly, emergency preparedness aided Alexandria, Virginia, to cope with disastrous flooding (Harman, 1984), and citywide drills for ambulance drivers also provided effectiveness in handling the Hyatt Regency disaster in Kansas City, where a skyway collapsed killing 114 people (Ross, 1982).

In times of crisis, local police, fire, ambulance services, and public works departments can provide the needed structure and preparedness. They are the critical human resources whose effective use is paramount in a disaster or crisis (Kartez, 1984). The leadership of these resources at the time of the crisis determines the effectiveness of the organized response to disaster. Most effective is when the organizations maintain their own identity and do not depend on outside volunteer help. Least effective is when only an amorphous organizational structure is in place.

Already it was noted that the transformational leadership components of charisma, inspirational leadership, intellectual stimulation, and individualized consideration contribute to effective leadership under stress (Bass, 1985). For instance, charismatic transformational leaders tend to keep their cool when faced with threats to their lives. Thus, Mahatma Gandhi, Franklin Delano Roosevelt, Kemal Atatürk, Benito Mussolini, Kwame Nkrumah, Charles de Gaulle, and Ronald Reagan displayed presence of mind and composure when faced with assassination attempts. They were not easily frightened or disconcerted. They remained calm, maintained their sense of humor, and were not thrown off balance in the face of danger or crisis (Willner, 1968). Combat heroes tend to come from the same mold. When 77 Israeli medal winners in the Yom Kippur War were contrasted with ordinary soldiers, the medal winners exhibited more emotional stability. They also showed aspects of transformational leadership: perseverance under stress, decisiveness, and devotion to duty (Gal, 1985).

Coping With Stress in the Military

In combat, visible inspirational leadership may make the difference between complete victory and overwhelming defeat. "A rational army would run away," declared Montesquieu. A twitch of emotion may change an intact command into an army in rout (Keegan, 1976). A visible transformational leader can make the difference between a rout or a rally. Civil War General Philip Sheridan riding back to rally his retreating troops illustrated the importance of a leader's visibility in sharing the risk and turning attention away from *sauve qui peut* to moving forward to attack the enemy. The Israeli Defense Force requirement that leaders be in front of their troops to be able to say "follow me" likewise points to the significance of the leaders' importance in visibly supporting their units and setting the example to be followed in risky situations (Gal & Jones, 1985).

Repeated observations indicated that the disruption of leadership during combat was one of the factors responsible for psychiatric breakdowns in battle, along with other aspects promoted by transformational leadership, such as group identification and group cohesiveness. Again, Steiner and Neuman (1978) noted that following the 1973 war, Israeli soldiers suffering psychiatric breakdown lacked trust in their leadership and did not feel they belonged to their combat units. Their self-esteem for their military performance was low. Clearly, transformational leadership was missing for them.

Another aspect of charisma that is important in the military is confidence in the leader. Confidence in their commanders was critical to Israeli soldiers' morale in the 1982 Lebanon excursion. This confidence derives from the demonstrated professional competence of the commander (charisma), from belief in his credibility (inspiration), and from the soldiers' perception that the commander cares about his troops (individualized consideration). Again, transformational leadership was the key; the three elements inspiring confidence in the commander according to Kalay (1983) were belief in the commander's professional competence, belief in the commander's credibility, and perception of how caring he was.

Coping With Stress in Business and Industry

In the 1990s the CEO of Silicon Graphics illustrated the importance of a transformational leader in stressful, crisis, and chaotic conditions.

Silicon Graphics was one of the fastest growing computer companies in the United States, in an industry and age in which international competition was fast and ferocious. The CEO created within the organization a relaxed, individually considerate, corporate atmosphere, where people were allowed to dress casually and have offbeat fun. He maintained a steady low-key personality, while intellectually stimulating employees to think creatively. Trust was emphasized as a way to make it possible to thrive on chaos. Silicon Graphics survived these very turbulent times and continues to be a strong company in a volatile business environment.

An important source of stress in all types of organizations is conflict. An important leadership function is managing the conflict and accompanying stress that occur within the work group. The transformational leader envisions superordinate goals for the conflicting parties—ways in which they both can gain from agreement and cooperation. The leader points to the inability of one party to get along without the assistance of the other. Yet the freedom of action of each party is maintained. Transactional elements may be introduced with creation of an organizational restructuring satisfactory to both parties that eliminates the sources of the conflict. Ways are sought to increase the trust of the parties in their guarantee to keep the agreement. The nature of the conflict is clarified, along with available creative alternatives to resolve it. Each side is helped to understand the other's position. Both parties are encouraged to avoid and to overcome rigid positions.

Thomas (1976) suggested that when quick and decisive action is vital to resolving the conflict between parties, assertive, dominating leadership may be most appropriate. This may also be true when unpopular actions such as cost-cutting are needed and cooperation from the parties is not being sought. For the transformational leader, such assertiveness may be required when superordinate organizational interests take precedence.

The intellectually stimulating leader moves the parties toward a solution that integrates the efforts of the parties in conflict into a collaborative solution. The conflict is turned into a mutual problem to be solved. A transactional leader searches for expedient compromises that are immediately rewarding, are temporary settlements, and avoid disruptions. Even laissez-faire leadership seems appropriate for certain cases when the leader decides to avoid dealing with the conflict because it is a trivial matter, when the descriptions or costs of the only solution outweigh the benefits, or when the two parties may need to calm down before they can deal more rationally with their mutual conflict.

In some instances, the conflict is between the leader and the follower. Cognitive resources theory suggests that highly intelligent but inexperienced managers/leaders are ineffective when in conflict with their boss. Much more effective are the experienced, but not as highly intelligent, leaders facing the same conflict with superiors (Fiedler, 1986). Consistent with cognitive resource theory, Gibson, Fiedler, and Barrett (1993) showed that experienced, rather than highly intelligent, leaders are intellectually stimulating in that they promote creativity in the groups they lead when the leaders are under stress due to conflict with their immediate superior. In such circumstances, paradoxically, the more intelligent leaders are less intellectually stimulating, as evidenced in this research by the lack of creativity of the group. Additionally, the intelligent but inexperienced leaders actually inhibit the group's functioning. There is much babbling by the leaders and the group members—much more talk and many fewer ideas generated under such stressful conditions.

Coping With Mergers and Acquisitions.   When one organization is acquired by another in a merger, in general, the employees in the acquired company may be disturbed by the loss of identity and purpose. Anxiety, anger, depression, and helplessness may occur. Resignations and forced departures occur, along with threats to employees' own security. As a result, survival in the merged organization may become an obsession. Transformational leadership is needed to deal with the merging of the cultures of the acquired organization and the organization taking over, transcending both organizations. The future system of contingent reward needs to be clearly communicated along with feedback on how well it works. Support, consideration, and commitment are needed in helping to cope with the stress of the merger.

Marks and Mirvis (1998) argue that leadership of organizations undergoing mergers or acquisitions needs to possess insight, inspiration, and involvement—core elements of transformational leadership—to help members deal with the stress and uncertainty. Marks and Mirvis assert that, along with keeping employees informed, leaders must use inspirational appeals to make both the intellectual and emotional case for why people should accept the new, combined organization. They also suggest empowering employees, consistent with notions of intellectual stimulation. Individualized consideration is also necessary, providing employees with awareness of the stress they will experience and providing suggestions on how to deal with it. Leaders "get information about the acquiring organization for their subordinates; identify counterparts in the other . . . and make contact and help subordinates to understand that their counterparts in the acquiring firm are not the 'bad guys' and, in many cases, are in a situation similar to their own" (Schweiger, Ivancevich, & Power, 1987, p. 135).

Transformational leadership can help followers and colleagues smooth the tensions of disengagement, disidentification with the old situation, disenchantment with the new arrangements, and disorientation without anchors to the past or the future. Individually considerate leaders can help colleagues and subordinates work through their denials and anger. An attractive vision of the future by the inspirational leader can promote acceptance of the new situation (Tichy & Devanna, 1986).

Coping With Stress in Teams

There are a number of ways that transformational leadership can contribute to the resolution of conflict within teams and small groups. For example, the leader's inspirational motivation creates a positive, optimistic environment for identifying the source of stress and an expectation of its resolution. When the stress results from conflict within the team, the leader may use appeals to superordinate goals to help factions within the team move beyond the differing objectives of the opposing parties.

The intellectually stimulating leader moves the team to define the crisis or conflict, to identify the facts and opinions, to determine the desired results, and to obtain open statements of opinions (for which trust of the transformational leader is needed). Different solutions with transforming superordinate goals need to be kept in mind, in addition to how the solutions will be implemented and evaluated (Atwater & Bass, 1994).

To the extent that leaders provide specific strategies or support in coping with individual team member's stress, individualized consideration can come into play. In a study by Sosik and Godshalk (2000), it was found that mentors who engaged in transformational leadership behaviors had a significant impact on alleviating proteges' felt stress. A dissertation by Rose (1998) found that high-quality leader–member relationships led to lower incidence of burnout and health problems.

After reviewing some of the literature, Burgess, Salas, Cannon-Bowers, and Hall (1992) formulated training guidelines for leaders of teams under stress. The strategies they presented included such transactional approaches as contingent rewarding and management-by-exception, double-checking of team member performance, focus on the task at hand, provision of feedback, monitoring of member performance, and troubleshooting to locate and correct errors. Equally present in their strategies were implementing transformational strategies for handling possible crises in the future, ensuring individual member competence, understanding the mission, aligning individual member's goals with those of the team, establishing trust and cooperation, and providing support.

Coping With Stress in the University

Neumann (1992) pointed out how college presidents can use the college budget to induce feelings of financial stress, which heightens the budget's symbolic meaning for the faculty. He found that the faculty expects and calls for transformational leadership to deal with the pressure. In one case of financial crisis, the university president emphasized intellectually stimulating meaning and challenge in his leadership. He laid out the steps that might be taken and sought a faculty consensus. In a different case of financial crisis at another university, the president was more transactional and focused attention on documentation, numbers, codes, and technical terms; he did not try to organize or mobilize the faculty's thinking on what was to be done. The first president who provided interpretation, meaning, structure, and implications for the future was seen as more effective by the faculty in dealing with the financial crisis than was the second president, who concentrated on financial analyses.

In 20 departments of two universities, Katz (1977) found that when conflict was high within the departments, transactional leadership was seen as needed for helping the departments to be effective. In those departments that were in conflict, the leaders were judged to be more effective if they initiated structure, clarified the rules, and suggested ways to get things done. But if conflict was absent in departments, such leadership was unnecessary. An experiment confirmed this finding. In the experiment, participants had to work on a routine coding task. If conflict was high among the subjects, initiating structure correlated .46 with their productivity; if conflict was absent, initiating structure correlated −.62 with their productivity (Katz, Phillips, & Cheston, 1976).

STRESS, CRISES, AND SUCCESSFUL LEADERSHIP

By leadership that is effective in coping with stress, we mean leadership that results in rationally defensible quality decisions; appropriate use of available information, skills, and resources; and enhanced performance of followers in reaching their goals, despite the threats and obstacles to doing so (see House & Rizzo, 1972). Such effective coping with stress may come from changing the leaders (Hamblin, 1958; Lanzetta, 1953) but more often results as a consequence of transformational leadership.

Transactional leadership can service the structure of relationships and readiness that is already in place, whereas transformational leadership adds to the structure and readiness by helping followers transcend their own immediate self-interests and by increasing their awareness of the larger issues. The transformational leaders shift goals away from personal safety and security toward achievement, self-actualization, and the greater good. Transformational leaders may have the charisma to fulfill the frustrated needs for identity and lack of social support felt by followers. Bradley (1987) found that the presence or absence of charisma in a commune's leadership affected the commune's survival. Communes did not survive if their members sought charismatic leadership that was not provided.

Transactional leaders manage emergencies with structures that have already been set up by actively managing-by-exception. They can supply solutions for immediate needs perceived by their followers. There is immediate satisfaction with such leadership but not necessarily long-term positive effectiveness in coping with the stressful conditions. What may be necessary are transformational leaders who evoke higher level needs, such as for the common good, and who move followers into a fully vigilant search for long-term readiness. As noted before, when Mulder, van Eck, and deJong (1971) examined patterns of leadership in a Dutch navy flotilla on active duty, the transactional interpersonal and task-oriented factors emerged as of some importance, but what distinguished effective leadership in crisis compared with noncrisis conditions was intense, powerful, self-confident leadership that characterized charismatic transformational leadership. In contrast, mild person–leader relationships were successful and effective in noncrisis situations.

Personalized (Pseudotransformational) Versus Socialized Transformational Leadership Approaches

As discussed earlier, inauthentic, pseudotransformational leaders are concerned with their own power, authority, and self-aggrandizement. They may be charismatic, inspirational, intellectually stimulating, and individually considerate, but it is for their own sake rather than for the sake of their followers. In contrast to socialized leaders who are truly transformational for the sake of both their followers and themselves, such personalized leaders display a different way of influencing their followers when the followers are faced with stressful conditions. For instance, followers may feel personally inadequate because of the gap between their self-perceived images of what they are and what they ideally should and would like to be. Stress is increased if they feel they cannot reduce the gap. Their own frustration may result in aggression and feelings of dependency on others. To help followers cope with their frustration, self-aggrandizing personalized leaders concentrate on their own charisma to make themselves the object of identification for their followers (Downton, 1973), but socially transformational leaders use individualized consideration to provide opportunities for their followers to develop themselves (Levinson, 1980).

The truly transformational leader manifests individualized consideration and converts crises into developmental challenges. The truly transformational leader uses intellectual stimulation to foster followers' thoughtful, creative, adaptive solutions to stress rather than hasty, defensive, maladaptive ones. True transformational leadership does not replace the transactional leadership that has provided the necessary structure for readiness. Rather, transformational leadership adds to transactional leadership (Waldman et al., 1990) because without the transformational components the transactional leadership may prove inadequate.

Why Transformational Leadership Is Needed

Directive, rapid decision making is sought from leaders by ready-to-be-influenced groups under stressful or crisis conditions. Consider the

U.S. Congress's quick adoption of the U.S. Patriot Act following the September 11, 2001, terrorist attacks. Legislators seemed willing to suspend their normal critical debate and readily accept the administration's arguments that the steps were "necessary" to maintain antiterrorist security. However, to be effective in stressful situations, leaders must organize the efforts of their followers in ways that promote vigilance, thorough search, thorough appraisal, and contingency planning to avoid defective coping with threat. Bolstering—each member assuring the others about the correctness of their opinion and solution—can be minimized by the leader playing the devil's advocate. Quick and easy decision making can be avoided by forming a decision-making group with members who differ in background and opinion (Janis, 1982).

To be effective in crisis conditions, leaders must be transformational—able to rise above what their followers see as their immediate needs and appropriate reactions. Such leaders need to arouse inert followers to the significance of threats and the group's lack of preparedness. The leaders need to alter inert followers' willingness to live with frustration, rather than make efforts to deal more adequately with obstacles in their path to reach positive objectives. Similarly, to be effective, instead of catering to the group's immediate needs and fears, leaders need to calm the demands for hasty change. To be effective, leaders need to be truly transformational in identifying and publicizing the inadequacy of defensive pseudosolutions. To be effective for hypervigilant followers in a state of panic, leaders need to be truly transformational in providing goals transcending self-interests. To be effective when panic is imminent, leaders need to provide clear, confident direction. The transformational leader's vision for the future may set the stage for effective planning ahead; nevertheless, transactional leadership may also be important in planning efforts.

Planning Ahead.   Effective political leaders prevent crises or their stressful effects by planning ahead (Yarmolinsky, 1987). Effective transactional leaders practice active management-by-exception by setting up early warning mechanisms to avoid surprises produced in last-minute, hasty, ill-conceived behavior. Potential crises are recognized rationally without emotional upset. Appropriate searches for information can be instituted without hasty defensiveness. However, it takes a transformational leader to articulate the need for an early warning system and to mobilize the organization to prepare for an acute crisis (Tichy & Devanna, 1986). In advance, such leaders devise tactics to be employed to avoid or defuse the crisis, to persuade followers to accept the proposed tactics and mobilize support for them. In this sense, the leadership takes on an important teaching function (Yarmo-linsky, 1987). By anticipating potential crises, by preparing with active management-by-exception in advance for them, and by long-range, proactive, envisioning transformational leadership, leaders are more effective than if they only engage in dealing with immediate problems (Katz, 1951).

Further Evidence of the Impact of Transformational Leadership

Direct survey evidence of the effects of transactional and transforma-tional leadership were obtained by Seltzer et al. (1989) from 285 to 296 MBA students holding full-time jobs who completed the Personal Stress Symptom Assessment (Numerof, Cramer, & Shachar-Hendin, 1984). The MBAs indicated how often they experienced headaches, fatigue, irritability, loss of appetite, insomnia, and inability to relax. They also completed the Gillespie–Numerof Burnout Inventory (Nu-merof & Gillespie, 1984), responding to such items as "I'm fed up with my job" and "my job has me at the end of my rope." Felt stress and burnout correlated .58. The respondents also described their immedi-ate superior with the MLQ Form 5R (Bass & Avolio, 1997).

Table 5.1 shows the first-order correlations of the transformational and transactional leadership ratings scores of the superiors and the felt stress and burnout of their subordinates. As seen in Table 5.1, stress was modestly, but significantly, reduced by charisma (–.17), intellec-tual stimulation (–.11), and individualized consideration (–.18), and burnout was reduced much more (–.52, –.46, –.36). Contingent reward also helped reduce burnout (–.43), but management-by-exception did the opposite (.22). Seltzer et al. (1989) concluded that 14% of the effects in reported symptoms of stress among the subordinates and 34% of the effects in feelings of burnout could be attributed to the lack of trans-formational leadership and contingent rewarding and more frequent management-by-exception. They also found that if the other factors were held constant through multiple regression analysis, reported stress and burnout were less if one worked under a charismatic and individually considerate leader. However, stress and burnout were somewhat higher if the MBAs worked at their full-time job under an intellectually stimulating leader. With the other factors held constant,

TABLE 5.1
First-Order Correlations of Transactional
and Transformational Leadership of Superiors
and the Experienced Stress and Burnout
Among Their Subordinates

	Symptoms Felt	
Leadership	Stress N = 285	Burnout N = 296
Transformational		
Charisma	−.18*	−.52*
Individualized consideration	−.18*	−.46*
Intellectual stimulation	−.11	−.36*
Transactional		
Contingent rewards	−.18*	−.43*
Management-by-exception	.09	.22*

*p < .01.
Note. From "Transformational Leadership: Is It a Source of More or Less Burnout or Stress?" by J. Seltzer, R. E. Numerof, and B. M. Bass, 1989, *Journal of Health and Human Resources Administration, 12,* pp. 174–185. Copyright 1989 by Pennsylvania State University at Harrisburg. Adapted with permission.

contingent rewarding was modestly associated with less stress and management-by-exception with more stress and burnout. Overall, transformational leadership and contingent rewarding by leaders were effective in reducing feelings of stress and burnout; management-by-exception accomplished the opposite.

Transforming Crises Into Challenges

Intellectually stimulating transformational leaders can halt crises by questioning assumptions and disclosing opportunities, fostering unlearning, and eliminating fixation on old ways of doing things (Nystrom & Starbuck, 1984). Inspirational leaders inspire courage and stimulate enthusiasm. The cyanide lacing of Tylenol on store shelves struck Johnson and Johnson in 1982. The company's public relations department had no plans to deal with such acute crises, yet the CEO provided transformational direction. He rejected glossing over the disaster. Rather, he converted the marketing disaster into an opportunity to gain credit for good citizenship. He regained the firm's market share by deciding to introduce—as quickly as possible—a tamper-proof

Tylenol bottle at a time of great public consciousness and publicity about the problem (Snyder & Foster, 1983).

McCauley (1987) pointed to a number of both transformational and transactional ways leaders can convert a stressful situation into a challenging one. The leader practices contingent rewarding by ensuring that there will be positive outcomes, and followers know what these are. Clear and attainable goals are set. Interim rewards for progress are given. More generally, using intellectual stimulation, taxing conditions are converted into problems to be solved. Inspirational leadership is employed to increase self-confidence. Envisioning, enabling, and empowering followers provides greater tolerance for ambiguity, uncertainty, and working with new and unfamiliar conditions. Situations beyond one's control are recognized, but the situations may need to be redefined, and goals may need to be changed.

Pines (1980) summarized the ways that transformational leaders can provide the support that makes for hardy followers, quality performance, and effective decision making, despite the presence of distressful conditions. Leaders can present dramatic changes as challenges, not as threats. Leaders can select followers who prefer a vigorous, fast-paced lifestyle and have the cognitive capacity and readiness to prepare themselves for coping adequately with the stress. Leaders can increase their followers' sense that they are the masters of their own fate. Followers' involvement and commitment can be increased by their empowerment to offset focusing on the deleterious effects of the stress. The intellectually stimulating leader can introduce the metaphor of mountain climbers who do not look down the vertical cliff face and contemplate their dangerous exposure but instead concentrate on the holds and grips available immediately in front of them.

It is important for the leaders themselves to believe they face a challenging problem rather than a crisis. They are more open to ideas and suggestions from their subordinates. More effective decisions are reached as a consequence. Thus, Tjosvold (1984) arranged an experiment for students acting as managers to lead other students acting as subordinates. The subordinates were actually confederates of the experimenter. The managers were the actual subjects of the research and supposedly had to deal with an issue of job rotation. They were told they were in a crisis condition, a challenging condition, or a situation of minor consequence. The managers who believed they were in a crisis were the most close-minded. They disagreed the most with their subordinates and were least interested in hearing more from them.

These managers exhibited the least knowledge of their subordinates' arguments and were least likely to change from their original position. Contrarily, those managers who thought they were in a challenging situation were most likely to explore and incorporate subordinates' views into their own. They were most likely to integrate their subordinates' opposing opinions into their own decisions, and they indicated most often the desire to hear more arguments.

Enhancing Cohesion

Transformational leaders reduce stress among followers by creating a sense of identity with a social network of support. Experienced stress is reduced as the follower is made to feel part of a larger entity. The insecurity of feeling isolated is replaced by the security of a sense of belonging. The loss of social ties through ostracism and isolation can be deadly among primitive peoples. Pines (1980) listed numerous examples of effects found for people with the social support of close friends, relatives, and group associations in comparison to those without such social support. For instance, they had lower mortality rates than those without such social support. Again, children in Israeli *kibbutzim* were less anxious during prolonged bombardments than were Israeli urban children.

Ganster, Fusilier, and Mayes (1986) reported that for 326 employees of a large contracting firm social support from supervisors, co-workers, family, and friends buffered the experience of the strains of depression, role ambiguity, role conflict, frustrating underuse of skills, and sleep troubles. Child-care crises could be handled most effectively according to 30 child-care workers with leadership that was supportive, respectful, calm, and confident. Such leadership clarified the situation and prepared for future crises. The children were dealt with ineffectively by leadership that was authoritarian and did not provide support, control, or good communications (Nelson, 1978).

Illustrating the importance of supportive individualized consideration in treating stress in combat is a card of information prepared for British noncoms to carry in a breast pocket. Included in ways to help others with acute symptoms of stress are the following strategies: Do not overreact, remain calm yourself, do not ridicule, calm the soldier, reassure the soldier, show understanding, and team up with him for a while. If possible, give him a warm drink and give him a specific task. If the stress reactions continue, keep the soldier with his unit but away from battle; allow him to sleep; treat him as a soldier, not a patient; have someone stay near him, such as a supervisor; try to have members of his unit take interest in his welfare; and have him help with small jobs.

CONCLUSIONS

In small groups and teams as well as in large business, military, and educational institutions, transactional leadership, particularly management-by-exception, can be a source of conflict, burnout, and stress; transformational leadership is more likely to help in resolving and reducing conflict, burnout, and stress. Charismatic leaders may owe their reputation to the success with which they find radical solutions to crises. Intellectually stimulating leaders help their followers to create better ways to cope with conflict. Individually considerate leaders may help to set up a social network of support to overcome the feelings of stress and burnout. But whether the leadership emerges and whether it is of consequence are contingent on situational circumstances.

6

Contingencies
of Transformational
Leadership

U.S. Civil War General George B. McClellan was loved and idealized by those in his command. He was highly effective in training and organizing his troops. However, in the different situation of combat, he was completely ineffective—almost laissez-faire. He was unable to win battles. In his campaigns to try to seize Richmond, the Confederate capital, he avoided as much as possible putting his troops in harm's way. Instead of advancing with his superior forces and doing battle with Lee, he retreated. Had he ordered the advance, it could have reduced the length of the Civil War by 2 years. The style of his leadership, and its effectiveness, was contingent on whether he was training troops or leading them into combat.

How stable is transformational leadership? Is transformational leadership more effective in certain situations? If so, what are those situations? In the ongoing organization or society, understanding of the leader's behavior requires examining a stream of causality. The effective leader is transformational or transactional as conditions change.

Burns (1956) noted that Franklin Delano Roosevelt was a practical, transactional experimentalist, as well as a charismatic with principles about social betterment. On assuming office, he moved the electorate inspirationally from the pessimism of the deep economic depression to feelings of hope, expectation, entitlement, and demand, as he succeeded in putting into place many remedial programs ranging from rural electrification to social security.

At the same time, many of his efforts, such as the National Industrial Recovery Act (NRA), ran into the Supreme Court's conservative views of the Constitution, resulting in his ill-considered scheme to pack the Supreme Court. Later on, knowing that the United States would eventually have to fight Germany, but that he could not overcome the isolationist opposition, he began to take as many escalating transactional, manipulative steps as he could to help Britain. Because Britain was near bankruptcy and could not purchase the military goods the United States could sell to them, he initiated a lend–lease program. Roosevelt arranged to lend the planes, tanks, and ships to Britain in exchange for offshore bases in the Bahamas, Bermuda, and other British colonies. He facetiously agreed, when asked, that the matériel would be returned when the war was over.

Harry Truman succeeded to the presidency on Roosevelt's death, "without experience, without knowledge, without prestige" according to *The New York Times*. He had been a transactional politician, but assuming the presidency, he became highly transformational. He framed American global participation and initiated the North Atlantic Treaty Organization, the Truman Doctrine to defend Greece, the Marshall Plan to bring about European recovery, the massive airlift to fly over the Soviet blockage of Berlin, and the Korean "police action." Truman also used his power of office to boldly dismiss America's most popular general, Douglas MacArthur, for the latter's refusal to accept constitutional civilian control of the military (Gardner, 1987).

CONTINGENCIES OR ONE BEST WAY?

Theory and research support a variety of contingency theories of leadership. Fiedler's (1967) work explained that task-oriented leaders are most effective when faced with circumstances that either offer a great deal of situational control to the leader or very little situational control. Relations-oriented leaders do best when situational control is moderate. Esteem and power of the leader and structure of the situation contribute to the favorableness of the situation to the leader. Equally researched is House's (1972) path–goal theory. The effective leader clarifies the transactional exchange and the path the subordinate needs to follow for goal attainment. Contingencies include the motivation and expectancies of the follower and the structure of the situation.

Numerous other situational leadership theories, such as those of Hersey and Blanchard (1969) and Vroom and Yetton (1973), posited different leadership and decision styles for different kinds of situations. Nevertheless, despite the vast array of contingent findings, overall the best leaders are described as those who integrate a highly task-oriented and a highly relations-oriented approach (Bass, 1990a). The best leaders demonstrate their ability to clarify the path to the goals. The general findings likewise have been that the best leaders are both transactional and transformational. Although Bass (1985) speculated on the individual and organizational constraints that would be conducive to more transactional or more transformational leadership, few empirical experiments have been attempted.

There is considerable evidence that those leaders described by their followers as more frequently transformational are likely to be both subjectively and objectively more effective and satisfying than those more frequently transactional leaders who exchange promises of rewards for appropriate role enactment by subordinates. In turn, such more frequently reward-oriented leaders are more effective and satisfying than those who more frequently manage-by-exception or are laissez-faire and abdicate their leadership responsibilities (Avolio, 1999; Bass & Avolio, 1990a, 1993a). Situational contingencies make a difference but nevertheless do not override completely the more general findings concerning the effectiveness of transformational leadership behaviors (Bass, 1997).

Suppose we were to ask which particular leadership behaviors would be most likely to emerge and to be most effective in differing circumstances. Would a contingent model be in order? For example, by definition, charismatic leaders are expected to emerge in times of crisis. If the same leaders and groups underwent alternating periods of stress and steady states, would more transformational leadership emerge in crisis conditions and more transactional leadership in steady states? Would the leaders be most effective and satisfying if they matched the stress/no-stress situation with transformational leadership under stress and transactional leadership with no stress? Would it be a matter of being just a bit more of one than the other when conditions changed?

In ongoing organizational life, transformational leadership generally has its impact regardless of situational circumstances. The hierarchy of effects that shows that transformational leadership is most effective, contingent reward next most effective, management-by-exception next most effective, and laissez-faire leadership the least effective holds, regardless of contingencies. But specific contingent conditions can have some impact on the effects of transformational and transactional leadership. For example, contingent reward broke up as a factor among employees in a Chinese state enterprise (Davis et al., 1994), and transformational leadership failed to have any impact in Chinese virtual teams. Contingent reward also involved different behaviors in Japan than elsewhere (Yokochi, 1989) and had a less-than-usual impact on effectiveness among Canadian field grade officers (Boyd, 1988). The empirical question is whether the effects are more than marginal and have practical consequences for selection, training, development, and placement. Does the best leadership use both transactional and transformational elements in varying amounts over any given period of time?

Consider the following scenario: A service supply company hires unskilled labor for the simple task of cleaning offices. A contingent model would suggest that for supervising such simple, unskilled work with less educated employees, transactional leadership emphasizing contingent rewards and management-by-exception is most likely to be necessary and effective. Nevertheless, one cleaning firm found great payoff from treating the employees as if they were well-educated professionals. Inspirational leadership in the firm's management provided the cleaners with meaning and challenge in their work and commitment to it. Intellectual stimulation promoted their creative improvements of how the work can be done better. Individualized consideration focused on their individual needs for personal recognition and improvement. All this is added to the extrinsic contingent rewarding of contests and prizes for performance. So on the one hand, contingent theory supports a transactional approach. Yet, as is generally true if there is investment in transformational leadership, it still adds considerably to the effectiveness of the less-frequently needed transactional leadership (Waldman, Bass, & Einstein, 1985).

SITUATIONAL CONTINGENCIES

Howell (1992) offered a list of organizational and task conditions likely to affect the emergence of transactional leadership as an exchange relationship and of transformational leadership as charismatic, inspirational, and intellectually stimulating. Table 6.1, adapted from Howell's

TABLE 6.1

The Likelihood of Exchange (Transactional) and Charismatic
(Transformational) Leadership Emergence Under Different
Environmental and Organizational Conditions

Situational Conditions	Likelihood of Exchange Leadership	Likelihood of Charismatic Leadership
Environmental		
Stable	High	Low
Unstable	Low	High
Political/legal	High	Low
Not political/legal	Low	High
Collectivistic	Low	High
Individualistic	High	Low
Organizational		
[Behavior] consistent with cultural values	Low	High
Inconsistent with cultural values	High	Low
Mechanistic	High	Low
Organic	Low	High
Reactive processing	High	Low
Proactive monitoring	Low	High
Hierarchical authority	High	Low
Dispersed authority	Low	High
Centralized decision making	High	Low
Decentralized decision making	Low	High
Vertical communication	High	Low
Lateral communication	Low	High
Task characteristics		
Standardized, routine	High	Low
Complex, changing	Low	High
Well-defined performance	High	Low
Poorly defined performance	Low	High
Goals		
Ambiguous performance	Low	High
Extrinsic rewards	High	Low
Intrinsic rewards	Low	High
Leader–subordinate relations		
Leader power greater	Low	High
Follower power greater	High	Low
Leader information greater	Low	High
Follower information greater	High	Low

Note. From "Organization Contexts, Charismatic and Exchange Leadership," by J. M.
Howell, 1992, *The Environment/Organization/Person Contingency Model: A Meso Approach to the
Study of Organizations,* edited by H. L. Tosi, Greenwich, CT: JAI. Copyright 1992 by JAI Press.
Adapted with permission.

original study, shows the organizational and task characteristics she expects would generate high or low frequencies of transactional or transformational leadership.

Given the behaviors involved in transactional and transformational leadership, one can also propose the task/goal conditions, characteristics of the subordinates and the leader that are most likely to correlate with each component of the Full Range of Leadership (FRL) model. For instance, as shown in Table 6.2, laissez-faire leadership is most likely

TABLE 6.2
Task/Goal, Subordinate, and Leader Conditions
Fostering the Emergence of the Full Range of Leadership

Emergent Leadership	Reinforcements/ Tasks/Goals	Subordinates	Leader
Charisma	Uncontrolled, conflict, stress	Inexperienced, low self-esteem, low self-efficacy	Realistically self-confident, determined, unconventional
Inspirational motivation	Ambiguous	Inexperienced	Articulate, flexible, emotional, perspicacious
Intellectual stimulation	Problems to be solved	Experienced, high	Rational, unconventional, perspicacious
Individualized consideration	Unmet individual needs	Inexperienced, career-oriented	Caring, empathetic, relations-oriented
Contingent reinforcement	Controlled by leader	Inexperienced, materialistic, not idealistic	Materialistic, conventional, not idealistic
Active management-by-exception	Objectively measurable performance	Inexperienced	Task-oriented
Passive management-by-exception	Uncontrolled, controlled by organization	Experienced	Reactive
Laissez-faire	Unimportant	Experienced	Distracted, indifferent, uncaring

Note. From "Organization Contexts, Charismatic and Exchange Leadership," by J. M. Howell, 1992, *The Environment/Organization/Person Contingency Model: A Meso Approach to the Study of Organizations,* edited by H. L. Tosi, Greenwich, CT: JAI Press. Copyright 1992 by JAI Press. Adapted with permission.

to emerge when the tasks and goals are unimportant, the rewards are low, discipline is lax, the subordinates are experienced, and the leader is distracted, indifferent, and uncaring. Some evidence to support this overall notion is available. For both nonprofessionals (Podsakoff, Niehoff, Mackenzie, & Williams, 1993) and professionals (Podsakoff, Mackenzie, & Fetter, 1993), investigators found evidence that the effects of transactional leader behavior were moderated by situational variations. Similar to findings for blue-collar employees, for 411 professional, managerial, and white-collar employees, contingent reward, noncontingent reward, and punishment leadership, as well as instrumental and supportive leadership of the employees, accounted for 12% of the variance of the general satisfaction level of employees. Effects of the form of leadership on satisfaction could be attributed to some extent to differences in follower characteristics, differences in tasks, or differences in organizational characteristics.

Environmental Contingencies

Among environmental variables of consequence to transformational and transactional leadership may be the environment's stability or turbulence and whether it is heavily collectivistic or individualistic in culture.

Stability Versus Turbulence. More transactional leadership is likely to emerge and be relatively effective when leaders face a stable, predictable environment. More transformational leadership is likely to emerge in organizations and be effective when leaders face an unstable, uncertain, turbulent environment. For Ansoff and Sullivan (1991), turbulence in the environment is characterized by complexity, lack of the leaders' familiarity with likely events, rapidity of change, and lack of visibility of the future. Leaders' strategies for coping with the environment require that they match their organization and their behavior with the level of environmental complexity. The five levels of stability–turbulence posited by Ansoff and Sullivan give rise to the suggestion as to how much transactional or transformational leadership would be required to match the environmental demands.

At the highest level of stability is the repetitive environment without change. It calls for stable leader reactions based on precedents—mainly transactional leadership. At the next level is a slowly

TABLE 6.3

Effects of Stable and Unstable Environments
on Leaders' MLQ Scores

	Stable	Unstable
Transformational leadership		
Charisma	2.2	2.6
Inspirational motivation	1.7	2.1
Intellectual stimulation	2.0	2.4
Individualized consideration	2.3	2.8
Transactional leadership		
Contingent reward	1.7	2.0
Managing-by-exception	2.3	2.2

Note. From "Leadership in the Twenty-First Century: A Speculative Inquiry," by R. J. House, 1995, *The Changing Nature of Work,* edited by A. Howard, San Francisco: Jossey-Bass. Copyright 1995 by Jossey-Bass. Adapted with permission.

expanding, incrementally changing environment. It requires leaders who use experience to react to changes—again the reaction of active management-by-exception appears adequate. At less stable levels where the environment changes more rapidly, the leader has to become more anticipatory or somewhat transformational. As change becomes discontinuous, the leader must seek opportunities for change. Finally, at the level where the environment is surprising, novel strategies and creativity need to be intellectually stimulated.

Pawar and Eastman (1997) suggest the stable-turbulent–unstable dichotomy can be conceptualized as whether the organizational environment is one focused on efficiency versus adaptation, hypothesizing that transformational leadership is more effective under an adaptation-oriented environment. The Center of Leadership Studies gathered data on Multifactor Leadership Questionnaire (MLQ) scores of leaders as found under various contingencies. Results for several thousand cases comparing stable and unstable environments were in line with expectations. As shown in Table 6.3, transformational leadership means were higher in unstable environments. Transactional management-by-exception was slightly higher in stable conditions.

In some cases, leaders may create the contingent conditions requiring their leadership. Pseudotransformational leaders may actively generate the need for their charismatic leadership by manufacturing environmental crises (Willner, 1984). But transformational leaders may effectively deal with environmental problems. Employees may come from populations who are indifferent or disenchanted with their lot. When organizational members experience alienation anomie in the existing social order, Boal and Bryson (1988) suggested that transformational leaders may emerge to create a new and different world that links the members' needs to important purposes, values, and meanings. Such inspirational leaders articulate a compelling vision. The leaders can show how the followers' behavior can contribute to fulfillment of those purposes, values, and meanings.

As noted in chapter 5, conditions of crisis, uncertainty, and turbulence make the emergence of charismatic leadership more likely than would occur in stable, routine conditions (Bass, 1985). Although he was willing and able to respond charismatically to several national crises that occurred during his terms in office as president, Theodore Roosevelt bemoaned the fact that the United States was not involved in a war during his presidency, which would have maximized the use of his charismatic and inspirational talents. House (1995) reported, as expected, that the tendency for the charisma of 24 entrepreneurial chief executive officers (CEOs) to correlate with the commitment of their followers depended on the uncertainty of the environment. The correlation was .16, .00, .26, and .06 in 4 successive years when the environment of the CEOs was low in uncertainty for a subset of CEOs and was .36, .47, .38, and .52 when it was high in uncertainty for another subset in those same years.

Inspirational leaders may reframe opportunities so that the environment is transformed from a situation of threat into a situation of opportunity. The environment threatening General Electric was reframed by CEO Jack Welch into General Electric's need to compete worldwide and to quickly and creatively exploit changes in market conditions and technology. Welch restructured and reoriented the corporation toward a vision of speed, simplicity, and self-confidence (Howell, 1992): "We have a real opportunity to shift from a [transactional] mode where we control, measure, catch, snitch, and follow, to [a transformational] one where work is exciting and people feel empowered and energized to grow and create" (Welch, 1989, p. 3).

Collectivistic Societies. Jung, Sosik, and Bass (1995) argued that more transformational leadership was likely to emerge in a collectivistic society than in an individualistic one. In a similar vein, Pawar and Eastman (1997) refer to organizations having a "clan mode" of governance, being more receptive to transformational leadership. To begin with, in collectivistic societies, people tend to view their group and organization as an essential part of their lives (Hofstede, 1991). Consequently, they are more attached to their groups, organizations, and societies than are those in individualistic societies. They are more willing to subordinate their self-interests for the sake of their larger collectives (Triandis, 1993). Emphasis is on group accomplishment. Individual aggrandizement is a threat to the collective. Depending on group performance for goal attainment, there is commitment to more long-term goals. Such commitment is seen as the dimension of Confucian dynamism (Hofstede & Bond, 1988), which is prevalent in Japan and among the "five tigers" of South Korea, China, Taiwan, Singapore, and Malaysia. Leung and Bozionelos (2004) found that in a Confucian culture the notion of attentive leadership is similar to the qualities of transformational leadership.

In collectivist cultures, group norms and values are more strongly adhered to and therefore provide a more powerful social control mechanism. Deviant behavior is less tolerated. At the same time, individual attitudes and personality are less likely to be correlated with explicit behavior. There is little need for theories that explain leadership in terms of personality contingencies in collective cultures. Group harmony—particularly, in-group harmony—is prized along with individual modesty (Triandis, 1993). Goal attainment depends on group collaboration. Exchanges are specific, such as involving the exchange of status for love and service. They are less likely to involve universal exchanges such as money for information and goods. The organization is likely to be viewed as an extended family in which paternalism provides in-group harmony (Markus & Kitayama, 1991). Promotion is based on seniority. There is a strong attachment to the organization, and individual goals are readily subordinated for the sake of the group ones. Work values are central. Most employees have a long-term relationship with the organization that first provides them with a full-time job when first hired; their interpersonal skills are viewed as more valuable than specific job knowledge and techniques. In-group solidarity is stressed (Lee, Yoo, & Lee, 1991).

Management controls depend on group norms and social values rather than written rules. Followers themselves can more easily identify with the leader based on a mutual belief in a common purpose and when the followers already are group oriented. Thus, the work teams within a Japanese organization were seen to have clearer identities and a shared view of events than groups of workers reporting to the same supervisor in Western countries (Smith, Misumi, Tayeb, Peterson, & Bond, 1989). As a consequence, Jung et al. (1995) proposed four explanations about the more ready emergence and facilitation of transformational leadership in the collectivist societies of East and Southeast Asia. Charismatic leadership is facilitated because of the ordinary high level of respect, trust, loyalty, and obedience to higher authority of the paternal, father figure. Followers already have a sense of shared fates with their leaders and organizations. Inspirational motivation is facilitated in collectivist cultures because followers already are committed to collective accomplishment, group goals, and the meaningfulness of their own participation. The transformational realignment of individual values is accomplished through realignment of the group's values. Thus, inspirational leadership is easier to bring about in a collectivistic culture because already present is a willingness to put forth extra effort on behalf of the organization and a high level of commitment to the collective accomplishment.

Although the creativity of individual followers may be inhibited in collective societies, the long-term strategies of the leadership for the collective may enhance the patience required to achieve success with products, systems, and long-term goals. Furthermore, the willingness of the leaders to turn their groups toward adapting and improving on Western technologies is illustrative of intellectual stimulation. The avoidance of things "not invented here" in Britain resulted, in 1 year alone in the 1970s, in Britain exporting 14 times more patents than it imported. The reverse was true for Japan. Yokochi (1989) found a high level of intellectual stimulation in the MLQ ratings of 135 senior managers in 17 large Japanese firms. The Japanese leaders' strong emphasis on intellectual stimulation was explained by Yokochi as due to the Japanese culture that values lifelong, continuous learning and the pursuit of intellectual activities. Walumbwa and Lawler (2003) found that collectivism moderates the effect of transformational leadership on work-related outcomes.

Individualized consideration is also important and relevant in collectivistic cultures, making it easier to effect. There is much paternalism. Leaders have personal responsibility for caring for their followers' career development and personal problems (Steers, Shin, Ungson, & Nam, 1990). As expected, MLQ ratings by their subordinates of the individualized consideration of senior Japanese managers were high compared to the results found in Europe and the United States

(Yokochi, 1989). As noted earlier, particular exchanges of affection, emotional attachment, status, and service are more common. Hence, there is frequent use of individualized consideration to help followers reach collective goals:

> The leader–member exchange that has been traditionally based on emotional engagement and leaders' *individualized consideration* to their followers has been taken for granted in collectivistic cultures . . . [The strong vertical interdependence in collectivistic cultures] . . . imposes a moral responsibility on the leaders to listen to and share followers' concerns and on the followers to pay back their indebtedness by meeting leaders' expectations. (Jung et al., 1995, p. 13)

In the collectivistic culture, transformational leadership emerges more readily because of its consistencies with the values of the culture. Likewise, if the organization's mission is consistent with the dominant values of society, leadership within the organization is facilitated. Shamir et al. (1993) noted that in the United States high-tech industries and investing can be linked to the U.S. societal values in scientific and economic progress. The tobacco industry would be an example of the opposite setting.

Organizational Characteristics

The type and qualities of a particular organization offer another set of contingencies that influence the effectiveness of transformational leadership. The basic organizational structure may be more or less amenable to transformational leadership. The sector in which the organization resides may play a part. Finally, the type of organizational members may determine whether transformational leadership is a good fit for the organization.

Organizational Structure. A classic distinction is made between mechanistic and organic organizational structures (Burns, 1961). Mechanistic organizations feature bureaucracy—elaborate control systems and strong hierarchies. Organic organizations feature decentralized decision making and adaptive learning. We expect that management-by-exception would be easier to pursue in mechanistic organizations, and transformational leadership and contingent rewarding will emerge more frequently in organic organizations (Bass, 1985). Mechanistic organizations discourage change and inhibit individual differences, motives, and attitudes (House, 1992), making management-by-exception easier to accomplish.

Organic organizations are open to more variation and experimentation with attendant greater risk taking, fitting better the prescription for transformational leadership. Mechanistic organizations work better in stable, predictable environments. Organic organizations work better in unstable, uncertain, turbulent environments.

Besides structure, the size of the organization may moderate the effects of transformational leadership. One study that examined the impact of the leader's vision for the organization on followers found that the impact of a transformational leader's vision on followers was more positive in smaller as opposed to larger organizations, presumably because the leader had more direct contact and influence on followers in the smaller organizations (Berson, Shamir, Avolio, & Popper, 2001). This is consistent with work by Shamir (1995) and Howell and Hall-Merenda (1999), which suggests that transformational leaders need to have considerable face time with followers to provide followers with individualized attention and develop close working relationships with them to be effective.

Organizational Sector. Perhaps building on assumptions that public sector organizations are more mechanistic-bureaucratic than the private sector, Lowe et al. (1996) expected that public sector leaders would be less transformational than those in the private sector. However, contrary to their expectations, the meta-analysis comparing MLQ scores of leaders in public versus private sector organizations found that the public sector leaders (primarily leaders in educational institutions and the military) were more transformational than those in the private sector. The more recent meta-analysis by Dumdum et al. (2002), however, found no significant differences in the MLQ scores of public and private sector leaders.

A meta-analysis (Gasper, 1992) of 32 published studies completed a specific comparison of 947 military MLQ respondents with 577 to 2,141 civilian counterparts describing their superiors. Table 6.4 displays the mean differences in correlations obtained with outcomes in perceived effectiveness, satisfaction, and objective measures of performances. Overall, the correlations with objective outcomes and perceived effectiveness are stronger in the military than civilian sectors. But satisfaction with the leadership is about the same or slightly greater in the civilian sector.

TABLE 6.4

Significant Military–Civilian Differences in Outcomes
Correlated With MLQ Factor Scores

MLQ Factor Scores	Objective Performance		Perceived Effectiveness		Satisfaction	
	Military	Civilian	Military	Civilian	Military	Civilian
Transformational						
Charisma	.53	.28	.75	.57	.71	.72
Intellectual stimulation	.46	.26	.51	.47	.52	.56
Individualized consideration	.57	.29	.59	.48	.58	.61
Transactional						
Contingent reward	.46	.20	.46	.50	.46	.58
Management-by-exception						
Active	.26	−.27	Differences not significant		Differences not significant	
Passive	.32	−.07	Differences not significant		Differences not significant	

Note. From *Transformational Leadership: An Integrative Review of the Literature*, by S. Gasper, 1992, unpublished doctoral dissertation, Western Michigan University. Copyright 1992 by S. Gasper. Adapted with permission.

The mean correlation with objective performance of the MLQ transformational factor scores ranged from .46 to .57. The comparable results for civilians ranged from .26 to .29. Military transformational leadership components correlated with subjective effectiveness and satisfaction from .57 to .75. For civilians, the figures were from .47 to .57. For the military, transactional contingent reward correlated .46 with both objective performance and perceived effectiveness. For civilians, contingent reward correlated .20 with objective performance and .50 with perceived effectiveness. For the military, active management-by-exception correlated .26 with objective performance and .32 with passive management-by-exception. The comparable correlations for civilians were −.27, and .07. Similar but not significant military–civilian differences emerged when perceived effectiveness was the criterion outcome.

More recently, it was hypothesized that leaders of nonprofit organizations would be more transformational than leaders of for-profit organizations, although there is no direct evidence of support (Riggio et al., 2004). It is assumed that the strong focus on the mission of many nonprofit organizations would make these organizations more conducive to transformational leadership (Thiagarajan, 2004). In a similar vein, Lafferty (1998) suggests that transformational leadership is a better fit with the requirements of managers of hospice care workers. In one study comparing leaders of nonprofit and for-profit companies in the environmental sector, it was found that nonprofit environmental organizations did indeed seem more conducive to transformational leadership than in their for-profit counterparts, even though the actual transformational leadership qualities of the two sets of leaders did not differ (Egri & Herman, 2000).

Type of Organizational Members. Certain types of followers, or the composition of the group of followers, may be more positively affected by transformational leaders. Wofford et al. (2001) found that followers who had greater need for autonomy and followers who were high on growth need strength (workers who want to be empowered and to grow on the job) were more positively influenced, and more satisfied with, transformational leaders than were followers who lacked these motivational characteristics. Another study of Dutch employees found that followers with a high need for leadership were more positively affected by the leader's charismatic/transformational qualities than were employees with a low need for leadership (De Vries, Roe, & Taillieu, 2002).

Based on interviews with more than 200 employees in 20 organizations, Loden and Rosener (1991) noted the importance of transformational qualities in those responsible for leading diverse multicultural groups. Effective leaders of multicultural groups are inspirational in that they envisage and support diversity at all levels in their organization. They use symbols and traditions to attest to the value of diversity. Moreover, their individualized consideration is built on their knowledge of multicultural issues, the adaptability of the language they use to communicate to their diverse followers, and their focus on respect for cultural differences. They encourage criticism from their followers. They are ethically and morally committed to fairness. They openly advocate the elimination of ageism, ethnocentrism, racism, and sexism. They mentor, coach, and empower their diverse followers and provide them with opportunities to make use of their unique competencies.

Task Characteristics of the Situation

There has been some research focusing on how characteristics of the task influence the effectiveness of transformational leadership. We can point to two studies of consequence—one by Moss (1992), which compared work groups with study groups, and the other by Keller (1992), which compared research and development groups at different phases of product development.

Work Versus Study Groups.   Moss (1992) asked 188 New Zealand subordinates of 63 workplace leaders to rate their leaders using the MLQ (Short Form 8A). Then, 44 of these same leaders who were participating in university study groups were rated again by 196 of their study group peers. These leaders received similar scores on contingent rewarding, active management-by-exception, and passive management-by-exception, regardless of whether they were being rated by followers in their actual work groups or by peers in the university study groups. However, some statistically significant mean differences emerged for the transformational and laissez-faire factors for the study and work groups. Of practical note was that leaders tended to display greater amounts of transformational leadership behaviors in their actual work groups than in their study groups. This suggests that the same leaders may display different levels of transformational leadership behaviors when in their actual work setting than in nonwork settings. Interestingly, these leaders also exhibit higher levels of laissez-faire leadership in the workplace than in their study groups—a puzzling result. Perhaps the demands of the study group situation were such that displays of laissez-faire leadership were frowned on by other members.

More suggestive of the contingent effects were the low correlations between leadership scores in the work and study settings obtained for the 36 to 40 leaders for whom complete data were available: charisma (.30), inspirational motivation (.30), intellectual stimulation (.27), individualized consideration (.80), contingent reward (.02), active management-by-exception (.17), passive management-by-exception (.10) and laissez-faire leadership (.08), even when corrected for attenuation of the scales due to the estimated unreliability of the short forms.

Research Versus Development.   A specific example of a task contingency was uncovered by Keller (1992) in the differential degree of effectiveness of transformational leadership in the research and development of a product. He studied 66 project groups containing 462 professional employees from three industrial research and development (R&D) organizations. Transformational factors of charisma and intellectual stimulation of the project leaders were measured. Overall, these factors predicted the quality of the projects completed and the tendency to meet budget and scheduling requirements as evaluated by both the team members and higher management. At the same time, the effects of the transformational leadership on project quality was greater for those R&D groups engaged in research than those R&D groups engaged in the product development that followed. The effects of the transformational leadership were contingent on the stage of research or product development in which a project team was involved.

Leader–Follower Relations

Using small space analysis, Shapira (1976) showed that whether a leader was directive or participative depended on whether the leader or the follower had the information and power in the situation. It can only be a matter of speculation at this time, but it is expected that where the leader has the power and information charismatic, inspirational, or intellectual stimulating leadership is likely to emerge. Where the follower has the power and information, it behooves the leader to be more individually considerate or transactional with the need to negotiate an exchange. This may help to explain why leading virtual teams depends solidly on the transactional exchange relationship between leader and team members (Sosik, Avolio, & Kahai, 1997; Sosik, Kahai, et al., 1998).

What differentiates transactional from transformational behavior can suggest potential contingencies of leadership required for success and effectiveness in different situations. When coaching, special labor-saving ideas, quality performance, and appreciation of the role of the employee in the large organizational picture are needed, leaders must be more transformational. When the needs include clarification about what needs to be done (as often occurs in leading virtual teams), the rewards for doing so, and the corrections necessary to accomplish the tasks, leaders must be more transactional.

CONCLUSIONS

Whether transformational or transactional leadership emerges and is successful and effective depends to some extent on the environment, the organization, the tasks and goals involved, and the distribution of power between the leaders and the followers. Thus, for instance, we find some differences in the military and civilian situations and in different cultures, although the concepts and general propositions about transformational and transactional leadership proffered in the next and subsequent chapters remain relevant and applicable. They need to be suitably adjusted to take account of specific circumstances.

7

Transformational
Organizational Cultures

In their best-selling book on successful, visionary companies, *Built to Last*, Collins and Porras (1994) suggest that these durable organizations thrive because they possess a culture that balances the continuity of core ideals and the inevitability of change. Organizations such as General Electric, Disney, Hewlett-Packard, and Marriott are successful partly because of the work of their founders and subsequent leaders but mainly due to their visionary and transformational culture.

Organizational culture is a learned pattern of behavior, shared from one generation of members to the next (Deal & Kennedy, 1982). It includes the values and assumptions shared by members about what is right, what is good, and what is important. Shared in addition are heroes, stories, and rituals that provide expressive bonding of the members. Organizational culture is the glue that holds the organization together as a source of identity and distinctive competence (Bass, 1992; see also Schein, 1992). In an organization's decline, its culture can become a constraint on innovation because of its roots in the organization's past.

Can organizational cultures usefully be described in terms of how transactional or transformational they are? The shared values within the organization persist over time and shape the norms and behavior of the groups and individuals within the organization and its reputation among insiders and outsiders. The organizational culture is maintained by its traditions even as the members change. Elite military forces, such as the Green Berets, the British Life Guards, and the Israeli

Commandos, illustrate those with strong cultures, as do firms such as Exxon, IBM, and Nordstrom.

LEADERSHIP
AND ORGANIZATIONAL CULTURE

Founders often create an organizational culture from their preconceptions about an effective organization. The founders' and successors' leadership shape a culture of shared values and assumptions, guided and constrained by their personal beliefs. For example, Disney and Kellogg are organizations whose cultures were largely shaped by their founders. Successive leaders have often viewed themselves as stewards of the organizational culture begun by the founder. Yet the organization's survival depends on how well those beliefs match up with the organization's continuing opportunities. As Collins and Porras (1994) suggest, it is indeed a balance between continuity of shared ideals and adaptation to change.

Organizational culture and leadership interact with each other. Leaders create and reinforce norms and behaviors within the culture. The norms develop because of what leaders stress as important, how they deal with crises, the way they provide role models, and whom they attract to join them in their organizations.

An organizational culture affects its leadership as much as its leadership affects the culture. If an organizational culture has in place values and guides for autonomy at lower levels, management will be unable to increase its personal powers. Decisions about recruitment, selection, and placement within the organization will be affected by the organization's values and norms. Leaders need to be attentive to the rites, beliefs, values, and assumptions embedded in the organizational culture. They can help or hinder efforts to change the organization, when it must move in new directions as a consequence of changes in the internal and external environment of the organization.

Adaptive Organizational Cultures

When the organizational culture fits with the demands on it, it is more likely to be effective. When demands change, a strong culture may find it difficult to change itself to match the changes in its markets, its suppliers, technological developments, the economy, governments, and available personnel. Old commitments, values, traditions, regulations, and rites may get in the way of flexible demands on the organization for new solutions. Xerox pioneered the development of the personal computer, but in 1974 its management could not appreciate a purpose for personal computers in business, and so it had to play catch-up with Apple, which made important developments in introducing personal computers to businesses, education, and home users in the 1980s. On the other hand, if the strong culture is adaptive and flexible, it will contribute to the organization's effectiveness. Microsoft and Motorola are examples of firms with strong organizational cultures that are also highly adaptive.

Because demands on most organizations are unlikely to be absolutely steady and stable, Kotter and Heskett (1992) found that "only cultures that can help organizations anticipate and adapt to . . . change will be associated with superior performance over long periods of time" (p. 44). The adaptive culture of Kotter and Heskett paralleled what Avolio and Bass (1991) designated a transformational culture.

Of 12 adaptive firms studied by Kotter and Heskett (1992) during the period between 1976 and 1986, all seem to have originated with transformational founders: Adolphus Busch at Anheuser-Busch, C. R. Smith at American Airlines, Sam Walton at Wal-Mart, Marion and Herbert Sandler at Golden West, Charles Sanford at Bankers Trust, Donald Kendall at PepsiCo, William Hewlett and David Packard at Hewlett-Packard, Michael Harper at Con-Agra, Joseph Albertson at Albertson's, the Daytons at Dayton Hudson, and Elliot Springs at Springs Industries.

In contrast to the leaders in most of the unadaptive firms, the leaders of the adaptive firms did as follows:

> [Leaders] got their managers to buy into a timeless philosophy or set of values that stressed both meeting constituency needs and leadership or some other engine for change—values that cynics would liken to motherhood, but that when followed can be very powerful. Those people and their successors then perpetuated the adaptive part of their cultures—the values/philosophy part relating to constituencies and leadership—because they worked at it. (Kotter & Heskett, 1992, p. 55)

Preserving the adaptive culture was deliberate. The transformational founders and their successors saw themselves as custodians of the corporate culture, as preserving the firm's core values, writing and speaking about them frequently. They hired, promoted, rewarded, and disciplined people consistent with the core values of their adaptive culture. New systems that were introduced needed to be adaptable.

Thus, we are likely to see adaptive firms led by transformational leaders who endorse assumptions such as people are trustworthy and purposeful; complex problems can be delegated to the lowest level possible; and mistakes can be the basis of how to do a better job, rather than a source for recriminations. Transformational leaders articulate a sense of vision and purpose to followers. They align the followers with the vision and empower followers to take responsibility for achieving portions of the vision. When necessary, the leaders become teachers; personal responsibility is accepted by the leaders for the development of their followers to the followers' full potential.

Three components were identified by Kotter and Heskett (1992) in the firms with unadaptive cultures. First, the firms' management had a dominant position in their markets, and they were seduced by their prior success in growth and profits. For instance, during the decade from 1976 to 1986 at Texaco, there was no encouragement to look outside the firm for better ways of doing things. Second, the management did not value their customers, stockholders, and employees. At Coors, when customer complaints were received about difficulties in opening their cans, the response was that Coors produced the best beer available; the complaining customers would find a way to get to the beer inside the cans. The third component was hostility to leadership and change. Thus, when executives at General Motors, Winn-Dixie, and Fieldcrest Cannon showed "too much leadership," they were not promoted.

Kotter and Heskett (1992) suggest that adaptive firms change to unadaptive ones as the leaders become solely managers or, in terms of this text, the mainly transformational leaders become mainly transactional. In the transactional organization, the leadership accepts no deviation from standard operating procedures: It manages-by-exception and rewards followers contingent on their correct application of the rules. The organization is likely to be highly mechanistic rather than highly organic. Transactional organizations are less able to adapt to changed demands from their internal and external environments.

TRANSACTIONAL AND TRANSFORMATIONAL CULTURES

The extent to which organizations maintain transactional or transformational cultures can be described by their members and reliably measured. Within this framework, organizations are likely to have cultures that vary from each other in both modes. Nonetheless, most organizations benefit from moving in the direction of more transformational aspects in their cultures, while also maintaining a base of effective transactional tendencies.

Transactional Mode

A transactional culture concentrates on explicit and implicit contractual relationships. Job assignments are in writing, accompanied by statements about conditions of employment, rules, regulations, benefits, and disciplinary codes. The stories that make the rounds repeatedly, the jargon used, the values emphasized, the assumptions shared, and the reinforcement systems in the transactional culture usually set a price for doing anything: "Everyone has a price." Motivation to work is a matter of trade-offs of worker effort in exchange for rewards and the avoidance of disciplinary actions. Commitments remain short term, and self-interests are underscored.

The partly transactional organization is an internal, competitive marketplace of individuals whose rewards are contingent on their performance. Additionally, management-by-exception is often actively practiced. Employees work independently. Cooperation depends on the organization's ability to satisfy the self-interests of the employees. The employees do not identify with the organization, its vision, or its mission. Leaders are negotiators and resource allocators in which the power and politics behind a request may be as important as its merit. Innovation and risk taking are typically discouraged. This is a recipe that can lead to scandals, such as those in 2002 and 2003 that destroyed firms such as Enron and Tyco. The transactional organization lends itself to excessive compensation for its top management and leads its workforce to question their reasons for loyalty to the organization. Individual rewards greatly outweigh concern for the larger organization in an "every person for him- or herself" culture.

Transformational Mode

In the organizational transformational culture, there is a sense of purpose and a feeling of family. Commitments are long term. Mutual interests are shared, along with a sense of shared fates and interdependence of leaders and followers.

Leaders serve as role models, mentors, and coaches. They work to socialize new members into the epitome of a transformational organization culture. Shared norms cover a wide range of behaviors. The norms are adaptive and change with changes in the organization's environment. Emphasized are organizational purposes, visions, and missions. In this pure organizational culture, challenges are opportunities, not threats.

As with leadership, transformational culture can build on the transactional culture of the organization. The inclusion of assumptions, norms, and values that are transformationally based does not preclude individuals pursuing their own goals and rewards. This can occur at the same time if there is an alignment of individual self-interests with a central purpose, and there is accompanying coordination to achieve the integrated goals. Leaders and followers go beyond their self-interests or expected rewards for the good of the team and the good of the organization.

In theory, transformational cultures should be more conducive to transformational leaders. It is a better fit. Groves (2004) found that charismatic/transformational leaders were more effective if the followers, and presumably the organizational culture, were more open to change and adaptation. On the other hand, a primarily transactional organizational culture could benefit from an effective transformational leader who provides the sort of leadership that can move the culture in a more transformational direction. Yet changing an existing organizational culture is a delicate operation that requires the leader to first investigate and understand the existing culture and then realign the old culture with the new vision and goals (Bass, 1985; Bass & Avolio, 1993b).

MEASUREMENT OF TRANSFORMATIONAL ORGANIZATIONAL CULTURES

Because organizational culture can have both direct effects on organizational outcomes and interactive effects with leadership, it is important to understand the nature of an organization's culture. The Organizational Description Questionnaire (ODQ; Bass & Avolio, 1992) is a 28-item survey questionnaire that can be completed by members of an organization. Transactional elements in the culture's assumptions, processes, and expectations are found in 14 items such as the following:

- You get what you earn—no more, no less.
- We bargain with each other for resources.
- Rules and procedures limit discretionary behavior.

Transformational elements of the organization's culture are presented in 14 items such as the following:

- People go out of their way for the good of the institution.
- Individual initiative is encouraged.
- We trust each other to do what's right.

The ODQ generates a transactional culture score (TA) and a transformational culture score (TF). A first factor analysis of the responses of several hundred organizational members of 69 organizations uncovered two distinct factors, one transformational and the other transactional. Respondents indicate whether each of the 28 statements is either true or false about their organization's culture, or they indicate that they cannot say. Scores are +1 for true, −1 for false, and 0 for cannot say. Thus, total transformational and transactional scores for each respondent ranged from −14 to +14. Coefficient alphas for the 14-item transactional scale were .60 and .64 for 169 leader participants from almost as many different organizations and .64 for their 724 subordinates. The corresponding alphas for the transformational scale were .77 and .69 (Bass & Avolio, 1990b).

Organizational Types

Organizations may be typed according to the mean scores from respondents about the organizations as shown in Table 7.1. These types are described in this section.

A predominantly transformational organizational culture receives highly positive ODQ transformational leadership scores and negative transactional ODQ scores from its members. The culture can be characterized by the four I's of transformational leadership. The organization is likely to be constantly discussing purposes, vision, values, and fulfillment. Absent are the transactional elements, such as formal agreements and controls that may make it difficult to be certain about what people will do. If the organizational score becomes a bit more transactional (a lower negative number), the culture places more value

TABLE 7.1

Frequency and Percentage of Types of Cultures
According to the ODQ Scores for 171 Leaders of Organizations

Transformational Mean Scores	Transactional Mean Scores		
	−14 to −6	−5 to +5	+6 to +14
+6 to +14	Predominantly transformational 19 (11.1%)	Moderately transformational 32 (18.7%)	High-Contrast 5 (2.9%)
−5 to +5	Loosely guided 17 (9.9%)	Coasting 46 (26.9%)	Contractual 13 (7.6%)
−14 to −6	Garbage can 1 (6%)	Pedestrian 17 (9.9%)	Predominately bureaucratic 21 (12.3%)

Note. From *Evaluate the Impact of Transformational Leadership Training at Individual, Group, Organizational, and Community Levels,* by B. J. Avolio and B. M. Bass, 1994, Final Report to the W. K. Kellogg Foundation, State University of New York at Binghamton University. Copyright 1994 by B. J. Avolio and B. M. Bass. Adapted with permission.

on exchanges and specific rewards for performance. In general, teamwork is accented.

As in most well-functioning families, expressiveness among members is high. The organization's structure is flat, loose, and decentralized. It is informal, flexible, adaptive, and dynamic. Highlighted are bottom-up decision making and the encouragement of individual and organizational growth and improvement. Creativity is high. Questions are raised continually about methods needed to achieve more effectiveness. Because transactional scores are extremely negative, newcomers and outsiders may have a problem knowing what to expect. A company "skunkworks," in which project developers are set off by themselves to carry on flexibly without much attention to the organization bureaucracy, is also illustrative of a highly transformational culture.

The moderately transformational organizational culture receives a transactional score that is less negative or somewhat positive. The culture sets more value on agreements, exchanges, and rewards for performance. Here we have the organization that is likely to be highly effective. On the one hand, it contains the transformational qualities needed for extra effort, commitment, and satisfaction. Yet it also may have enough transactional structure to provide predictability of relationships and requirements without falling into bureaucratic traps.

Probably, Kotter and Heskett's (1992) adaptive organizations are closest to this organizational type.

A high-contrast organizational culture receives high ODQ ratings from respondents in transformational character coupled with a similarly high level of ratings for transactional character. There is a great deal of both transactional management and transformational leadership but often with conflict over the best ways to proceed. Much of the conflict is likely to be constructive. Trust is available to maintain balance between the rule-based old ways of doing things and the needed innovations. This is particularly true where trade-offs must be made between short-term gain and individual rewards for the long-term benefit of the group and organization.

The well-run, small, elite military organization fits this high-contrast type. Members are highly committed, and extra effort is normal. The leadership is highly transformational. At the same time, the success of these elite forces depends on tight structures and highly predictable communication systems. Examples include the U.S. Special Forces, such as the Navy Seals, and the British Strategic Air Systems (SAS). The military academies also tend to have these high-contrast characteristics. Élan is combined with attention to the rules.

The loosely guided organization is one that is moderately transformational but without much structure. It is an alliance of members who may not be strongly committed to the central organization and are mostly able to do what they please. The organization is highly unstructured and characterized by great flexibility but low predictability. Accomplishments in the loosely guided organization are most likely due to informal leadership efforts. A university department, a professional services firm, or a confederation of independent sovereign states may fit this description.

A coasting organizational culture falls between the extremely transformational and extremely transactional cultures. External controls are balanced against efforts favoring self-control. Transactional management and transformational leadership are moderate in frequency. The organization coasts along and does not optimize the use of its resources and opportunities. Although there may be dissatisfaction with the old ways, changes are not sought. Such is the organization most commonly found. Members feel that much more can be done, nevertheless the organization fails to adapt to new realities until it is forced to. Detroit motor companies were content to coast along into the 1980s making autos that failed to match up with the quality that was provided by Japanese and German competition. Apple may be an example of a coasting organizational culture. Apple's culture of entrepreneurial innovation leads to numerous technological innovations that the company has been unable to capitalize on in capturing the business market (Hawn & Overholt, 2004). Apple seems unable to shift out of the entrepreneurial mode to deliver the products they invent, although the recent success of their I-Pod may mean that they have finally broken out of this pattern. The U.S. government also seemed to have a coasting culture, doing little in the face of intermittent terrorist attacks in Beirut, Yemen, and Africa, until the September 11, 2001, assault on the U.S. homeland.

Highly transactional, contractual organizational cultures and bureaucracies are characterized as attending more to self-interest than to the interest of the organization, as such. Members guard their own turf. Short-term goals are the rule. There is much attention to enforcement of agreements, codes, controls, directions, and standard operating procedures. The organization is an internal marketplace in which much is negotiated according to the rules and regulations. The organization's structure is tall, tight, stable, mechanistic, and centralized. There is a clear, top-down chain of command. Employees have little discretion and are monitored, driven, and controlled. The large civil service agency is illustrative of this contractual or bureaucratic organizational culture. This organization tends to be flattened by the use of electronic networks. Virtual teams are generally horizontal networks.

The somewhat mechanistic pedestrian organization is moderately transactional with little or no transformational qualities. Little gets done that is not a consequence of formal agreements; little change is observed, and risk taking is avoided. There is a general sense of structure and procedure, but it is less complex and well organized as in a true bureaucracy. The organization's leaders are handicapped by having little discretion. Work is routinized. There is little commitment to the organization by either the leaders or members. Many volunteer agencies tend to be pedestrian, lacking the transformational qualities required to arouse its members to extend themselves. Military forces that lose their sense of purpose and relax their rules to allow more play and less work become pedestrian organizations.

The "garbage can" organizational culture, so named by March and Olsen (1976), tends to be lacking in either transactional or transformational leadership; consensus is absent, and everybody "does their own thing" so that the organization is a garbage can of fruitless activities.

Little cooperation among members is observed. Agendas depend on who attends meetings and the problems they personally have as they wait for an arena in which to air their grievances. The organization is formless, confused, shapeless, and without either clear purposes, values, or rules and regulations. Interdepartmental faculty committees often take on this garbage can type of culture. Many of the complaints about committees in industry and government are about such garbage cans.

ORGANIZATIONAL CULTURE
AND QUALITY IMPROVEMENT

To better understand the relationship between organizational culture and effectiveness, a program was developed to explore the role of culture in improving the quality of performance. The ODQ was completed by 130 leaders from a variety of sectors including industry, education, and health care and 877 of their subordinates. The participants were taking part in a community leadership development program, had volunteered for the research, and were mainly from different organizations and a variety of levels in the organizations.

Twenty-seven additional questions were asked that dealt with the same issues of total quality improvement that corporation contestants for the Malcolm Baldridge Awards must answer. The 27 questions were clustered into five factors: organizational vision, information sharing, quality assurance, customer satisfaction, and working with others. Table 7.2 shows the correlations between ODQ ratings of transformational and transactional organizational culture and the five quality improvement factors.

As seen in Table 7.2, organizational vision, information sharing, and perceived customer satisfaction were higher in transformational organizations for both the program participants and their subordinates. Quality assurance and good working relations were also seen as higher by the subordinates but not by the program participants in transformational organizations. The subordinates tended to exhibit slightly more negative correlations with perceived quality improvement ($-.17, -.12, -.11, -.13, \& -.12$). Correlations between transformational cultures and quality improvement for the subordinates were $.23, .23, .24, .22$, and $.17$. In all, those organizations described as transformational appeared more likely to also be seen as doing more to improve their quality of

TABLE 7.2

Relations Between Transformational and Transactional
Organizational Culture and Quality Improvement According
to 130 Community Leaders and Their 877 Subordinates

	Culture			
	Program Participants (N = 130)		Subordinates of Participants (N = 877)	
Amount of Quality Improvement	Transactional	Transformational	Transactional	Transformational
Organizational vision	−.07	.21	−.17	.23
Information sharing	−.08	.15	−.12	.23
Quality assurance	−.12	−.11	.21	.24
Customer satisfaction	−.11	.17	−.13	.22
Working with others	−.04	.06	−.12	.17

Note. From *Evaluate the Impact of Transformational Leadership Training at Individual, Group, Organizational, and Community Levels*, by B. J. Avolio and B. M. Bass, 1994, Final Report to the W. K. Kellogg Foundation. Binghamton, NY: Binghamton University. Copyright 1994 by B. J. Avolio & B. M. Bass. Reprinted with permission.

production and service. Those described as transactional seemed to be doing less well (Avolio & Bass, 1994).

It is important to note that the ODQ, and the typology of organizational cultures derived from it, are useful tools for both better understanding the nature of particular organizations and for understanding how transformational and transactional leadership interact with elements of organizational culture. Although the ODQ has been used extensively as a tool in leadership development programs, it has been underused as a research tool. Indeed, examination of the interaction of leadership and organizational culture has been a neglected research topic. We revisit this issue later.

A BAROMETER OF LEADERSHIP TRAINING

Eighty-seven of the previously mentioned participants and 168 of their subordinates used the ODQ to describe their respective organizations first during training in the Full Range of Leadership (FRL) program (Avolio & Bass, 1991) and again approximately 6 months to 2 years later.

The trained leaders' perception that their organization was transactional decreased from −3.72 to −4.40 from the first to the second administration. After they returned to their home organizations, the subordinates' perceptions of their organization's transactional culture increased from −3.32 to −2.41 from the first to the second administration. The subordinates saw more structure being introduced by their leaders that the leaders did not see. On the other hand, there was strong agreement about the increase in transformational qualities in the different organizations. For the leaders, mean organizational transformational scores rose 6.80 to 10.41; for the followers, the comparable scores rose from 6.60 to 8.70. The changes were statistically significant as well as of practical importance because the overall variations in the distributions of scores tended to be small. As a whole, the scores were concentrated on middle-of-the-range coasting (Avolio & Bass, 1994). We return to the topic of leadership training in chapter 10.

CONCLUSIONS

Organizational cultures can be transformational. They can be transactional or a combination of both or neither. The members of a high contrast, elite professional group or military unit tend to behave as transformational, as well as transactional, leaders toward each other and to the other constituencies of the organization. In the consummate bureaucracy, much transactional leadership is the rule. Both kinds of leadership are missing in the garbage can organization and somewhat more frequent in the coasting organization. Finally, we have found that transformational organizational cultures are more likely to bring about quality improvements.

8

Transformational Leadership of Men and Women

Historically, the vast majority of noted leaders have been men. This is particularly true for those labeled charismatic-transformational—Gandhi, King, Mandela, Kennedy, and even the notorious ones, Hitler, Stalin, Bin Laden. By comparison, only a handful of charismatic female leaders easily come to mind: Eleanor Roosevelt, Queen Elizabeth I, Golda Meir. Yet if the elements of charismatic-transformational leadership are analyzed, they suggest that women might be more likely to engage in transformational leader behaviors and be more effective transformational leaders than men.

For example, the ability to inspirationally motivate followers is largely dependent on skill in emotional communication to effectively and accurately communicate inspiring emotional messages. Consistent research evidence suggests that women as a group are better emotional communicators than men (DePaulo & Friedman, 1998; Hall, 1984). Similarly, providing individualized consideration and being intellectually stimulating require good interpersonal skills, other areas where women may have some advantages over men (Riggio, 1992). Indeed, for more than a decade, popular writers and the mainstream business magazines have been touting the female advantage in leadership (Helgesen, 1990; Rosener, 1990, 1995; see Eagly & Carli, 2003, for a review).

The issue of leadership advantages or disadvantages, and the related issue of similarities and differences in the leadership of men and women, are complex and controversial topics. Are differences in men and women leaders real differences or merely perceived differences influenced by biases and stereotypes of men and women? How have changes in the leadership role—for example, moving from the leader as a power wielder to a more relationship-based approach—influenced how men and women perform in leadership positions? Most important for our purposes, what are the implications of gender differences for transformational leadership?

MEN AND WOMEN AS LEADERS

The issue of how men and women lead has been of interest to scholars for decades. There are two key questions: Do men and women lead differently? That is, do male and female leaders exhibit different forms of leader behavior? The second question concerns whether men or women, as a group, are the more effective leaders, and under what circumstances?

A generation ago, when leaders in business, government, and the military were predominantly male, the few women who were able to succeed were believed to have adopted masculine behaviors and attitudes (Brenner & Bromer, 1981; Kruse & Wintermantel, 1986). They were presumably promoted for demonstrating masculine virtues of ambition, competitiveness, and task orientation. Accordingly, successful female executives were thought to have adopted male characteristics through training or socialization, as they progressed upward in the organization. Although few women were expected to penetrate the glass ceiling and enter the top ranks of management (Morrison, White, Van Velsor, et al., 1987), the successful 40-year-old female manager was expected to behave no differently as a leader than her 40-year-old male counterpart who was another rising star in the organization (Denmark, 1977; Osborn & Vicars, 1976). There is some research evidence to support this notion that the requirements of the leadership role shaped the behavior and styles of female (and male) leaders.

Early research focused on the traditional dichotomy of task-oriented versus relations-oriented leader styles. The prevailing stereotype was that task orientation was a more masculine style, whereas relations orientation, particularly evidenced in nurturing, consideration, and caring, was regarded as more feminine (Eagly & Crowley, 1986; Eagly, Mladinic, & Otto, 1991). A meta-analysis by Eagly and Johnson (1990) of studies from 1961 to 1987 showed that in laboratory experiments, student leaders demonstrated leadership styles that were consistent with stereotypes. That is, female leaders tended to show more relations-oriented and democratic styles than men, with male leaders showing more task-oriented and autocratic styles. However, in studies of male and female managers in actual work organizations, there were no significant differences. An important conclusion that can be drawn from this work is that the role of manager/leader overrode any preexisting gender effects. Women and men in actual leadership positions behaved much the same, due either to role requirements or role expectations that shaped their behavior. As Eagly and Johannesen-Schmidt (2001) note, "leadership roles, like other organizational roles, provide norms that regulate the performance of many tasks, which would therefore be similarly accomplished by male and female role occupants" (p. 784). In addition, female managers in the workplace a generation ago had primarily male managers as their role models for managerial/leadership behavior.

That workplace male and female leaders' task versus relations styles did not differ was actually consistent with the prevailing thinking of leadership scholars about what it takes to be a successful leader. Regardless of their sex, the best leaders were characterized at the time as those who integrated their task and relations orientation in their behavior toward their colleagues and subordinates (Bass, 1990a; Blake & Mouton, 1982; Hall, 1976; Misumi, 1985). The balancing required of task and relations orientation led to the proposition that the best leadership may be found in androgynous attitudes and behaviors (e.g., Porter, Geis, Cooper & Newman, 1985).

Since this earlier work, there have been significant changes in both the population of leaders and in how leaders lead. The proportion of female leaders is rapidly increasing, in work organizations, in government, and elsewhere (Eagly & Carli, 2003). Women now hold about half of the managerial and professional positions in the United States (U.S. Bureau of Labor Statistics, 2003). In addition, half of the 4,000 delegates to the 2004 Democratic U.S. presidential nominating convention were women. Despite that women still face a glass ceiling when it comes to upper level leadership positions (women represent only a small percentage of corporate officers and chief executive officers [CEOs] of large corporations), there is a growing acceptance of women as leaders (Carli & Eagly, 2001; Vecchio, 2002). At the same time, the flattening of organizational hierarchies, the empowerment of followers, and the growing emphasis on quality leader–follower relations have all influenced leadership style. To be effective in today's world, leaders need to be more transformational. And there is growing evidence that women, as a group, are more disposed to transformational leadership behaviors.

EVIDENCE OF SEX DIFFERENCES
IN TRANSFORMATIONAL LEADERSHIP

Anecdotal, research, and meta-analytic evidence all point to the greater tendency for women in leadership positions to be somewhat more transformational and to display less management-by-exception and laissez-faire leadership than their male counterparts. Concomitantly, they are seen by their subordinates and colleagues as slightly, but significantly, more effective and satisfying as leaders.

Anecdotal Evidence

In 1985, in an early training workshop on transformational leadership composed of 12 women and 12 men in upper levels of management of a Fortune 50 firm, Bass (1985) observed (during a survey feedback session) some potentially intriguing sex differences in transformational leadership ratings. Three to five subordinates described each of these 24 leaders using the Multifactor Leadership Questionnaire (MLQ; Form 5R). The profiles for each leader were identified by code numbers only. In the workshop exercise, without knowing their names or gender, Bass selected 4 of the 24 managers with the highest MLQ charismatic leadership scores, which accounts for the greatest percentage of variance in transformational leadership, to participate in a team exercise. The probabilities were that 2 of the 24 would be men, although stereotypes and the literature until then would have suggested that all 4 would be men (see, e.g., Frank & Katcher, 1977; Kruse & Wintermantel, 1986). However, contrary to expectations, all four top-rated charismatic leaders were women, and they were top-rated leaders by a sizable margin. During the exercise, they revealed unusual competencies, presence, and self-confidence.

Around this same time, Riggio was working with a U.S. company that manufactured and distributed hair and skin care products. The upper management team of a dozen leaders consisted of 9 men and 3 women. Two of the three women received the highest scores on measures of charismatic leadership potential (Riggio, 1987). No doubt, these women were also the most transformational of the company's leaders. Shortly thereafter, both women left the company, with one moving to a direct competitor. The loss of these two influential leaders was quite dramatic and coincided with a decline in the company's performance.

Survey Evidence

Clearly, the unexpected anecdotal results could have been due to chance. Nevertheless, the pattern Bass found with the Fortune 50 company's managers was consistent with results found previously in New Zealand with two samples of leaders. In a study completed in 1984, 23 New Zealand educational administrators were evaluated by their direct reports using an earlier form of the MLQ (Form 4). Female supervisors were rated higher on each of the four respective transformational leadership components compared to their male counterparts (Bass, 1985).

A similar pattern was found for transformational leadership ratings for 45 New Zealand professional administrators and managers. Female leaders were rated higher on transformational leadership when compared to their male counterparts. At the same time, men were found more likely to practice management-by-exception.

MLQ (Form 5) data from four separate investigations gathered between 1986 and 1992 supported the conclusion that women display more transformational and less transactional leadership (Bass, Avolio, & Atwater, 1996). In the first study, the majority of leaders assessed— 79 females, 150 males—were middle- to upper level managers from six, mainly high-tech Fortune 500 firms. Subordinates who rated these managers—219 females, 658 males—were typically selected by the focal managers themselves. In the second study, MLQ data were gathered about 38 female and 58 male first-level supervisors. For the second study, the subordinates—147 females and 124 males—who completed the ratings were selected randomly. For the third study, 154 female and 131 male focal leaders were drawn from not-for-profit groups such as small health care, social service, government, and other local agencies as well as small businesses. These focal leaders selected their own 532 women and 381 men as raters before participating in a leadership training program for the leaders. In the fourth study, the subjects—10 female and 36 male leaders—were superintendents, principals, and staff members from public school districts who had asked 81 women and 50 men direct reports to rate their leadership styles.

Some of the differences favoring the female leaders in transformational leadership were small and some failed in statistical significance as individual studies. Nonetheless, in all four studies, the female leaders attained higher scores for all four components of leadership: charisma, inspirational motivation, intellectual stimulation, and individualized consideration. The same was true for contingent reward, although the effects generally were not statistically significant in the separate studies. As for management-by-exception and laissez-faire leadership, no differences emerged between male and female leaders, except in the case of the first-line supervisors of the second sample, where, significantly, women more actively managed-by-exception, and, significantly, men more passively managed-by-exception—the reverse of any expectations based on stereotypes about the behaviors of women and men. Figure 8.1 displays the results of the first study, and Fig. 8.2 does the same for the second study to illustrate the sex differences.

Female raters were more generally lenient in their MLQ assessments of both male and female leaders, but again, contrary to expectations, whether the subordinate providing the MLQ rating was a man or a woman made no difference. This was the same kind of outcome that Komives (1991) found. Her data showed that whether female or male resident assistants of university dormitories reported to a person of the same or different sex made no difference in their view of supervisory leadership or satisfaction with it. Regardless, the interaction of gender dyad composition on leader behavior and effectiveness needs to be researched further.

Corroborative Survey Results

The results favoring women as transformational leaders were confirmed by Druskat (1994), who conducted an MLQ (Form 8Y) survey of 3,352 sisters, 1,541 brothers, and 1,466 priests in the Roman Catholic Church in the United States. Form 8Y, a 40-item version of Form 5, was used. Respondents were instructed to describe the person or group in their congregation to whom they considered themselves accountable.

Transformational leadership divided into a factor of charisma combined with individualized consideration and an inspirational–intellectual stimulation factor. Transactional leadership factors that emerged were contingent reward, active management-by-exception, and a combination of passive management-by-exception with laissez-faire leadership.

(Study 1)

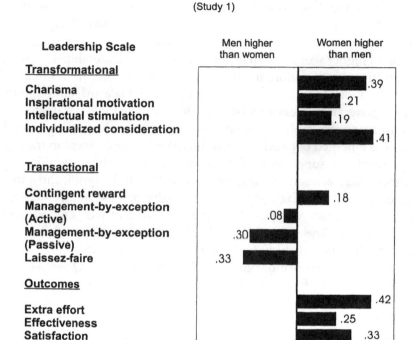

FIG. 8.1. Mean differences among men and women managers in MLQ scores when rated by subordinates. (*Note:* From "Shatter the Glass Ceiling: Women May Make Better Managers," by B. M. Bass and B. J. Avolio, *Human Resource Management*, 1994, *33*, 549–560. Copyright © 1994 by John Wiley & Sons, Inc. Reprinted with permission.)

As expected, for priests, brothers, and sisters, all were rated higher in transformational leadership than the norms for the general population. However, the female leaders were rated as more highly transformational in leadership by their collegial sisters than were the priests and brothers, who were both rated by their male counterparts as highly transformational. Thus, in the aggregate, the sisters were rated more highly transformational than were the brothers and priests. At the same time, however, both brothers and priests earned higher transactional scores than did the sisters. These findings are confounding given that women generally are more lenient raters, and leniency correlates slightly with assigning more transformational ratings and less ratings of passive management-by-exception (Bass & Avolio, 1989).

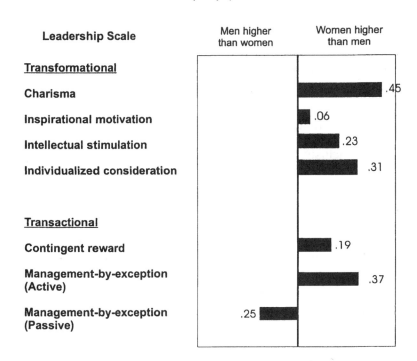

FIG. 8.2.   Mean differences in MLQ scores among men and women managers when rated by subordinates. (*Note:* From "The Transformational and Transactional Leadership of Men and Women," by B. M. Bass, B. J. Avolio, & L. Atwater, 1996 *International Review of Applied Psychology, 45,* 5–34. Copyright © by Psychology Press. Adapted with permission.)

Self-Rated Leadership. Indirect corroboration was provided by Bachman and Gregory (1993). Mentoring is an important aspect of individualized consideration. A survey of 1,736 Kaiser Permanente management employees by Bachman and Gregory found female mentors were somewhat more likely to provide role models for both male and female employees and to be somewhat easier to talk to. Further indirect corroboration was seen in Air Force Academy data. Although only 5 of 40 Air Officer Commanders (AOCs) rated as transformational and transactional by 4,400 cadets at the Air Force Academy were women, strong positive correlations were found between the cadets' ratings and the AOCs' self-assessments with an adjective checklist. Self-assessed feminine attributes of the AOCs correlated .53 with cadet-assessed charisma and .54 with intellectual stimulation. Self-assessed masculine attributes correlated −.11, −.16, and −.04, respectively, with the cadet-assessed transformational scores (Ross, 1990). However, a disconfirming result was reported by Komives (1991). Forty-three female residence hall directors appraised themselves as less transformational, particularly on intellectual stimulation, according to a comparison with 31 men who served as resident hall directors.

Meta-Analytic Evidence

The most conclusive evidence for sex differences in transformational leadership comes from the recent comprehensive meta-analysis by Eagly, Johannesen-Schmidt, and van Engen (2003). This meta-analysis included 45 studies and examined sex differences in all of the leadership behaviors in the Full Range of Leadership (FRL) model, from transformational to transactional to laissez-faire leadership. Although many of the studies used the MLQ, a number of other measures of leadership style/behaviors were also included (e.g., Transformational Leader Questionnaire, Posner & Kouzes's Leadership Practices Inventory). Included among the 45 studies was the very large study conducted at the Center for Leadership Studies, Binghamton University, to provide norms and psychometric data for the MLQ. Also coded were a number of potential moderating and confounding variables, ranging from the organizational level of leadership (supervisory, middle management, executive), the nationality of the leaders, the source of the study (e.g., published journal article, dissertation), the age of the leaders, and various qualities of the sample (e.g., organizational sector, random selection). Measures of leader effectiveness were also obtained where possible.

The results showed that female leaders were more transformational overall (using a composite score for transformational leadership) than were male leaders. As far as the specific components, women scored significantly higher than men on overall Charisma, Idealized Influence (attributed), Inspirational Motivation, Intellectual Stimulation, and Individualized Consideration. Female leaders also scored higher than male leaders on the transactional leadership dimension of contingent reward. Male leaders, on the other hand, received higher scores than female leaders on both Management-by-Exception, passive and active forms, and on Laissez-Faire leadership (see Figure 8.3).

It is important to note, however, that although some of these differences were quite small, the findings were robust. Eagly et al. (2003)

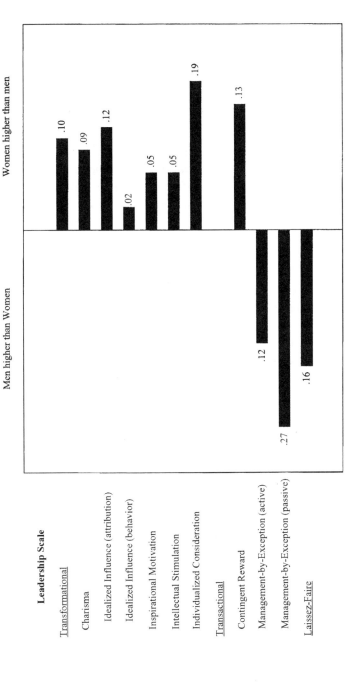

FIG. 8.3. Mean differences in MLQ scores among men and women managers. (Adapted from "Transformational, Transactional, and Laissez-Faire Leadership Styles: A Meta-Analysis Comparing Women and Men," by A. H. Eagly, M. C. Johannesen-Schmidt, & M. L. van Engen, 2003, *Psychological Bulletin, 129*, 569–591.

separately analyzed studies using the MLQ and studies using other measures of charismatic/transformational leadership and received similar results. The pattern of results was also largely unaffected when outliers were removed or included. In addition, there were some moderators. The female "advantage" in transformational leadership increased in educational settings and decreased in business settings. The sex difference also went more strongly in the female direction with older as opposed to younger leaders. Importantly, more recently published studies showed a more pronounced sex difference in transformational leadership than did studies published earlier. Eagly et al. (2003) suspect that this is because "women are gradually becoming freer to manifest leadership behaviors that differ from men's behaviors" (p. 585). In other words, there is greater acceptance of transformational leader behaviors, and this allows female leaders to more freely display this leadership style.

WHY THE DIFFERENCES
IN TRANSFORMATIONAL LEADERSHIP?

An explanation for the male–female differences in transformational leadership may be partly attributable to the tendency for women, as a group, to be more relations-oriented—at least when they are not influenced by the demands of the traditionally "male" managerial role, as mentioned earlier (Eagly, 1991). At the same time, there is a strong component of developmentalism in transformational leadership. By definition, transformational leaders focus on developing and raising the awareness of their followers about the importance of satisfying higher order growth needs (Burns, 1978). Transformational leaders also place heavy emphasis on differentiating among the varying developmental needs of their followers. They attempt to understand the needs of followers and then develop them to higher levels (Bass & Avolio, 1990b). Providing indirect support for this latter position, female leaders see themselves on the Myers-Briggs Type Indicator as more "feeling" (Myers & McCauley, 1985) than men do. Eagly and Johnson (1990) described female leaders as more interested in others than their male counterparts and as more socially sensitive. Female leaders appear to display qualities more in line with transformational leadership. Beyond this, they are also more likely than their male counterparts to attribute their transformational leadership to their relational qualities (Komives, 1991). Additional evidence suggests that female leaders develop unique, individual relationships with each follower, suggesting that they may be better in one-on-one interactions and more devoted to individual follower development than their male counterparts (Yammarino, Dubinsky, Comer, & Jolson, 1997).

Another reason for expecting female leaders to be more transformational is the component of moral value in transformational leadership (Kuhnert & Lewis, 1987), and, when reasoning morally, women highlight responsibility and care; men highlight rights and justice. Again, women may be more transformational because they tend to be less self-serving authoritarians than men in leadership style (Eagly & Johnson, 1990).

It is important to mention that some of the apparent female advantage in transformational leadership may be perceptual. Women may be perceived by subordinates (the persons who are completing many of the measures of transformational leadership, such as the MLQ) as more transformational because of stereotyped notions about how women leaders behave in general. This is the obverse of earlier stereotypes equating traditional notions of the "leader" with male stereotypes (e.g., Lord, Foti, & DeVader, 1984; Lord & Maher, 1993).

One cannot ignore some personality traits favoring transformational leadership in male leaders because, as with men in general, transformational leaders are less conforming, more self-confident, and more likely to take risks (Bass, 1985). Women generally are more conforming, less self-confident, and less likely to take risks (Hennig & Jardim, 1977). In this regard, Hackman, Furniss, Hills, and Paterson (1992) showed in data from 71 men and 82 women in New Zealand that both feminine factors and masculine factors were positively correlated with perceptions of transactional and transformational leadership. The investigators concluded that transformational leadership required a gender balance rather than the traditional leadership stereotype of masculinity.

The Changing Nature of the Leadership Role

Perceptions of the leadership role and sex role stereotyping have both played a large part in contributing to the glass ceiling for women, limiting the number of women who rise to positions of leadership (Eagly & Karau, 2002; Heilman, 2001). The perception of leaders was that they should be aggressive, competitive, and tough—a perception that is changing but one that many still believe (Bersoff, Borgida, & Fiske, 1991; Boyce & Herd, 2003). Yet female leaders who behave this way are often disliked and create dissatisfaction among colleagues and subordinates (Eagly, 1991; Eagly, Makhijani, & Klonsky, 1992; Ridgeway, 2001). District Attorney Marcia Clark, the prosecutor in the O. J. Simpson case, was faulted for her aggressive prosecutorial style. Perhaps the most egregious case was that of Ann Hopkins, a consultant for Price Waterhouse, who won a U.S. Supreme Court discrimination case because she was advised to "act more feminine."

Yet this perception of leaders as tough and aggressive power wielders is changing, with contemporary approaches to leadership focusing more on establishing collaborative relationships and sharing power with followers (e.g., Lipman-Blumen, 1996; Pearce & Conger, 2003). At the same time, flattening of organizational structures, the encouragement of teamwork, and an emphasis on creating learning organizations have made the organizational leadership environment more conducive to transformational leadership and the leadership style more stereotypically conceived of as feminine (e.g., nurturing, socially sensitive, relations oriented). Fortunately, society is changing. Women have become generally more assertive, less dependent, better educated, and more career oriented.

CONCLUSIONS

As suggested, women as a group may be more likely than men to develop the kinds of relations-oriented and socioemotional behaviors that are critical to the development of transformational leadership. At the same time, work organizations are changing the requirements of the leadership role. For more than a decade, organizational cultures have increasingly emphasized caring and concern for others without diminishing the importance of completing the work to be done (Offerman & Gowing, 1990). So it seems that women might have some slight advantage over men in terms of developing transformational leadership characteristics.

On the other hand, although women have achieved gains in middle-level positions of leadership, there is still a glass ceiling that makes it more difficult for women to reach the top-level leadership positions in business, government, the military, and elsewhere. Yet there is growing evidence that this too may change. Young women are demonstrating greater aspirations to positions of leadership, and they are becoming more concerned with issues of power, prestige, and risk-taking behavior (Eagly & Carli, 2003). Those of us in higher education are seeing increasing proportions of women ascend to leadership roles in student government and other areas and increasing numbers of women in MBA programs and programs focused on leadership. Women now make up a sizeable percentage of soldiers in the U.S. military. One has already achieved the rank of lieutenant general in the U.S. Army. As Eagly and Carli (2003) note, this trend helps enlarge the pool of talented individuals from which organizations can select and develop their leaders, leaders who will be particularly effective in meeting the challenges of today and the future.

9

Implications of
Transformational Leadership
for Organizational Policies

Each year *Fortune* magazine publishes its list of the 100 best companies to work for. Some of the companies regularly make the list because of their compensation packages, including extensive and liberal employee benefits and perks. For example, SAS Institute boasts, in addition to high salaries, multiple employee cafeterias, two Montessori child-care centers for employees, an on-site fitness center, and a host of other benefits. This suggests that some of what makes a company a great place to work is transactional in nature. However, perennial best companies include Microsoft, Cisco Systems, and Starbucks. No doubt, part of the reason is the transformational leadership of chief executive officers (CEOs) Bill Gates, John Chambers, and Howard Schultz, respectively. Sometimes, the transformational qualities of the organization are more subtle and are not necessarily linked to charismatic leaders or to extensive transactional wages and benefits.

The 2004 top company to work for is J.M. Smucker, a 107-year-old family business that is best known for its jams and jellies. Based in Orrville, Ohio, Smucker is not all about salaries and benefits and perks. Instead, co-CEOs Tim and Richard Smucker make sure that employees are rewarded, and they also provide individualized consideration, following their father's code of conduct, which includes listening to employees, valuing them, and making them feel like an integral part of the organization (Boorstin, 2004). In a very subtle way, the Smuckers have displayed transformational leadership, keeping employees

126

committed and satisfied even as the company has grown and acquired other food manufacturers.

Leadership makes its presence felt throughout the organization and its activities. We have found that employees not only perform better when they believe their leaders are transformational, but they are more satisfied with the company's performance appraisal system (Waldman, Bass, & Einstein, 1987). Evidence suggests that this may be due to the individualized consideration and intellectual stimulation components of transformational leadership that help employees feel a strong connection to the company and efficacious in their jobs and careers (Parry, 1999, 2002). Even very early research supports this notion; mass downward communications directed toward all workers have a greater impact if the messages are reinforced face to face by their supervisors (Dahle, 1954).

What are the implications of transformational leadership for organizational policies? Where it is in short supply, transformational leadership should be encouraged because it can make a big difference in the organization's performance. Executives, supervisors, administrators, and military officers need to do more than focus on the exchange of material, social, and personal benefits for adequate performance. The inspirational charismatic leader, such as Steve Jobs or General George S. Patton, can instill a sense of mission and articulate a vision of possibilities. The individually considerate leader, such as the Smuckers or Eleanor Roosevelt, can lead followers to merge their self-interests with higher level concerns. The intellectually stimulating leader, such as Bill Gates, questions assumptions that result in revolutionary innovations. This is not to say that charismatic/transformational leaders are always prosocial in their efforts (Conger, 1990); many, like Napoleon Bonaparte and J. P. Morgan, Sr., fulfilled grandiose dreams at the expense of others.

Unless it is already predominantly transformational, the overall amount of transformational leadership in an organization can be increased substantially by suitable organizational and human resources policies. Transformational leadership at all levels in a firm should be encouraged because it can make a big difference in the firm's performance if it is nurtured at any level, not just at the top level of leadership.

Transformational leadership presents opportunities for improving the organization's image, recruitment, selection, promotion, management of diversity, teamwork, training, development, and ability to innovate. It also has implications for the organization's strategic planning and the design of its jobs and organizational structure. Policies can be set in place that arrange for a desirable mix of transformational and transactional styles to appear in the leadership displayed by the individual members of an organization. Such policies can influence the norms, values, and culture of the organization itself. As a consequence, various aspects of the organization, ranging from strategic planning to employee selection, will be favorably affected.

THE CASCADE EFFECT

Leadership in organizations usually begins at the top. There is a tendency for transformational leadership to cascade downward in an organization. The cascading effect of transformational leadership, particularly charismatic leadership, has a number of implications (Bass, Waldman, Avolio, & Bebb, 1987). Training in transformational leadership must be provided at multiple successive levels of the organization, starting at the top. Engaging the higher levels in the mentoring and coaching process is helpful. Higher levels would provide role models for lower levels:

> [M]anagers should be observant in noticing how their behaviors and characteristics are being modeled to ensure that their leadership is cascading effectively. For example, a middle-level manager may demonstrate transformational leadership to a subordinate, lower-level supervisor by delegating important, challenging work assignments and decision making. This lower level supervisor may, in turn, delegate important assignments and decision making indiscriminately to subordinates who are not willing or able to handle such responsibility. The middle-level manager should provide the first-level supervisor with coaching as to how and when delegation can be used effectively. However, *charismatic* leaders . . . may come on "too strong" for some or all of their best subordinates . . . *charismatic* first-level supervisors require fewer *charismatic* qualities in their own superiors. It may be useful to "tone down" one's *charismatic* behavior particularly with those subordinates who are also deemed to be *charismatic* themselves. (pp. 85–86)

In similar fashion, individualized consideration reflected in organizational policies that promote the health and welfare of the organization's members stimulate individualized consideration among the individual members, among the individual units of the organization, as well as among the organization itself (Bass & Avolio, 1990a).

IMPLICATIONS
FOR STRATEGIC PLANNING

The degree to which an organization is based on transformational or transactional leadership affects the openness and control of the flows of information, the importance of organizational rules and procedures, the centralization or decentralization of power, and the bases of power (expert vs. legitimate vs. esteem). All of these will likely affect the organization's strategic planning.

Shrivastava and Nachman (1989) categorized the strategic planning observed in organizations into four clusters: entrepreneurial, bureaucratic, political, and professional. It can be seen that the transformational–transactional paradigm at the individual and organizational levels could account for much of what was found in the 27 organizations they studied. In the entrepreneurial cluster, a confident, entrepreneurial, energetic, knowledgeable individual "uses his personality and *charisma*" (p. 14) to set up the roles for others and control their performance. Examples of these individuals are Howard Head of Head Ski; Marcel Bick of Bic Pen; John Connolly of Crown, Cork, & Seal; and e-Bay's founder Pierre Omidyar. Their businesses would most likely fit the high-contrast or moderately transformational types described in chapter 7.

The second cluster is bureaucratic, which is akin to our highly transactional organizational type:

> Strategic direction and thrust . . . is guided by . . . the bureaucracy . . . standard operating procedures and policies shape the strategy. . . . Members are accustomed to adhering to existing rules and regulation. . . . They take preassigned organizational roles as guides to behavior. (Shrivastava & Nachman, 1989, pp. 54–55)

Specified are the nature and amounts of information, the kinds of analyses that must be completed, and the elaborate ratification and authorization procedures that must go into problem solving and decision making. Texas Instruments is cited as a representative case.

The third cluster is political. Organizational decisions emerge as a consequence of coalitions among the managers, each with functional authority over some part of the organization. Jointly negotiated interests and goals of a dominant coalition of managers determine policies, strategies, and plans. Again, much transactional leadership is apparent. It can be collegial, constructive, and supportive, such as in the case of hospital affiliates closest to our contractual type of organization described in chapter 7, or it can be destructive and fragmenting as in the case of the defunct *Saturday Evening Post*, where jockeying for the top position and lack of control (more akin to our garbage can organization) led to the demise of the organization.

The fourth cluster is professional, and includes, for instance, an R&D organization with a staff of professionally educated and trained specialists whose influence depends on their expertise. There is collegial maintenance of standards, identification with professional peers, and concerns for autonomy and commitment. Small groups devise their own procedures: "strategy making is guided by . . . knowledge-based discourse . . ." (Shrivastava & Nachman, 1989, p. 57). Much of the cultural character here is transformational. Delta Electronics is given as an illustration of such an organization. Hewlett Packard and Microsoft, particularly in their early years, might also fit this model.

Waldman and Javidan (2002) outlined how the charismatic element of transformational leadership might influence strategy. In particular, they discuss the process of how charismatic leaders both build enthusiasm and inspire commitment toward a strategic goal, and they emphasize how environmental uncertainty may enhance this process, as anxious followers look to the charismatic leader for direction (Waldman, Ramirez, House, & Puranam, 2001).

In a study of mid-level managers in a telecommunications firm, Berson and Avolio (2004) found that transformational leaders were more focused on company expansion into new markets. Moreover, transformational leaders were better able to get followers committed to organizational goals, presumably due to their better abilities to communicate with followers.

IMPLICATIONS FOR CORPORATE IMAGE

An organization that is permeated with a suitable pattern of transformational and transactional leadership from top to bottom provides an image, to its own cadres as well as to financial backers, suppliers, customers, clients, and the community at large, of an organization that is oriented toward the future, that is confident about its capabilities, that has personnel who work together for the common good, and that values highly its intellectual resources, flexibility, and the development of its people and products.

Hickman (2004) and others (Austin, 2000; Chrislip & Larson, 1994) discuss a certain form of transformational organization that involves an organization-wide emphasis on social responsibility. Several companies have established partnerships with nonprofit organizations to demonstrate this commitment to the greater good and have enhanced their corporate images in the process. Examples of such organizations are Timberland and its linkage with City Year, an urban service organization; the longstanding partnership between Starbucks and CARE; and the unusual collaboration between Georgia-Pacific and The Nature Conservancy. Hickman (2004) suggests that organizations that have embraced this higher purpose foster greater transformational leadership throughout their organizations, while increasing profitability.

It is no accident that many excellently managed firms today contain a large proportion of transformational leaders. Conversely, the poorly managed "dinosaurs" need to develop a lot more transformational leadership in their organizations. By "a reasonable frequency" of transformational leadership, our frames of reference are the transformational scales of the Multifactor Leadership Questionnaire (MLQ). As has been seen in chapters 3 and 4, all correlate with effectiveness, performance, commitment, and satisfaction.

IMPLICATIONS
FOR RECRUITING

We opened this chapter with a discussion of *Fortune* magazine's list of best companies to work for. All too often, recruiters and job applicants focus on the transactional elements (salary, benefits, perks) when looking for a job and a company in which to work. Greater attention should be paid to the organizational culture, to the company's mission and philosophy, and to its quality and form of leadership.

Organizations with high levels of transformational leadership and a transformational organizational culture should attract better recruits. Candidates are likely to be drawn to an organization whose head is charismatic and inspirational and who is known to be confident, successful, and optimistic. Moreover, prospects are likely to view the

organization more favorably if the interviewer displays individualized consideration. Better educated and brighter prospects will be
impressed in meeting with intellectually stimulating representatives
of the organization during the recruiting process.

IMPLICATIONS FOR SELECTION
AND PROMOTION

The leadership components of idealized influence, inspirational motivation, intellectual stimulation, and individualized consideration
that describe transformational leaders can be incorporated into assessment, selection, and promotion programs (see chap. 11). And as
leadership performance at one level is likely to forecast performance
at the next, followers, peers, and superiors can be used to describe the
current leadership behavior with the MLQ of prospective candidates
for promotion or transfer into positions of increasing supervisory responsibility (see Cannella & Monroe, 1997). Feedback of MLQ results
can also be used for mentoring, counseling, coaching, and training
(Bass & Avolio, 1990a; see chap. 10).

Again, because charismatic and inspirational leaders display various personality attributes, such as high energy, self-confidence, determination, intellectual and verbal skills, strong ego ideals, and an inner
locus of control, measures of such traits can provide valid screening instruments. In the same way, underlying individualized consideration
are coaching skills, preference for and use of two-way communication,
empathy, and willingness to use delegation. Intellectual stimulation
involves general intelligence at lower organizational levels and cognitive creativity at higher levels. Each of these traits and abilities can be
assessed in advance and used as part of larger selection batteries as is
discussed in chapter 11.

When employees rate their managers on the MLQ, they describe
new business leaders as significantly more transformational than established business leaders. Thus, MLQ scores might be used profitably
to identify executives to head new ventures (Bass, 1990b). The parallel
in the military may be sorting out the better garrison from the better
combat commanders. Bass (1985) found that field grade combat officers
were more transformational than those in noncombat assignments,
likely due to the differences in the demands of the two assignments
rather than the officers themselves. Nevertheless, the more transfor-

mational officers in combat are likely to be more effective leaders in combat, but the effects are less likely at home sites.

In a study designed to identify prospects for executive positions in international organizations, Spreitzer, McCall, and Mahoney (1997) found that many of the qualities of transformational leaders, particularly dimensions related to individualized consideration and intellectual stimulation were important for international executives. In addition, these international leaders needed to be flexible, willing to take risks, and willing to learn and grow on the job.

IMPLICATIONS FOR PERSONNEL DEVELOPMENT

A management trainee's first supervisor makes a big difference in the individual's subsequent career success. Vicino and Bass (1978) found that 6 years after a sample of more than 400 managers had joined Humble Oil, those who were more highly rated for merit by superiors at the end of the 6 years reported that they had been given challenging assignments by their initial supervisor (i.e., they had been inspired and intellectually stimulated and had received individualized consideration). The managers were also more highly rated at the end of the 6 years if they had been assigned to initial supervisors with good reputations in the firm. They could model their own leadership style after that of their initial supervisors. For instance, if immediate superiors are more charismatic, their subordinates will also be more charismatic in their leadership (Bass, Waldman, et al., 1987).

Organizational policy must support an understanding and appreciation of the maverick who is willing to take unpopular positions, knows when to reject the conventional wisdom, and takes reasonable risks (Bass, 1990b). The designer of the stealth fighter had to overcome ridicule and disbelief before getting approval to proceed. Policy should encourage the nurturing of intellectual stimulation as a way of life in the organization. In the information age, the best and the brightest should be encouraged and nourished, whereas ordinary members are empowered likewise to fully participate in the efforts for continuous improvement. Innovation and creativity should be fostered at all levels of the organization. Effective reengineering and total quality management programs will depend much on this striving for excellence (see LeBrasseur et al., 2002).

IMPLICATIONS FOR TRAINING
AND DEVELOPMENT

Transformational leadership is a widespread phenomenon (Bass, 1997). As is detailed in chapter 10, it occurs only slightly more frequently at the top than at the bottom of an organization. The gradient was rather small, when comparisons were made among 700 North Atlantic Treaty Organization (NATO) field-grade officers and when U.S. Navy lieutenants were compared with captains and their superiors. It has also been observed by many personnel in their first-level supervisors. As is the subject of chapter 10, transformational leadership can be taught and learned. Shop stewards in correctional institutions, project leaders, first-line supervisors, middle managers, and senior executives in industry, hospitals, education, and elsewhere have benefited from training in transformational leadership (Bass, 1999; Bass & Avolio, 1990a).

IMPLICATIONS FOR LEADERSHIP
EDUCATION

There has been a veritable explosion of leadership education and development programs in U.S. higher education and throughout the world. Nearly every business school offers some sort of leadership development program, and many large companies either offer their own leadership education/training or import them from business schools or consulting organizations (Ayman, Adams, Fisher, & Hartman, 2003). However, what is truly dramatic is the increase in undergraduate leadership education, including programs that offer credentials or degrees in leadership (Riggio, Ciulla, & Sorenson, 2003). Featured prominently in many of these education programs are the theory and concepts of transformational leadership, along with other prominent leadership theories (Ayman et al., 2003). Students learn not only about leadership theory but also about its measurement, including measurement instruments, such as the MLQ. At the U.S. Air Force Academy in Colorado Springs, the MLQ scales are used to show that the transformational leaders among the instructors and staff provide role models for their students. The faculty and students discuss the questionnaire results and their implications (Curphy, 1990).

Clearly, education and training can seldom turn an exclusively transactional leader into a highly transformational leader. Moreover, some leaders, while striving to be transformational leaders, can misuse their training. Their pseudotransformational efforts only further the leader's self-interest and values. Under the influence of such a leader, followers can be directed away from their own best interests and those of the organization as a whole.

For too long, leadership development has been seen mainly as a matter of training, as such, and skill development. But leadership—particularly transformational leadership—should be regarded as an art and a science likely to be enhanced with a quality education process.

IMPLICATIONS
FOR CAREER DEVELOPMENT

There are three ways that the encouragement and application of transformational leadership can help in career development. First, it pays to introduce the concept of transformational leadership by example early in the careers of new personnel and then to provide continuing support for it. Second, its diffusion flows from the top down. Third, the organizational culture should support its development and maintenance. Transformational leadership and the underlying philosophy can become an integral part of an organization's career development program. Pounder (2003) suggests that the concept of transformational leadership can be used as a framework for designing management development programs.

In support of the first point, as previously noted, the first supervisor of a new recruit can make a big difference in the subsequent career success of the recruit (Vicino & Bass, 1978). A policy of individualized consideration at all organizational levels encourages a renewal among individuals to achieve their maximum potential throughout their careers in the organization. In support of the second point is the cascading effect. Managers tend to model their own transformational leadership on that of their immediate superiors or mentors. As higher-ups become more transformational, we see more transformational leadership cascading downward (Bass, Waldman, et al., 1987). To illustrate the third point, policies should be in place so that intellectual stimulation is nurtured and embedded as a way of life in the organization's culture. Organizational policy must support an understanding and appreciation of those who are willing to take unpopular positions at early stages in their careers, know when to reject conventional wisdom, and can accept reasonable risks. There must be a right to fail.

IMPLICATIONS FOR JOB DESIGN AND JOB ASSIGNMENT

As we have noted, highly rated managers had challenging tasks delegated to them by their supervisors when they first joined the company. Jobs should be designed to provide greater challenges. Employees should be able to see themselves as part of a process that provides a product or service in which they may be trained to handle a variety of the jobs required, as needed, to complete the process. This is in contrast to feeling responsible for only a single bundle of tasks (Cascio, 1995). For instance, in assembly work, instead of one person being responsible for the supply of parts, another for joining the parts, another worker for inspecting them, and a fourth person for packaging them, all four persons should be members of a team, trained to handle any of the tasks as needed. A transformational leader who is focused on the individual development of subordinates designs jobs so that they allow people to learn, grow, and be creative. Employees perceive their work as meaningful, are given responsibility for their own work, and see the results of their efforts (see Hackman & Oldham, 1976, 1980).

In chapter 14, we discuss substitutes for leadership. One likely substitute for inspirational motivation is being assigned a challenging task. Individualized consideration should be provided through delegation with guidance and follow-up. This should become an individualizing and developmental way of life in the organization.

Transformational leaders show individualized consideration by paying attention to the particular development needs of each of their followers. Jobs are designed with those needs in mind as well as the needs of the organization. Some followers could profit from the experience of leading a project team. Others need an opportunity to reinforce what they have learned in an advanced training class. Their individually considerate leader assigns them tasks accordingly.

Leaders can be intellectually stimulating to followers if the leaders' own assignments give them the discretion to explore new opportunities, to diagnose organizational problems, and to generate solutions. On the other hand, if leaders are given assignments from a higher authority that involves the leader spending large amounts of time solving small, immediate problems or tasks unrelated to the followers, there will be implications for the quality of transformational leadership of the team. Such leaders are likely to be less intellectually stimulating than those who have the discretion to envision what is needed, who have time to think ahead and to devote time to stimulating followers' thinking.

IMPLICATIONS FOR ORGANIZATIONAL STRUCTURE

Transformational leadership is not a panacea. In many situations, it is inappropriate, and transactional processes are indicated. In general, organizations and agencies that are functioning in stable environments can afford to depend on their one-minute managers to provide the necessary, day-to-day leadership. If the technology, workforce, and environment are stable as well, then things are likely to move along quite well with managers who simply promise and deliver rewards to employees for carrying out assignments. And in stable organizations, even active management-by-exception can be quite effective if the manager monitors employee performance and takes corrective action as needed. Rules and regulations for getting things done, when clearly understood and accepted by the employees, can eliminate the need for leadership under some circumstances.

But when the organization or agency is faced with a turbulent environment; when its products and services are born, live, and die within the span of a few years; or when its current technology can become obsolete, then a rigid organizational structure of rules, regulations, job specifications, and passive management-by-exception becomes the kiss of death. Transformational leadership needs to be fostered at all levels in the organization. To succeed, the organization needs to have the flexibility to forecast and meet new demands and changes as they occur—and only transformational leadership can enable the firm to do so. The ill-structured problems faced by such organic organizations call for leaders with vision, confidence, and determination. These leaders have to move followers to assert themselves, to join enthusiastically in organizational efforts and shared responsibilities for achieving organizational goals. The leaders arouse followers' collective consciousness about what they are attempting to accomplish. Charismatic-inspirational qualities, attention to individualized consideration and to intellectual stimulation are to be sought and encouraged in organizations that must live with continuing demands for renewal and change. More organizations today are of this type—existing in a turbulent, uncertain, and constantly changing environment.

Problems, rapid changes, and uncertainties call for a flexible organization with determined leaders who can inspire employees to participate enthusiastically in team efforts and share in organizational goals. In short, charisma, attention to individualized development, and the ability and willingness to provide intellectual stimulation are critical in leaders whose organizations are faced with demands for renewal and change. At these organizations, fostering transformational leadership through policies of recruitment, selection, promotion, training, and development is likely to pay off in the health, well-being, and effective performance of the organization.

With the cohort of recent and new recruits, the successful organization is the place where individual needs are recognized and enhanced rather than brought into conformity with the old way of doing things. Within the constraints of organizational requirements, the dreamers are allowed to dream and to test the absurd in problem exercises. The leaders know that the best form of leadership builds followers into disciples who take responsibility not only to accept a vision but also to expand that vision even further than their leaders anticipated.

IMPLICATIONS FOR ORGANIZATIONAL DEVELOPMENT

Transformational leadership has direct application to group and organizational development and to management of an increasingly diverse workforce. Following both processes to their logical extreme, a transformational leadership training and development program should be evaluated as successful if the organization has been transformed to a level where it challenges followers to develop themselves as well as others around them. The program should be evaluated as successful if leaders develop themselves so that they can inspire their followers, intellectually stimulate them to solve problems in unique and creative ways, and exercise individualized consideration. If such transformations have occurred both individually and at the group and organizational levels, the stage is set for furthering the organization and its members' achievement of their full potential.

The advantages of transformational leadership can be reinforced by organizational policies, structure, and culture, thus greatly improving the overall performance of both individual members and the organization as a whole. Increased transformational leadership and its effects can occur at every organizational level.

Team Leadership

Leaders need to be individually considerate in dealing with followers from different functional areas and backgrounds and must show sensitivity to these differences. They must avoid glossing over the different constraints faced by their diverse subordinates who may be on different career ladders, have different superiors to whom they report, be of a different race and sex, and who have different needs and different skills and strengths. Individually considerate leaders must show they recognize the multiple identities of their team of diverse followers. They should delegate opportunities to make it possible for followers to represent the team in meetings with other teams, with higher authority and outside agencies. Team leaders need to be sensitive to the demands placed on individual members of the organization from different functional areas, their reputation, and the quality of the relationships in their different functional areas. The effective transformational team leader is culturally sensitive. Offerman and Phan (2002) discuss the culturally adaptive or culturally intelligent leader and suggest that individualized consideration plays a key part in this aspect of effective leadership.

In addition to understanding cultural issues, the team leader must know the capabilities of each team member. Intellectually stimulating leaders take advantage of diverse backgrounds and experiences of their team members, using this understanding to promote greater creativity. Because no team leader can be an expert in all areas represented by the members of the team, the intellectually stimulating leader should serve as a catalyst for creative activity. The leader should move the members to unearth their diverse assumptions and to problem solve in orderly stages. However, the team leader needs to be directive when necessary, clarifying, summarizing, and testing for consensus.

IMPLICATIONS FOR DECISION MAKING

Team and organizational decision making ideally involves scanning, problem discovery, diagnosis, search, evaluations, choice, innovation, authorization, and implementation (Bass, 1983). It should proceed in an orderly forward fashion from scanning to implementation, but it seldom does. For instance, without adequate diagnosis and search, many an ineffective team or organizational leader first makes a choice, then asks for a justifying evaluation of the preempted choice.

The process may flow in a reverse direction. We may observe direct and indirect links and reversals among each of the phases from scanning to implementation. Thus, failed attempts at innovation may result in a need to return to the diagnostic and search processes.

Intellectual stimulation may be necessary when seemingly unresolvable problems of conflicts among the diverse interests of the members arise from the divergent interests of the members. Basic assumptions need to be tested, and alternative viewpoints, procedures, and perspectives need to be developed. Inspirational team and organizational leaders need to promote understanding of the team and the organization's mission and importance. They need to describe what should be done in language that the diverse members find readily understandable. Inspiring leaders remain optimistic about likely outcomes and boost their team's and organization's confidence. Simple words are employed, which permit understanding across the boundaries between the functional areas and the diverse backgrounds of the members. A common language is sought. Technical jargon is avoided wherever possible if it is limited to usage to only a few of the members. Despite the diversity of interests and backgrounds, team and organizational leaders must inspire a clear sense of purpose and direction. They must be keepers of the vision. Team leaders should promote cooperation and alignments of individual, team, and organization.

Ideally, it should be possible to attribute some charisma to the persons who lead the team or organization. They should have a reputation for integrity, capability, and success. In turn, such charismatic leaders should provide a role model for working well with others of different opinions. The leaders, ideally, should be those whom the diverse members will want to emulate.

Not to be forgotten is the need for team and organizational leaders to be transactional as they cope with necessary technical controls and personnel practices. The more they can be constructive and active in their exchanges, the more likely the team or organization will progress as an effective decision-making body.

CONCLUSIONS

Transformational leadership can contribute to improvement in strategic planning, corporate image, recruitment, selection, and transfer of personnel. It also has implications for job and organizational design as well as for decision making and organizational development. Yet how much can individuals improve their performance as transformational leaders through experience and training? This is the topic of the next chapter.

10

The Development
of Transformational
Leadership

Can transformational leadership be developed, taught, and learned?
The quick answer is yes. But to truly understand how individuals become transformational leaders, we need to start with early life experiences, continue with examination of how early leadership experiences
and life experiences may affect later leadership development, and look
at how managers and leaders are trained and developed in organizations. The first part of this chapter addresses some of what is known
about the experiences in one's earlier development that affect one's
ability to become a more transformational leader later in life. Then,
we briefly discuss the elements of training managers and leaders to be
more transformational, describing, in depth, the Full Range Leadership
Program (FRLP), and discuss successful training of transformational
leadership in other programs. The evidence for the effectiveness of
transformational leadership training is presented. Finally, we discuss
the training of transformational teams.

As Day (2000; Day & O'Connor, 2003) and others (Ayman et al.,
2003) noted, there is a distinction between leader development and
leadership development. Leader development focuses on the enhancement of the individual leader, whereas leadership development looks
at how the leaders and followers—the group or organization as a
whole—can develop shared leadership capacity. Early in the chapter,
we focus primarily on the development of individual transformational

142

leaders, but we move on to study a more systemic approach to developing shared leadership.

TRANSFORMATIONAL LEADERSHIP DEVELOPMENT

Personal Background and Early Experiences

Collectively, our leadership centers have hosted hundreds of leaders from all walks of life. When speaking about the most important influences in their personal leadership development, the vast majority mentions the role of one or both parents. Is this simply filial loyalty, or is there something to this?

Micha Popper and his colleagues (Popper & Mayseless, 2003; Popper, Mayseless, & Castelnovo, 2000) noted both the role that parents play in developing transformational leadership as well as the similarities in the behavioral style of good parents and authentic transformational leaders. Similar to good parents, transformational leaders promote followers' maturity and conviction to ideals. They promote concern for others and for society; they encourage independent, critical thinking; and they enhance followers' sense of self-efficacy and self-worth. "[T]ransformational leaders, like good parents, develop self-efficacy and competence by being there for their proteges, by providing challenges, by conceiving high expectations, and by monitoring and providing the kind of scaffolding needed for success without being overbearing" (Popper & Mayseless, 2003, p. 53).

In an interesting study of high school student athletes, it was found that adolescents who rated their parents as more transformational, using the Multifactor Leadership Questionnaire (MLQ), were rated by their peers and coaches as displaying more transformational leadership behaviors, and they were rated as more effective and satisfying team leaders (Zacharatos, Barling, & Kelloway, 2000). This provides additional evidence that suggests that the roots of leadership may begin early in life.

Differences in Life Histories.   Even very early research emphasized the predictive use of using biodata (life history data) to forecast subsequent leadership performance. For example, Cox's (1926) study of the biographies of 300 geniuses focused on elements of life history that contributed to these individuals' success. Evidence from biographical accounts about the development of 69 famous world-class transformational and transactional leaders was reported in anecdotes by Bass (1985) and empirically by Bass, Avolio, and Goodheim (1987).

Owens and Schoenfeldt (1979) in studying job interviewees (primarily male) report that leadership potential correlated with items such as age at the beginning of one's first steady paid job, volunteer work, swim lessons and bike riding, and rural or urban background; early experience as a supervisor; shooting a gun, hiking, camping, repairing cars, and engaging in athletics while in high school; and previous organizational and work experiences as a leader. However, Bettin and Kennedy (1990) showed that the experience had to be relevant to be predictive. Measures of experience, such as time in service and the diversity of experience (in terms of the different number of positions previously held), only added 1% to 5% to the prediction of the current military performance of 84 U.S. Army captains, based on ratings by two superior officers (the battalion commander and the battalion executive officer). What was highly predictive, however, was the relevance of previous assignments and responsibilities assessed by a set of expert judges, which added 20% to the prediction of the current assignments of the captains as company commanders, personnel officers, intelligence officers, operations officers, or logistics officers.

Earlier relevant experiences also appear to contribute to emerging as a more transformational leader in adult life. Among Digital Equipment senior executives, Avolio and Gibbons (1988) compared transactional and transformational leaders (according to MLQ ratings by their immediate subordinates). Differences in life history profiles were revealed in in-depth interviews that were completed with the executives. Interviews were conducted with executives who had been identified as high in transactional or transformational leadership, or low in both.

Highly transformational executives came from families who stressed high standards of excellence along with strong, supportive homes. Executives, rated by their immediate subordinates as highly transformational, reported in retrospective interviews that their parents provided them with challenges but also supported their children's efforts whether they resulted in success or failure, consistent with Popper's work. It was OK to fail as long as you tried your best. Mistakes were considered part of the learning process. Transformational leaders engaged in more leadership activities in high school and college. They did not play at being leaders; rather, their leadership behavior was an integral part of their persona, based on long-term development rather than a quick dose of training. On the other hand, primarily transactional leaders tended to take on particular leadership roles according to the situation they faced—the kind of leadership then taught in most short-term training programs.

Similarly, Yammarino and Bass (1990a) found that those junior naval officers who were rated as more transformational by their subordinates tended to be more involved in high school sports activities, particularly team sports. Again, for Virginia Military Academy cadets, adolescent athletic activities were a positive indicator of subsequent transformational leadership performance (Atwater et al., 1994).

In another retrospective analysis (Avolio, 1994), prior to their beginning a transformational training program, 182 community leaders from different organizations and agencies were asked to complete a questionnaire about their life before volunteering for the program. Included in the Life History Questionnaire were eight questions about their parents' interest, for example, how often did one or both parents "take an interest in how you were doing in your classes in elementary or high school?"

The moral standards and strictness of parents were queried, along with the extent the respondents wanted to emulate their parenting. Experience in high school athletics and other extracurricular activities were examined along with favorableness of attitudes toward school and one's first full-time job.

The 182 focal leaders completed the self-rated MLQ and were rated also by their 856 followers. Overall, a meaningful pattern was found of correlations between the retrospections of one's life history and self- and follower-rated MLQs. Scale scores on a factored cluster of items that recalled positive experiences in elementary and high school correlated between .19 and .24 with all four self-rated components of transformational leadership factored scale scores. Again, feeling positive about the work experiences in one's first full-time job correlated with MLQ self-ratings as follows: charisma, .24; inspirational motivation, .36; intellectual stimulation, .30; and individualized consideration, .27. High parental moral standards correlated .16 with individualized consideration.

Parental interest and parental high moral standards correlated significantly between .16 and .20, with charisma and individualized consideration as measured by followers' MLQ ratings. As would be expected, favorable school experiences correlated .17 with intellectual stimulation as seen in the leader by their followers. Also, a scale based on factored items of frequent engagement in athletics and outside activities during high school correlated −.31 with self-rated intellectual stimulation.

Biodata Analysis. In addition to the empirical findings just described, in an unpublished analysis (Bass & Avolio, n.d.), an intuitive–empirical approach was applied to the biodata. The items and their alternatives had each been placed in the biodata questionnaire because intuitively it was thought that each contributed to at least one of the components of the full range model of transformational–transactional leadership. Table 10.1 presents the biodata items that were associated with each of the full range of leadership components. The criterion used was whether the rate of endorsement of each item was at least 6% greater for those community leaders who scored above the median on each of the MLQ factors. For example, for the charismatic-inspirational factor (a combination of inspirational motivation and idealized influence), leaders above the median were more likely to endorse the 20 items in Table 10.1.

The biodata results lend support to the psychoanalytic view that many celebrated leaders such as Pierre Cardin and Henry Ford were prisoners of their past. Pierre Cardin had a strong need to get even for the wrongs done to him as an Italian youngster growing up in France; there were upheavals in the family, but he had continued strong support from his mother. In response, he democratized fashion, creating a billion dollar *haute couture* for the common man. Henry Ford had a difficult relationship with his father, and he had a close, loving mother who died when he was 13 years old. As an adult, Ford had few real friends and was unable to accept ideas easily from others around him (Kets de Vries, 1994). In the same way the differences in the leadership styles between two such transformational military leaders as Dwight Eisenhower and Douglas MacArthur can be understood to some extent by Eisenhower's more humble beginnings and Douglas MacArthur's, as son of a famous Civil War general. MacArthur was the consummate charismatic; Eisenhower was a great coalition builder.

Transformational leaders in adult life do not just emerge accidentally. As already noted, they are shaped to some degree by the high moral standards set by their parents and parental interest shown in their early performance, particularly in school. Avolio and Gibbons (1988) reported that neither a severely disadvantaged nor highly privileged childhood was conducive to becoming a transformational leader. Most conducive was a childhood with some, but not too much, challenge. Consistent with this, Avolio (1994) found that feeling satisfied with home and school were important in retrospect. Engaging in athletics during adolescence forecasted subsequent transformational leadership among military cadets, yet it was not so for civilian community leaders because of the greater importance of physical competence to military performance and because none of the military cadets and 52% of the community sample was female. Of course, this difference may disappear with the increasing participation of girls in school athletic activities. Sports provide both sexes with experience in trying to overcome challenges, exerting extra effort, meeting high standards, and considering other team members—all behaviors involved in transformational leadership.

EDUCATING AND TRAINING TRANSFORMATIONAL LEADERS

Transformational leadership can be taught and learned. We have already seen how good parenting and early experiences can help develop leaders. In the previous chapter, we mentioned the rise of leadership education programs at the undergraduate and graduate (e.g., business school) level. However, Bennis and Nanus (1985) noted that traditional MBA programs were failing in this endeavor because they most often focused on learning to manage simple, stable situations. Porter and McKibbin (1988), in an influential review of business school curricula, found that little attention was paid to developing students' administrative and leadership skills. As a result of these and other criticisms, business schools have been paying greater attention to the development of leadership skills. More often, business schools and other educational programs concerned with the quality of leadership in their discipline (e.g., public and health care administration, educational administration/leadership) are using transformational leadership as a model for developing leadership skills in students (Pounder, 2003). In addition, the U.S. Air Force Academy has included aspects of transformational leadership training in their classrooms for some time (Curphy, 1990, 1992). In short, some transformational leadership development can take place through traditional college, graduate school, or military

TABLE 10.1
Biodata Items Associated With Each Full Range of Leadership Component

Charismatic Inspirational	Intellectual Stimulation	Individualized Consideration	Contingent Reward	Management-by-Exception	Laissez-Faire Leadership
• Both father and mother succeeded in being good parents, but "I'll do better." • Upbringing was strict but fair. • No, mother was not employed. Did not confide in mother. • Family never moved from one house to another. • Almost always a leader of the gang or "clique." • Usually picked near first for team games. • Participated in student government, fraternity, and social groups in high school. • One of the most active and popular students in high school.	• Father had a graduate degree. • Mother was a college graduate. • Several bookcases full of books available when growing up. • Liked school very much. • Somewhat above average student in high school. • Read one or more newspapers thoroughly each day. • Devoted much time to reading all kinds of material, including work related. • Bothered most by people who brag.	• Had positive relations on the job with immediate superior, coworkers, subordinates, and clients. • A major motivating force in life was to help others. • Had a happy rather than an unhappy childhood. • Was praised as a child as a reward for performance. • Had a mother who took much interest in their K–12 school. • Had well-intentioned but an overly possessive father or a highly formal father.	None	• Both parents were equal in providing discipline (only if respondent was raised by both parents).	• Father was not at all interested in K–12 performance. • Parents interested but did not know what career I wanted to pursue. • When you broke something as a child, parents usually said little or nothing about it. • Parents neither encouraged nor discouraged me to seek school or church offices. • Parents never gave me material rewards for good grades in school. • Was not elected to any offices in the past 5 years.

- Self-actualization most important.
- Liked most listening and creating new ideas on the job.

- Varied from uninterested to strongly interested in schooling.
- Wanted others to feel that "I was a nice person."
- Encouraged others to talk to them about their personal problems.
- Told personal problems by others.

- Preferred teachers hard to get a good grade from.
- Most bothered by other people's lack of initiative.
- Was quite confident of self in most activities.
- Dissatisfied with self once in a while.
- Most important was making the most of abilities (self-actualization).
- Most influencing career was accomplishing an ideal at work.
- Engaged in religious activity 1 to 3 hr a week.
- Read adventure stories, biographies, and historical novels.
- In past 5 years, held offices in clubs and committees.
- Held three to five elected positions in past 3 to 5 years.

education (Ayman et al., 2003). There has been exponential growth in college-based leadership development programs, including the awarding of degrees and certificates (Riggio et al., 2003). Business schools also offer executive education programs that can develop leadership skills, in general, and transformational leadership, in particular.

Another component of training transformational leaders involves counseling, feedback, and guidance to promote self-understanding, awareness, and an appreciation of the range of potential leadership behaviors used by effective transformational leaders. The MLQ can be used as one tool to provide feedback of the leader's self-rating, as well as follower ratings, on the Full Range of Leadership (FRL) components. Other relevant assessment instruments can be used as well. Executive/leadership coaches and counselors are also used to provide feedback and guidance to promote a leader's self-understanding and awareness.

Competencies to Be Learned

The greatest attention in leadership training involves the learning of core leadership competencies. However, it is important to emphasize that leader competencies only represent one (albeit an important) part of leadership development.

Conger and his colleagues (Conger & Benjamin, 1999; Conger & Kanungo, 1988) suggested that their definition of charismatic leadership, which includes the four components of transformational leadership, could be developed by learning five competencies.

1. *Critical evaluation and problem detection.* Practice problem solving coupled with feedback can promote improvement in this first competency. Perhaps the most intense way to develop problem-solving skills, according to Conger, is through action learning (Conger & Toegel, 2003).

2. *Envisioning.* Envisioning can be fostered in learning programs in creative thinking. These teach how to unlearn and to contemplate profound changes. The Quick Environmental Scanning Technique (QUEST) aids such learning. Here participants brainstorm about their organization's environmental circumstances and devise strategies for dealing with change.

3. *The communication skill for conveying a vision.* Rhetorical principles can be learned; practice is provided in trying to portray an

appealing future state, coupled with feedback about the performance.

4. *Impression management.* This reinforces the bases of transformational leadership. For this, one needs to learn how to use to best advantage exemplary behavior, appearance, body language, and verbal skills.

5. *How and when to empower followers.* This enables followers to complete the mission shared with the leader. Empowerment can be enhanced through the competence of transformational leaders in communicating high performance expectations, improving participation in decision making, removing bureaucratic constraints on followers, setting meaningful goals, and applying appropriate systems of reward.

Conger and Benjamin (1999) also emphasized developing the competencies of broad interpersonal skills, a global perspective, ability to build community, and sensitivity to diversity.

Of course, leadership development must go beyond mere skill training. The leader must be committed to developing his or her own leadership capacity. This takes dedication and commitment. It must be internalized. It is important to realize that the best of leaders are both transformational and transactional, but they are likely to be more transformational and less transactional than poorer leaders. Leadership development guides by Bruce Avolio (1999, 2005) emphasize the personal commitment and dedication needed for effective leader development.

FULL RANGE LEADERSHIP DEVELOPMENT

A very important meta-analysis by the Gallup Leadership Institute (2004) examined 100 years of leadership intervention research and determined that attempts to change and develop leadership are indeed effective. This goes for both older intervention programs based on early leadership theories as well as leadership interventions based on transformational and charismatic leadership theories.

A variety of popular programs, such as those of Kouzes and Posner (1987, 2003), the Center for Creative Leadership's Leader Labs, and Conger & Kanungo's (1988) training in charismatic competencies, introduce the transformational–transactional paradigm. The most research-based effort has been the Full Range Leadership Program (FRLP) of Avolio and Bass (1991). FRLP is described in some detail to answer the questions about what and how to train in the paradigm of the FRL, with emphasis on developing more transformational leaders. Much of what is presented is based on training hundreds of leaders in not-for-profit organizations and more than 2,000 leaders in profit-making firms.

Two core elements of the FRLP are feedback of MLQ results and creation of the personal development plan. These are typically done well before the FRLP workshop training. The use of MLQ feedback and development of a personal development plan can also be used to promote leadership development as a stand-alone training method.

Feedback of MLQ Results

For people to change their behavior, perceptions, and attitudes, they must be aware of the specifics that require changes and they must have the motivation to make such changes. A diagnosis is needed to establish appropriate changes in their behavior to improve the success and effectiveness of their leadership. Pile (1988) showed that results from the MLQ could be fed back to each leader beneficially in individual counseling arrangements. A computerized MLQ profile provides counselors and leaders with a comprehensive description of the leaders' performance according to themselves, their subordinates, or coworkers (and their superiors when the 360-degree approach is employed; Bass & Avolio, 1997).

The data are interpreted by the counselors to the leaders. Comparisons are drawn: how the leaders' scores compare to the general norms for other leaders, how the leaders' self-ratings compare with ratings by subordinates or coworkers or superiors, and how the leaders' MLQ scores compare to other leaders in their own organization. On an item-by-item basis for each of the MLQ items, as well as the component factor scores, specific strengths and weaknesses are identified in each of the leaders' profiles.

Because each item does not necessarily identify all of the actions or behaviors that result in the rating, the leaders should give some thought to identifying events, incidents, or actions that can aid in their interpretation of the ratings. In addition to reviewing the normative results, leaders need to consider the absolute frequencies provided from the MLQ, ranging from 0 (*never*) to 4 (*frequently, if not always*)—some of the results may seem absolutely too high or too low. In absolute terms, it is suggested that counselees work to achieve 3.0 or higher in the transformational components, 2.0 or lower in management-by-exception and 1.0 or lower in laissez-faire leadership. At the same time, they should pick out the largest discrepancies between their self-ratings and the ratings received from others and the discrepancies between their own results and normative data that are provided them about their workshop group or their entire organization.

Overall, the feedback should move the leaders to target desired changes. Rather than spending too much time questioning their raters' intentions, leaders need to focus on their new awareness of the broad range of leadership components measured by the MLQ and the individual items within those components as described in chapter 1. Leaders become able to generate personal ideas for self-improvement and specific goals and objectives to be achieved in enhancing the effectiveness of their leadership potential. Priorities can be set along with the methods used to try to achieve the objectives.

A plan often seen is to try to increase one's individualized consideration and reduce one's passive management-by-exception. The focus on individualized consideration fits with seeing that one's self-development is consistent with increasing one's emphasis on developing others to their full potential. The skills and insights regarding self-improvement are the same skills and insights important to developing followers to their full potential. Moreover, a key element of charismatic leadership is role modeling desirable behaviors. Showing a willingness to change one's own behavior when it is counterproductive is likely to rub off on followers. Counselees must decide for themselves whether they are ready for change and, if so, in what directions to make such changes and the time in which they will make the attempts to change.

The Personal Development Plan

During the time period that follows an initial MLQ feedback session, profiled leaders work out their personal development goals and plans. The plan established for an individual leader often varies depending on the specific leader's needs. It may include workshops in areas that require strengthening, one-to-one counseling, observation of other leaders, or some combination of activities. Whatever plan is chosen, the focus is on building the leader's ability to function as a transformational and active transactional leader. In larger organizations, an on-site consultant in organizational development (OD) can serve a very useful role in facilitating the implementation of the leader's plan through process observations of one-to-one meetings between leaders and followers, by being a sounding board for ideas, and by providing support and reinforcement for changes the leader is attempting to implement. Executive coaches can play the same role.

Included in the plan should be a continuation of specific follow-up evaluations. A rather straightforward follow-up might involve readministering the MLQ survey to followers or colleagues of the leader, the leader's superior, and the leader at some designated point in the future. In some situations, it may be appropriate to observe the leader interacting with followers or to interview followers, superiors, and co-workers to get an estimate of the changes observed in the target leader. It should be kept in mind that the process of change and development regarding the leader is generally a long-term one that requires continual updating, feedback, and modification. With most leaders, the changes identified in their developmental plans occur over time. Changes that are abrupt or inconsistent with past behaviors of the leader may be misinterpreted by followers, or even the superior, as well as be seen as threatening (Bass & Avolio, 1997).

As mentioned, although the planning process can take place on an individual basis, it also can be embedded in the formal FRLP training workshop. Resources are available from MindGarden, Inc. (www.mindgarden.com) to assist in training from the full range model.

The Full Range Leadership Program

The original and complete FRLP workshop runs 3 basic training days and 2 to 3 advanced training days with a 3-month interval between the basic and advanced programs. More recently, a briefer, 1- to 1.5-day basic workshop (8–12.5 hr of training time) has been offered, which contains the most critical, core training modules listed in Table 10.2 (available from MindGarden). Typically, a follow-up is planned for 1 year later. The workshops can be massed or spread across several days or weeks—customized to fit particular individual or organizational needs. Cases are also available for discussion (Avolio & Bass, 2002).

Unless the MLQ has been used in prior counseling as described earlier, the MLQ is distributed approximately 4 weeks before the first

TABLE 10.2
The Original FRLP Basic and Advanced Workshops

The Basic FRLP Workshop

Introduction. FRLP begins with an appreciation of the multiple changes that have occurred to organizational life. For example, organizations have to become more responsive to change just to keep up with changing internal and external demands on them as well as to maintain and increase their effectiveness. The introduction also stresses that the participant needs to be both a good manager and a good leader. Good management provides predictability and order to meet the current requirements for products and services; good leadership also envisions new directions and motivates others to move in these new directions.

Module 1: My Ideal Leader and Classifying Leadership Characteristics. This module includes an examination of participants' implicit theories of leadership and leaders who have influenced them. Characteristics of these leaders are explored and clustered. What slowly emerges is that each cluster is one of the components of the transformational leadership model.

Module 2:Introduction to the Full Range of Leadership Model. Participants review each of the components of the Full Range of Leadership (FRL) model and how they relate to activity and effectiveness as leaders. Case studies and behavioral examples focus attention on the various leadership styles found in most organizations. Questions are posed about each component, such as how well it does or does not fit the participants' own behavior and that of their organization.

Module 3: The Many Roads to Transformational Leadership. This module contains a videotape depicting some key behaviors typical of various leadership components.

Module 4: Review MLQ Feedback. Participants receive their own detailed leadership profile based on the rating results of the MLQ. Participants use this to begin developing personal leadership development plans.

Module 5: Role-Playing Transactional and Transformational Leadership. Working in small groups, participants develop a videotape of two contrasting scenes, depicting transactional and transformational leadership, and review and discuss the results.

Module 6: Focus on Individualized Consideration. Participants learn to use delegation to develop their followers' potential. Many ways to make delegation more effective are presented.

Module 7: Peer Ratings. Group members rate their peers on the transformational and transactional leadership behaviors observed during the previous modules and discussions. Participants share feedback to the degree desired of the behaviors and discuss reasons for their ratings and implications for improvement.

Module 8: Leadership Blockages. Potential organizational blocks to the participants' leadership plans are addressed—supervisor, self, followers, and policies. Participants refine the objectives of their leadership plans developed in Module 4 and review strategies to overcome the potential blockages to carrying out their plans.

(Continued)

TABLE 10.2 *(continued)*

The 3-Month Interval Between Basic and Advanced Workshops

During the 3-month interval, participants have time to practice key skills within their own work environment. Advanced readings and cases studies are completed. Participants' leadership plans are tested and refined. The participants may formulate and evaluate specific objectives and assess their organizations' readiness for change. They may involve subordinates, coworkers, and supervisors in discussions about their leadership style. They identify as an organizational problem one that has been difficult to solve and attempt a solution in the Advanced Training Workshop after learning more about intellectual stimulation. They may experiment with different leadership styles. They may also collect survey data on their organizational culture (see chap. 7) from others with whom they work and meet with their supervisors to discuss their leadership development plans.

Advanced FRLP Workshop

Module 9: Review of Leadership Development Plans. The success-to-date of each participant's leadership plan is presented and discussed. Participants review their leadership plans individually and in teams. Reasons for successes and for failures are examined. Problems are discussed and plans revised.

Module 10: Values and Resource Allocation. Participants complete an exercise to understand how their values affect their resource allocation decisions. The four values examined are power, merit, equality, and need.

Module 11: Intellectual Stimulation and Problem Solving. During the 3-month interval, participants have prepared and submitted actual work problems that appeared difficult or impossible to solve. Emphasizing the use of intellectual stimulation, teams work out solutions to selected problems.

Module 12: Understanding Organizational Cultures. Participants focus on understanding the transformational and transactional characteristics of their own organizational cultures, using the Organizational Description Questionnaire (ODQ) described in chapter 7. They systematically examine desired changes and how to effect such changes.

Module 13: Inspirational Motivation. Ways of using inspirational motivation are presented and discussed. This module may be incorporated into Module 14.

Module 14: Charisma and Vision Alignment. This module deals with participants envisioning a near future in which the participants have aligned their own interests as leaders with those of their followers, colleagues, and organization. The relevance of charismatic leadership is considered.

Follow-Up Workshop. An optional follow-up, half day module can be conducted 6 months to 1 year later. A new MLQ feedback from colleagues is produced. Participants discuss the evidence for their successes and failures to improve as they had planned and the reasons why. They revise their plans accordingly and provide a synopsis of their intentions.

day of the Basic Training Workshop. The surveys are distributed to followers (and superiors) by a neutral party and returned anonymously. If circumstances preclude advanced distribution of the MLQ, self-ratings are completed at the start of training. Then, participants near the end of basic training or personnel staff are asked to distribute questionnaires to the followers of the participants for completion and anonymous return.

The FRLP provides education along with skill training. The philosophy of leadership involved in being transformational and transactional is discussed early on. Although the program contains some simulations and exercises, it mainly includes action learning, dealing with real issues, dilemmas, and problems faced back home. It is stressed that there are numerous ways to be a transformational and transactional leader—and that one must be both. It is a question, more often than not, of needing to reduce one's management-by-exception and increasing components of one's transformational leadership. The program proceeds from increasing awareness of the leadership paradigm to learning about alternatives that are conducive to improving oneself as well as well one's followers to adapting, adopting, and internalizing the new ways of thinking and acting.

In the original prototype program, there are 13 or 14 modules, 8 in the Basic Training Workshop of 3 days and 5 or 6 modules in the Advanced Training Workshop of 2 to 3 days. The interval of 3 months between the Basic and Advanced Training Workshops provides opportunities for trying and reinforcing planned changes before returning for the Advanced Training Workshop. The modules are presented in manuals for each participant (Avolio & Bass, 1991) and reviewed with certified trainers who complete a special training-of-trainers program. The original FRLP Basic and Advanced Training Workshops are presented in Table 10.2.

As mentioned, the original basic and advanced FRLP workshops have been completed by thousands of leaders from different sectors—business, government, health care, educational administration, and social services. Facilitators and educators from the United States, Britain, Italy, Denmark, Israel, South Africa, Australia, and elsewhere have been certified in training-of-trainers programs.

The 5- and 6-day workshops conducted with senior and middle managers in human resource management, marketing, manufacturing, finance, and R&D as well as with community leaders have provided considerable evidence that individuals can learn how to become more transformational in their behavior with positive effects on their colleagues' and followers' performance.

As part of the FRLP, self-reports and incidents routinely assess the impact of the program. For instance, as already noted, at the start of the Advanced Training Workshop, in Module 9, participants report on what they have been able to transfer back to their jobs, on what they have learned in the basic workshop, and on the obstacles they confronted. In the same way, the follow-up module 6 months to 2 years later provides the opportunity for a more extensive correlation of ratings and critical incidents that have occurred to the participants as they tried to change (Bass & Avolio, 1990b).

EFFECTIVENESS OF TRANSFORMATIONAL LEADERSHIP TRAINING

Two formal evaluations were conducted with the original FRLP training. One was a controlled field experiment using Canadian shop supervisors (Crookall, 1989), and the other a quasi-experimental field study of leaders from a variety of sectors in the Binghamton area (Avolio & Bass, 1994). These were followed by several field experiments.

Shop Supervisors

For a 3-day modified FRLP workshop, Crookall (1989) arranged to complete an evaluation to compare FRLP trainees with the Hersey and Blanchard (1969) situational leadership program trainees and two measurement control samples that remained untrained. The trainees were shop supervisors working in minimum, medium, and maximum security prisons in Canada. The supervisors worked directly with inmates employed in industrial shops to produce specific products for sale within and outside the prison systems. Each supervisor was rated by the inmates attending class in his shop, using a modified version of the MLQ Form 5. The form was adjusted to provide a reading level commensurate with the inmates' education levels. The experimental design tested the impact of the training programs on increasing the leadership of the supervisors and its resulting effectiveness in various industrial and vocational shops in the prison system.

Significant training effects were obtained on such outcomes as productivity, attendance, and the prosocial behavior of the inmates who worked for the trained supervisors. Specifically, compared with untrained supervisors, trained supervisors were found to be more effective leaders on a variety of specific measures of organizational- and individual-level outcomes. More dramatic effects were reported for FRLP than for situational leadership, although both forms of training were found to improve the shop supervisors' performance compared with the control groups of supervisors.

Although performances of both trained samples improved, in comparison to the three other groups of supervisors, those who were trained in transformational leadership did as well or better at improving productivity, attendance, and citizenship behavior among the inmates; they also won more respect from the inmates.

Community Leaders

A large-scale, quasi-experimental, pre- and postevaluation was reported by Avolio and Bass (1994, 1999). At the time of completion of the evaluation, covering a 3-year period, a total of 489 participants in the vicinity of Binghamton, New York, had finished the Basic Training Workshop, and 400 participants had completed the full program of the Basic and Advanced Training Workshops. They came from 183 organizations in the area served. A sample of 66 of the 400 had completed the follow-up module 6 months to 2 years after the advanced program. Additionally, 105 had completed postassessment evaluations at this time.

Interviews, open-ended questionnaires, and structured questionnaires of participants and their colleagues were methods used to evaluate the efforts. Participants were drawn from 10 sectors of the community. Pretest, posttest, and follow-up data included self-ratings and ratings from colleagues about the leadership, organizational culture, and performance on the job. Also, considerable biographical data, personality data, and leadership performance data were collected before, during, and following training. It was also possible to complete some analyses of change as a consequence of the training effort.

The 66 participants who attended the follow-up module sessions had been rated more transformational according to MLQ results than those who did not attend. All had finished the advanced workshop at least 6 months earlier. A limited number were invited and many did not attend because of conflicts in schedules. This created a ceiling effect that attenuated the overall effects of training. However, the sample of

66 was no different in age, sex, education, or type of their organization (government, industry, education, and health care) from the 489 who had completed the basic program.

Figures 10.1 and 10.2 show the changes in MLQ self-ratings and ratings by followers from before Basic Training Workshop to the follow-up module. As seen in Fig. 10.1, a significant increase of .26 of a standard deviation occurred for self-rated inspirational motivation, .14 for intellectual stimulation, and .23 and .26 for inspirational motivation and intellectual stimulation as assessed by over 300 subordinates. As expected, the biggest transactional shift occurred for management-by-exception, which was reduced by 11% of a standard deviation according to self-ratings and more than one half of a standard deviation (59%) according to subordinates. Rate-rerate comparisons, without intervening training, do not show such changes, and whereas self-ratings may reflect the bias of expectations from attendance in the training, pre- and postsubordinate ratings of subordinates back on the job are unlikely to be contaminated.

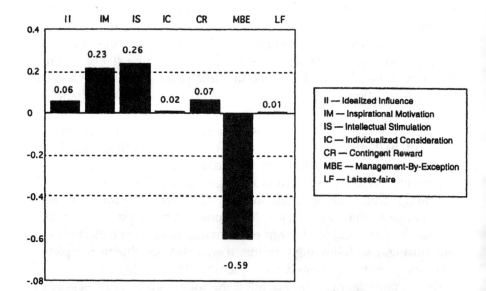

FIG. 10.1.   Standardized change in leadership styles according to self-ratings from before to after training of the leaders in the Full Range of Leadership Program ($N = 87$). (From *Evaluate the Impact of Transformational Leadership Training at Individual, Group, Organizational, and Community Levels*, p. 37, by B. J. Avolio and B. M. Bass, 1994, Final Report to the W. K. Kellogg Foundation, Binghamton University, Binghamton, NY.)

The gains were pinpointed more specifically. An MLQ component was more likely to rise from before the basic workshop to the follow-up module if the component had been included as a goal of the participant's leadership development plan. For instance, intellectual stimulation rose from a mean of 2.53 to a mean of 2.91 if it was a stated goal of the leadership development plan. If it was not, it remained unchanged at 2.74 before and 2.77 at the follow-up. The same effects appeared for the other components of transformational leadership.

A plurality of participants stated that implementation of their leadership development plans was aided by their own motivation, by their colleagues (34%), by knowledge obtained (13%), and through feedback (12%). Lack of self-discipline and time pressures were mentioned as the factors most inhibiting implementation of leadership development plans.

Open-ended evaluative comments were also obtained from the 66 participants of the follow-up module, 6 months to 2 years following their attendance in the Basic and Training Workshops. Of all the comments, 75% were positive, 23% were neutral, and 2% were negative. In addition, participants showed high levels of satisfaction with the FRLP

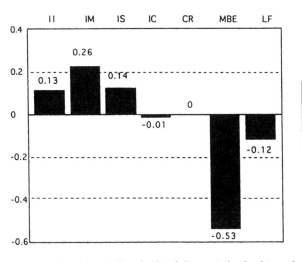

FIG. 10.2.   Standardized change in leadership styles according to 3–5 subordinate raters from before to after training of their leaders in the Full Range of Leadership Program (*N* = 87). (From *Evaluate the Impact of Transformational Leadership Training at Individual, Group, Organizational, and Community Levels*, p. 37, by B. J. Avolio and B. M. Bass, 1994, Final Report to the W. K. Kellogg Foundation, Binghamton University, Binghamton, NY.)

program, with satisfaction rates rising from 88% to 92% from the end of the basic to the end of the advanced program.

An additional 3-day workshop on transformational leadership was conducted for Israeli Defense Forces (IDF) military cadets (Popper, Landau, & Gluskinos, 1992). Transformational leadership still continues in IDF officer training school and was recently subjected to a rigorous evaluation of its effectiveness, which is described later in this chapter.

More Recent Evidence

A field experiment involving 20 bank branch managers also showed positive effects of transformational leadership training (Barling, Weber, & Kelloway, 1996). The managers were assigned to a training (9 managers) or a control (11 managers) condition, with trained managers undergoing a 1-day, group transformational leadership training (similar to the FRLP training), and four one-on-one booster sessions, where each manager discussed the progress of his or her personal development plan with the trainer. Overall, transformational leadership as rated by subordinates increased significantly for the trained leaders but was unchanged in the control group. The largest change was in intellectual stimulation, which was particularly emphasized in the training. In addition, bank workers under the trained leaders showed increases in their levels of organizational commitment, and the financial performance of their branches improved.

A field experiment was conducted with the cooperation of the IDF to both evaluate the ongoing transformational leadership training used by the IDF as well as provide evidence for the positive effects of transformational leadership training (Dvir, Eden, Avolio, & Shamir, 2002). A total of 54 platoon leaders were assigned to a 3-day transformational leadership training (again, based on the FRLP training) or to an eclectic leadership training that focused on leadership issues and models of leadership other than transformational leadership. These platoon leaders had both direct followers, noncommissioned officers (NCOs) who reported directly to the leaders, and indirect followers, who were the cadets reporting to the NCOs but under the command of the leaders. The results showed that leaders who underwent transformational leadership training had a more positive influence on their direct reports' development. Specifically, NCOs of transformationally trained leaders had higher levels of self-efficacy and a more collectivistic orientation, showed a more critical-independent approach to thinking, and reported more extra effort than did NCOs with leaders from the control leadership training groups. The evaluation also showed improved performance of the indirect followers of transformationally trained leaders on a number of military tasks, over the cadets led by leaders receiving the eclectic leadership training. These findings suggest that transformational leaders have strong effects on the development of their immediate followers, presumably through individualized consideration and intellectual stimulation, whereas the inspirational motivation or charisma of the leader motivates more distant follower performance, while, of course, demonstrating the effectiveness of transformational leadership training.

An additional evaluation of both transformational leadership training and counseling/feedback was conducted with 40 managers in a Canadian health care organization (mostly nursing or administrative supervisors). The results suggest that both training and providing feedback about supervisors' leadership style had positive effects on both the leaders' display of transformational behaviors and their rated performance (Kelloway, Barling, & Helleur, 2000).

Finally, Dettmann and Beehr (2004) used the FRLP approach to train 73 nonprofit leaders. Using a longitudinal, quasi-experimental design, they found that leaders perceived themselves as having become more transformational in the short term, but followers perceived the trained leaders as more transformational in the long term.

In summary, transformational leadership training, involving educating trainees about the FRL model, its implications, and its benefits, along with feedback about leadership trainees' existing style, coupled with building transformational leadership skills, seems to be highly effective. It is important to consider, however, the issues discussed in chapter 7 regarding the organizational culture. Transformational leadership training is more effective in organizations that embrace transformational leadership style—cultures that encourage employee development, empowerment, critical thinking, and creativity.

TRAINING TRANSFORMATIONAL TEAMS

Although there are many ways that the MLQ can be used by OD consultants, an advantage of the measure is that it taps constructs that can be dealt with at the individual, group, and organizational levels. As noted in chapter 2, a Team Multifactor Leadership Questionnaire (TMLQ) has been developed for assessing group-level transformational leadership (Bass & Avolio, 1996). As many organizations are changing from a steep hierarchical structure to a flatter, one with fewer levels and lateral multifunctional networks being stressed, teams are being formed to identify problems and propose solutions. High performance teams are sought. Although teams may make better decisions and increase commitment, the team leadership may over time include all members sharing the leadership to some extent. This concept of team leadership, also referred to as shared leadership, is attracting a great deal of attention of both scholars and practitioners (e.g., Avolio, Jung, Murry, & Sivasubramaniam, 1996; Kline, 2003; Pearce & Conger, 2003). It is predicated on the notion that all team members may need to develop the ability to facilitate, to coach, to mentor, and to teach and delegate to develop others. Knowledge of group processes is important to all the team members. High-performance team members display transformational leadership toward each other, and, under certain conditions, teams using shared transformational leadership can outperform teams led by more traditional, vertical leadership (Pearce & Conger, 2003; Pearce & Sims, 2002).

The Model of Expectations

When individuals are working in unstructured collectives, they are working below expectations as a group. When individuals are working in structured groups, they are working at expectations. The individuals in structured groups have well-defined roles. They are working beyond expectations when they form into highly developed, highly performing teams.

Unstructured Groups.   Just as we have been able to describe organizations as transformational or transactional, so can we do the same with reference to teams, but in somewhat more detail, using the TMLQ completed by each member of the group. The members in unstructured groups display behavior like laissez-faire and passive management-by-exception leaders. They are laissez-faire in that they fail to set clear agendas and are confused about responsibilities. As a consequence, there is disorganization and conflict among the individual members. The members display passive management-by-exception toward each other. Such members wait for problems to arise and are hesitant to offer ideas; they are reactive rather than proactive.

Structured Groups. Members in structured groups display, in varying degrees, active management-by-exception and enact constructive transactions. Structured group members monitor each other's performance for deviations and rule enforcement. There is an unwillingness to take risks.

As members become more constructive they increase their commitment, cohesiveness, and drive—they become more focused on their roles and recognition of accomplishments. The members provide agendas, assign tasks, and follow-up, and they become more cooperative and perform as expected.

High-Performance Teams. Members start behaving as a team when they display individually considerate and intellectually stimulating transformational leadership behavior toward each other. They also show individualized consideration, empathy, and alertness to the needs of the other members. They coach, facilitate, and teach each other and are willing to engage in continuous improvement.

As a team, members intellectually stimulate each other. They challenge assumptions and question the traditional ways of doing things, listen to each other's ideas, feel comfortable offering new ideas, and view problems as opportunities to learn.

In the high-performance team, the members inspire each other. They express optimism, excitement, and enthusiasm about the future of the team. High-performance members are confident that the team has the talent and the experience to meet and exceed its most challenging goals. They parallel the individual concept of charisma in that the members show a high degree of unity, pride in the team, loyalty to the team, identification with the team, cohesiveness, and commitment to the team's mission. The members are confident about the competence of each other and their trust in each other. They believe in the dependability, reliability, and integrity of each other and the team as a whole. Members influence each other by helping each other to align their individual interests with the general purpose of the team. They reorient their individual goals for the good of the team. Members serve as role models for each other. As team members move toward full agreement on a shared vision, they increase their level of commitment, become more cohesive, and increase their focus on achieving their team goals. They become highly productive and achieve more than expected. Research demonstrates that teams with high levels of transformational team leadership outperform teams lacking transformational team leadership (Sivasubramaniam, Murry, Avolio, & Jung, 2002).

Application to Training

The FRLP for team training first provides (in a condensed version) the individual training described before. Then team development, following the theory just presented, is centered around the members contracting a consensus about the group's goals, roles, norms, and leadership. Ninety undergraduates completed such team training, and the teams they developed proceeded as teams to complete community projects of their own choice. Industrial teams have been trained in the same way.

CONCLUSIONS

We have shown that early life experiences play a part in the development of transformational leaders. Family, school, and work are important. Additionally, the practicing leader can profit from receiving counseling and feedback about what can be done to improve the leader's profile—more transformational leadership and less management-by-exception. Successful development can also be achieved by the leader and by teams wanting to improve on those components of the FRL that are identified as needing improvement.

11

Predictors and Correlates of Transformational Leadership

Are there certain characteristics—personality, intelligence, temperament—that would predict who might be a more transformational leader? We have already seen in the previous chapter (chap. 10) that early developmental and life experiences seem to influence later transformational leadership. In fact, the U.S. Army uses a biodata inventory of personal experiences and background to help predict performance of its leaders (Atwater et al., 1994).

In this chapter, we review individual factors that have been correlated with the various leadership dimensions from the Full Range of Leadership (FRL) model, with particular attention to those associated with transformational leadership. In addition to the broad range of personality variables, we also explore how multiple dimensions of intelligence (e.g., IQ, emotional intelligence) are related to transformational leadership. Finally, we consider the broader picture of leadership, examining how individual differences might interact with situational factors in influencing leader effectiveness, and we make suggestions for investigating other possible correlates of transformational leadership.

PERSONALITY AND TRANSFORMATIONAL LEADERSHIP

There are a number of personality characteristics that can be theoretically linked to transformational leadership in general and to its specific components. For example, one would expect that the follower-oriented focus of transformational leadership would mean that transformational leaders should be outgoing, extraverted, and sociable. As with most effective leaders, we might expect transformational leaders to be confident and have high self-esteem. We anticipate that transformational leaders are positive, optimistic, and emotionally balanced, and we might suspect that they are able to cope with stressful and complex environments. Finally, we might expect, consistent with notions of charismatic leadership, that transformational leaderships are innovators and more likely to be risk takers than nontransformational leaders.

Extraversion/Sociability

Research has clearly demonstrated that extraverts—persons who are outgoing, talkative, uninhibited, and prefer group settings—are more likely to emerge as leaders in group settings (Bass, 1990a). So extraversion seems to be a characteristic of leaders generally, but it seems particularly relevant for transformational leaders. Judge and Bono (2000) in a study of hundreds of leaders recruited from community leadership training programs in the midwestern United States found a correlation of .28 between extraversion and transformational leadership as measured by Multifactor Leadership Questionnaire (MLQ) ratings from subordinates and supervisors. Moreover, extraversion was significantly correlated with all four components of transformational leadership. Subsequently, Bono and Judge (2004) found that extraversion was most strongly associated with the charisma components (combined idealized influence and inspirational motivation) than with the other two components of transformational leadership. Ployhart et al. (2001) also found that extraversion correlated in the .2–.3 range with ratings of transformational leadership of over 1,000 Asian military recruits being observed in leadership-oriented assessment center exercises. In a dissertation, Monroe (1997) also found that extraversion was positively correlated with transformational leadership in senior managers.

In another study of community leaders Avolio and Bass (1994) found significant correlations (.21 to .25) between measures of sociability and the charismatic and individualized consideration components of the MLQ. In this study, the Myers-Briggs Type Indicator (MBTI) scale of extraversion was significantly correlated only with individualized consideration (.19). Church and Waclawski (1998) found similar connections between transformational leadership and MBTI extraversion.

Ascendancy/Dominance

Ascendancy—the tendency to assume a leadership role in social situations—and dominance are two related constructs that have also been linked to leadership emergence. Avolio and Bass (1994) found that ascendancy, as measured by the Gordon Personal Profile, correlated significantly with all of the components of the MLQ (.19 to .23). It is important to note that both sociability and ascendancy also correlated significantly with the MLQ contingent reward scale in these community leaders. Ross and Offerman (1997) found a positive, but nonsignificant, correlation (.16) between dominance and transformational leadership.

Self-Confidence/Self-Esteem/Self-Efficacy

Effective leaders generally have high levels of self-esteem and positive self-regard (Bass, 1990a). One would expect that this would also be the case for transformational leaders. Particularly, self-confidence should be related to the idealized influence component of transformational leadership. House (1977), in particular, discusses the critical role of self-confidence for charismatic leaders to inspire followers' faith in the charismatic leader.

In a study of U.S. Air Force Academy cadets, Ross and Offerman (1997) found a strong positive correlation (.53) between the self-confidence scale of the Adjective Checklist (ACL; Gough & Heilbrun, 1983) and a composite measure of transformational leadership from the MLQ. Sosik and Megerian (1999) found a positive relationship between a measure of social self-confidence and self-rated transformational leadership but no significant relationship with subordinates' ratings on the MLQ. Using Neuroticism as a measure of lack of self-confidence, Judge and Bono (2000) did not find the expected negative relationships between neuroticism and the MLQ scales.

Self-efficacy is defined as a belief in one's own abilities and is related conceptually to self-confidence (Bandura, 1997). Bandura has argued that self-efficacy is domain specific, and Murphy and colleagues (Murphy, 1992, 2002; Hoyt, Murphy, Halverson, & Watson, 2003) have focused on leadership efficacy, finding that it is related to rated leader performance (Murphy, Chemers, Kohles, & Macauley, 2004). One would expect that leadership efficacy is stronger in transformational than in nontransformational leaders.

Openness to Experience/Risk Taking

Consistent with notions of charismatic leaders being risk takers, creative, and likely to engage in unconventional behaviors (e.g., Conger & Kanungo, 1998), several researchers have explored the relationships between measures of relevant personality constructs and transformational leadership. Using their observational coding of transformational leadership behaviors, Ployhart and colleagues (2001) found small but significant correlations between the Big Five's (NEO Personality Inventory) Openness to Experience scale and ratings of transformational leadership. Judge and Bono (2000) also found a significant correlation between the Openness to Experience scale and the MLQ measures of transformational leadership, suggesting that transformational leaders are creative, have a strong need for change, and are able to adapt to others' perspectives. Consistent with this notion, Bommer, Rubin, and Baldwin (2004) found that transformational leadership is negatively associated with cynicism about organizational change.

In a study of sales managers, Dubinsky, Yammarino, and Jolson (1995) found no significant relationships between managers' innovativeness and transformational leadership but did find small correlations between a measure of their risk taking and the MLQ transformational leadership scales (.18 to .25), with the correlation between risk taking and intellectual stimulation reaching significance (.25).

Locus of Control

Individuals having an internal locus of control—believing that they have personal control over their own lives—should be associated with charismatic and transformational leadership. Howell and Avolio (1993) found that internal locus of control, as measured by 13 items from Rotter's (1966) scale, correlated significantly with individualized consideration (.33), with intellectual stimulation (.25), and with charisma (.18). Gibbons (1986) also found concurrent validities for locus of control using Shostrom's (1974) Personality Orientation Inventory (POI). For example, the self-assessed inner direction, similar to an internal locus of control, correlated .37 with executives' subordinates ratings of their charisma (.37), individualized consideration (.44), inspirational motivation (.33), and contingent reward (.41). However, the correlations were −.04 with management-by-exception and −.27 with laissez-faire leadership.

Hardiness

Transformational leaders might be expected to be psychologically healthy and resilient individuals. Avolio, Bass et al. (1994) analyzed results for 141 Virginia Military Institute (VMI) cadets in their junior year, whose MLQ transformational leadership scores according to subordinates were forecast with a large battery of tests. Included were hardiness measures developed by Kobasa, Maddi, and Kahn (1982). Transformational leadership correlated with all three hardiness measures (rs = .23, .15, and .37). There was also a positive relationship between transformational leadership and measures of leader physical fitness (r = .21).

Dubinsky et al. (1995) investigated the relationship between the components of transformational leadership and both emotional and behavioral coping with stress, using items from Epstein and Meier's (1989) Constructive Thinking Inventory. Although these indices of effective coping were all positively correlated with the MLQ transformational leadership components, none reached significance.

Importantly, there is recent evidence that transformational leaders promote greater hardiness in their followers. In one study, all of the components of transformational leadership, with the exception of inspirational motivation, correlated positively and significantly with a measure of followers' resiliency (Harland, Harrison, Jones, & Reiter-Palmon, 2005).

MULTIPLE INTELLIGENCES AND TRANSFORMATIONAL LEADERSHIP

Historically, there has been considerable research interest in the intelligence of leaders, with early emphases on both general cognitive intelligence (i.e., IQ) and on social intelligence or interpersonal competence (Bass, 1990a). More recently, there has been renewed interest in the role that non-IQ elements of intelligence play in leadership, particularly social intelligence and emotional intelligence (e.g., Goleman, McKee, & Boyatzis, 2002; Riggio, Murphy, & Pirozzolo, 2002).

Cognitive Intelligence

Generally, leaders have needed to be more intelligent but not too much more intelligent than their followers, according to reviews (Ghiselli, 1963; Stogdill, 1948). However, Fiedler (1995, 2002) argues that although intelligence matters in leadership, the relationship is complex.

Atwater and Yammarino (1993) found small but significant correlations between the intelligence scale of the 16PF Inventory (Cattell, 1950) and both the transactional (.23) and transformational (.20) subordinate ratings of U.S. Naval Academy squad leaders. Using assessments of midlevel executives' intelligence (defined as "good judgment") made by a management committee's members, Hater and Bass (1988) found positive correlations with all of the MLQ transformational leadership factors.

Social Intelligence

Thorndike (1920) defined social intelligence as the ability to think and act wisely in social situations and to understand and manage people. This likely represents a broad range of skills that are critical for leaders, particularly transformational leaders. More recently, Zaccaro (2002) suggested that social intelligence is composed of social perceptiveness, social knowledge and reasoning, social influence skills, behavioral flexibility, and other dimensions. There is some evidence that elements of social intelligence are related to transformational leadership (Bass, 2002a). For example, Southwick (1998) found that persuasiveness correlated significantly with all of the MLQ transformational components and that social sensitivity correlated with all but intellectual stimulation. In a study of nearly 1,000 Israeli managers and workers in a manufacturing company, Berson (1999) found moderate (.3 to .4) to substantial correlations (.5 to .6) between transformational leadership and being open, frank, informal and being both careful listeners and careful transmitters of information. As further support of the connection between social intelligence and transformational leadership, Sosik and Dworakivsky (1998) found a small but significant correlation between self-monitoring (skill in social self-presentation) and the charismatic components (idealized influence and inspirational motivation) of the MLQ. Interestingly, Dettmann and Beehr (2004) found the opposite—that low self-monitors were more likely to be transformational leaders. This may have something to do with the issue of authenticity/transparency because low self-monitors are more likely to express their true inner feelings and values, rather than engaging in managing their display.

Emotional Intelligence

The still new construct of emotional intelligence has received a great deal of attention since its 1990 debut in the academic literature (Salovey & Mayer 1990), due in large part, no doubt, to the best-selling book by Goleman (1995). Emotional intelligence deals with a broad range of skills related to emotional awareness, emotional knowledge and understanding, emotional communication, and emotional regulation (Mayer & Salovey, 1997; see also Law, Wong, & Song, 2004; Wong & Law, 2002). Individual differences in constructs related to emotional intelligence/competence have been investigated in the leadership literature, including some research on transformational leadership. For example, in 1959, Mann reviewed 15 early studies that investigated empathy and leadership. Although these results were not conclusive, it is generally believed that empathy is a critical skill for transformational leaders, particularly when being individually considerate (Bass, 1990a). Ashforth and Humphrey (1995) suggest that whereas transactional leadership is primarily a cognitive process of determining fair exchanges, transformational leadership is a process of evoking and managing the emotions of followers—very consistent with concepts of emotional intelligence. Megerian and Sosik (1996) suggest that there should be relatively strong connections between emotional intelligence and transformational leadership. George (2000) suggests that emotional intelligence is related to charismatic leadership.

Gardner and Stough (2002) conducted a study of 110 high-level managers who completed a self-report measure of workplace emotional intelligence and who also completed self-ratings of their leadership using the MLQ. Moderate to large significant correlations were found between all of the transformational leadership scales and all of the emotional intelligence subscales (e.g., emotional management, emotional recognition and expression). There were also significant positive correlations between the MLQ contingent rewards scale and significant negative correlations between emotional intelligence and passive management-by-exception and laissez-faire leadership. Of course, one concern with this study was the use of self-reported leadership ratings.

In another study, charisma as assessed by the MLQ significantly correlated with some subscales of the Trait Meta-Mood Scale, a measure used to assess emotional intelligence (Palmer, Walls, Burgess, & Stough, 2001). In a study of dorm resident advisors and their supervisors, Sivanathan and Fekken (2002) found a positive relationship ($r = .40$) with MLQ transformational leadership scores, as rated by their dorm residents, and the self-report Bar-On emotional quotient inventory.

Groves (2005) investigated the role that skills in emotional communication and skills in social role playing, as measured by Riggio's (1989; Riggio & Carney, 2003) Social Skills Inventory, play in charismatic leadership. Not surprisingly, emotional expressiveness was predictive of follower ratings of charismatic leadership. In addition, skill in social role playing (similar to self-monitoring) also correlated with charismatic leadership ($r = .27$).

In a very recent study, emotion recognition ability, positive affectivity, and agreeableness all positively correlated with transformational leadership behavior (Rubin, Munz, & Bommer, 2004). In addition, emotion recognition ability—an important component of emotional intelligence—moderated the relationship between leader extraversion and transformational leadership.

Practical Intelligence

Sternberg and his colleagues (Sternberg, 2002; Sternberg et al., 2000; Sternberg & Wagner, 1986) have proposed that practical intelligence—knowing how to get things done—is a critical determinant of effective leadership. Conceptually, practical intelligence should be important for transformational leaders in knowing how to listen to and respond to followers.

A key component of practical intelligence is tacit knowledge, knowledge that is not explicitly taught but knowledge that is required to succeed in a particular setting or environment (Sternberg, 2002). Sternberg and his associates developed measures of tacit knowledge for managers and tacit knowledge for military leadership and found that both of these predict effective leadership (Wagner & Sternberg, 1991; Williams, Horvath, Bullis, Forsythe, & Sternberg, 1996).

Other Individual Differences

It is no surprise given the volume of research on transformational leadership that a number of additional individual difference variables are being investigated as possible correlates of transformational and charismatic leadership. For example, Crant and Bateman (2000) found that charismatic leaders tended to have more proactive personalities:

> People who are proactive effect environmental change; they identify opportunities and act on them, show initiative, and persevere until they bring about meaningful change. They transform their organization's mission, find and solve problems, and take it upon themselves to have an impact on the world around them. (p. 65)

On the other hand, certain characteristics are incompatible with transformational leadership. For example, criticalness and aggression have been found to be strongly negatively correlated with transformational leadership (Ross & Offerman, 1997).

PATTERNS OF TRAITS

Table 11.1 is a summary of personality and other individual differences that have been associated with the components of the FRL model, many of which were just reported. Some traits such as self-acceptance, ascendancy, sociability, and internal locus of control seem to differentiate transformational leadership and contingent rewarding from management-by-exception and laissez-faire leadership. Management-by-exception may be less predictable because it is less reliable as a measurement than the other factors and in revisions of the MLQ was separated into active and passive factors. Also, management-by-exception may be state based rather than trait based and may depend more on situational factors, such as the need for physical safety, than on a characteristic behavior of a leader.

Table 11.1 represents zero-order correlations between individual differences and leadership, but an important question is how these predictors might work in combination. In a regression analysis, Ross and Offerman (1997) found that a combination of leader self-confidence and dominance was a better predictor of transformational leadership than either trait alone ($R = .41$).

Atwater and Yammarino (1993), in their study of 107 (99 men) midshipmen at the U.S. Naval Academy who served as summer squad leaders, had the leaders complete a large battery of measures, including a biodata measure (the BIOLEAD index), the Epstein and Mayer Constructive Thinking Inventory, the Myers-Briggs (MBTI),

TABLE 11.1
Personality and Individual Differences
Significantly Associated With the Factors of the FRL

Transformational Factors

Charisma	Charisma-Inspiration	Inspirational Motivation	Intellectual Stimulation	Individualized Consideration
Ascendency	Self-confidence	Ascendency	Ascendency	Ascendency
Sociability	Personal	Sociability	Internal locus	Sociability
(Less) Thinking	Adjustment	Sensing	of control	Extraversion
Feeling	Pragmatism	Internal locus		Feeling
Internal locus	Need for change	of control		Internal locus
of control	Nurturance			of control
Self-acceptance	Femininity			Self-acceptance
	(Less) Aggression			
	(Less) Critical			

Undifferentiated Transformational Leadership

(Less) Thinking than feeling
(Less) Emotional in coping
Behavioral in coping
(Less) Superstitious thinking
Naive optimism
Intelligence
Conformity
Hardiness
Physical fitness

Transactional Factors

Contingent Reward	Management-by-Exception	Laissez-Faire
Ascendency	(Less) Self-acceptance	Emotional stability
Sociability		Personal relations
(Less) Thinking		Original thinking
(Less) Math		Math
Sensing		Biodata
Physical fitness		(Less) Moral reasoning
Internal locus of control		External locus of control
Self-acceptance		(Less) Self-acceptance

Undifferentiated Transactional Leadership

More thinking than feeling•
(Less) Emotional in coping
Behavioral in coping
Naive optimism
(Less) Negative thinking
Intelligence
Self-discipline

and Cattell's (1950) 16PF Inventory. In stepwise regression analyses, regression of subordinates' and superiors' MLQ ratings of the squad leaders on the various individual difference measures, found multiple Rs of .53 and .48, respectively. The results also produced stepwise multiple Rs of .53 and .48, respectively, from the personality assessments for subordinates' and superiors' MLQ ratings of the squad leaders. For the corresponding predictions of transactional leadership, the multiple Rs were .57 and .49. Significant predictors included more behavioral but less emotional coping, greater warmth and intelligence but less conformity (from the 16PF), more sensing and feeling (from the MBTI), and greater participation in varsity sports (from the BIOLEAD inventory). This pattern is somewhat consistent with the notion of transformational leaders, particularly male leaders in a military setting, as being resilient, empathic, cognitively and emotionally intelligent, and less likely to accept the status quo.

TRAITS VERSUS SITUATIONS

Following his review of the literature, Stogdill (1948) concluded that there were some personal dispositions associated with leadership, such as energy level, cognitive ability, persistence, and sense of responsibility (for the extended study, see Bass, 1990a, chap. 5). Nevertheless, he also argued that there needed to be a match between the leader's attributes and the needs of the group to be led. The analysis required attention to both the leader's individual attributes and the demands of the situation.

Bass (1960) concluded that the ANOVA model was the appropriate description of the person-situation issue. Some of the variance (and covariance) in any analysis is due to the leader as a person. No matter where you put some people, they will emerge and succeed as leaders. Universally, we are likely to see more determination in the personality of transformational than transactional leaders, regardless of the situation. Some of the variance is also due to the culture and organization. For example, due to their very different cultures, the transformational leader in Honduras might be more directive than the transformational leader in Norway. Beyond the main effects, some of the variance will also be due to the statistical interaction of person and situation. For example, Saddam Hussein (transformational to many of his Iraqi partisans) would become submissive to international authority when coerced by immediate military force or threat but returned to domineering whenever the force was lifted or the threat became less credible. The question is an empirical one as to how much of the variance is due to the three sources: person, situation, and interaction of person and situation. Multiple levels of analysis are required, and the statistical methodology is now available (e.g., Yammarino, Spangler, & Bass, 1993; Yammarino, Spangler, & Dubinsky, 1998).

Pre-Stogdill, the emphasis was on the person; post-Stogdill, on the situation. The emergence of organizational behavior as a field and of cross-cultural research is premised on the expectations that situations would make a difference. Thus, after Barnlund (1962) systematically recomposed groups with changing membership on successive tasks, he erroneously concluded that most of the variance in the emergence of one as a leader was due to the task circumstances. However, in the 1980s, revised analyses and new evidence turned the tide back toward the person. Thus, Kenny and Zaccaro (1983) reexamined Barnlund's results and found that 49% to 82% of the variance should have been attributed to the person in Barnlund's experiment. Many individual traits already have been tried as predictors of transformational–transactional leadership, and many of these are reviewed here. Although situational factors clearly affect the effectiveness of different leadership styles and behaviors, there is good reason to believe that individual differences play a part in the makeup of transformational (and other forms) of leadership. It has been argued elsewhere that the concept of transformational leadership is universal (Bass, 1997). It can be similarly argued that some of the personal characteristics of individuals make them more able to be transformational (or transactional or laissez-faire) in their leadership behaviors and style. The GLOBE project (House et al., 2004) showed that charismatic transformational leadership is seen as effective by middle managers in 62 countries, but the characterization of charismatic leaders may differ from one country or region to another.

ADDITIONAL PROMISING PREDICTORS

Untried but likely to have some validity for predicting transformational leadership is the Campbell Leadership Index (CLI). Positive correlations would probably emerge with the CLI Leadership Orientation Scale involving checking adjectives to describe yourself as competitive, forceful, adventuresome, risk taking, enthusiastic, inspiring, impressive, resourceful, savvy, well-connected, insightful, forward-looking, creative imaginative, convincing, fluent, active, and healthy. Scales that also might prove predictive include those assessing consideration, empowering, and friendly to predict individualized consideration as well as credible and optimistic for the transformational components of charisma and inspirational leadership.

Other uninvestigated predictors of transformational and transactional leadership include the popular tests of integrity and honesty (Camara & Schneider, 1994). In a similar vein, it would be important for better understanding of authentic transformational leadership to examine individual differences in ethical behavioral tendencies or ethical decision making (Messick & Bazerman, 2001; Trevino, Brown, & Hartman, 2003). The study by Turner et al. (2002) that found that leaders with higher levels of moral reasoning tended to be more transformational is promising. A focus on individual differences in cognitive style is important and would provide insight into how transformational leaders process information. The work of Wofford, Goodwin, and Whittington (1998) on the cognitions of transformational leaders is important pioneering work, as is the notion of transformational and transactional cognitions (Goodwin, Wofford, & Boyd, 2000). It is also important to better understand how followers can play a role in shaping the behavior of charismatic and transformational leaders (Howell & Shamir, 2005).

Greater attention might also be given to issues of role playing, particularly the ability to play competing roles (Hart & Quinn, 1993), and to issues such as the Persean consistency of belief and action (Raelin, 1993), working with paradox (Handy, 1994), and task and relations orientation (Bass, 1967). The effort should be driven by the expanding understanding of transformational leadership and its components. Also to be exploited is the line of investigation carried out by House and his colleagues (e.g., House, Spangler, & Woycke, 1991), Simonton (1988) and Deluga (1997, 1998, 2001), in which charismatic world-class leaders, such as U.S. presidents, are significantly discriminated from counterpart noncharismatic leaders. The discrimination is by objective analyses of the themes within their inaugural addresses or themes used by cabinet members' descriptions of the president's behavior. The validating appraisal of charisma is from the pooled judgments of historians.

A particularly carefully crafted historiometric study of the association of destructive behavior that discriminates personalized from socialized world-class leaders was completed by O'Connor, Mumford, Clifton, Gessner, and Connelly (1995). Ultimately, tests for prediction could be developed to follow from these fundamental studies.

CONCLUSIONS

There are many and varied predictors and correlates of transformational leadership. In addition to providing a better understanding of the psychological makeup of transformational, transactonal, and laissez-faire leaders, studying personality and other individual differences and their relationship to leadership can help us in leader identification, selection, and development. Clearly, however, there is much opportunity for research on this topic.

12

Rank, Status, and
Transformational Leadership

After heroic military victories, Napoleon Bonaparte was appointed to the position of Commander of the French Army in 1795, at the age of 26. Two years later, he was elected to the prestigious Institut de France. In 1802, he granted himself the title of consul for life and capped his rise in status by crowning himself emperor in 1804, which coincided with a senate proclamation and vote of the people—both of which Napoleon arranged.

As with Napoleon, rank and status—the importance and worth of one's position in a nation, group, or organization—can be by appointment, election, or self-authorization. How do rank and status—a very important contingency variable—affect the tendency and need to be more transformational? This question is addressed first by briefly looking at the issue of appointment to a leadership post by higher authority and contrasting it with elected positions of leadership. Next, we briefly discuss self-appointed leaders. Finally, we examine how rank and the level of one's position in an organization affect the tendency to be a transformational leader.

ELECTION VERSUS APPOINTMENT

Elected and appointed leaders derive their legitimacy from different sources, elected leaders from the members of their group or organization, and appointed leaders from higher authority. No data are available on whether appointment or election make a difference, but

it is likely that elected leaders may be more transformational, and appointed leaders may be more transactional. To remain in office, elected
leaders must retain their power as persons in the eyes of their constituents. Elected leaders must cultivate followers. It is difficult for them to
be purely transactional with their constituents. If a higher authority
appoints the leaders, it provides recognition, authority, and specific
responsibilities. This makes it easier for appointed leaders to practice
contingent rewarding and management-by-exception (Bass, 1960).

Self-authorized, emergent leaders may arise also as a consequence
of the personalities and characteristics of the leaders and their followers, but that is a matter of individual differences discussed in chapter
11. As already discussed, for example, leaders with more internal
locus of control are more likely to display transformational leadership;
leaders with more external locus of control are more likely to display
laissez-faire leadership. Likewise, there is some evidence that emotionally intelligent leaders are more transformational, with emotional
intelligence correlating negatively with management-by-exception
and laissez-faire leadership.

Sources of Power

Ordinarily, elected or appointed leaders initially would be expected
to enjoy relatively high status as a result of their appointment or election to the position of leader. Titles, perquisites, and symbols of office
and simple behaviors such as maintaining eye contact or speaking in
a firm voice with few hesitations would help to maintain the higher
status. Leaders who are appointed derive authority and power from
their position in the unit and organization. Specifically, appointed
leaders would be expected to have more of French and Raven's (1959)
legitimate, reward, and coercive power than elected leaders. It would
be expected that they could frequently make use of management-by-
exception if they choose. Elected leaders would be expected to derive
their power from their expertise and their referent power—their esteem as persons (Ben-Yoav, Hollander, & Carnevale, 1983). Of course,
both appointed and elected leaders can be transactional as well as
transformational, depending on their personal predilections and training. They can be successful or unsuccessful as leaders, depending on
their ability to function effectively with their followers and their ability
to meet their followers' important needs. Nonetheless, it is likely that
the elected leaders enjoy advantages over appointed leaders in cha-

risma and individualized consideration if the appointed leaders are unfamiliar to the followers and do not have the reputation or esteem of the elected leaders. Indeed, in one study of appointed leaders, a negative relationship was found between leaders' reward power base and how much they used individualized consideration with followers (Barbuto, Fritz, & Matkin, 2001).

Elected leaders may have emerged in closely contested elections, so much individually considerate patching up of feelings may be needed before the leaders and their constituents can move ahead. This was certainly the case in the 2000 U.S. presidential election, where George W. Bush lost the popular vote but won the presidency by a 5–4 decision in the Supreme Court. In the early days of his term, Bush's popularity was quite low, partly due to the turmoil of the highly contested election. By the end of his first term in 2004, Bush's popularity was evenly divided betweeen those who supported his reelection and those who disliked him intensely.

Elected leaders' advantages disappear if the elected leaders are unable to function effectively or are perceived as functioning ineffectively in the role. The electorate's strong expectations about popular, but incompetent, elected leaders intensify their dissatisfaction should the leaders fail.

Appointed leaders who are effective need to overcome resistance to being appointed rather than elected. In the long run, to remain effective, appointed leaders should avoid relying heavily on the formal authority derived from their appointment to lead primarily by management-by-exception instead of practicing more frequent transformational and contingent rewarding leadership. However, transformational leaders' use of the "harsher" power bases, such as their use of their legitimate authority or even coercive power ("do it because I say so"; "do it or suffer the consequences"), may be more accepted by followers. For example, in a study of police captains, officers reporting to transformational captains were more willing to comply with the leader's use of both "harsh" and "soft" power bases than officers who worked for nontransformational captains (Schwarzwald, Koslowsky, & Agassi, 2001).

Dealing With Follower Expectations

Whether elected, appointed, or self-authorized, leaders need to recognize that followers have shared expectations about their leaders' characteristics and behavior; their perceptions of their leaders' actions are influenced by these beliefs. Leaders need to be individually considerate and understand followers' expectations of the leaders. If, for instance, followers expected their leaders to be strong advocates when representing the followers' views to a higher authority, but the leaders failed to do so, the leaders would lose esteem and referent power in the eyes of their followers, despite the leaders' expertise in performing other functions. Followers might falsely conclude that their leaders would fail to meet expectations in other areas. At the same time, appointed leaders need to build and maintain credibility with followers.

Importance of Powers of Position and Powers of Person to Transformational and Transactional Leadership. Atwater and Yammarino (1989c) asked 285 employees reporting to 118 appointed supervisors in 45 smaller organizations to complete the Multifactor Leadership Questionnaire (MLQ) (Form 8) about their supervisors. The investigators also asked for ratings of the supervisors on 36 items about the bases of the supervisors' power.

Three powers derived from the supervisors' appointment and the status of their position: legitimate power (has authority to give you tasks or assignments), reward power (can provide important benefits and advantages), and coercive power (can get you dismissed from your job). These were in contrast to the two powers derived from the supervisor as a person: expert power (has expert knowledge in how to do your work) and referent power (has personal qualities you admire).

Table 12.1 shows the results obtained. The more the appointed leaders had legitimate power, the more they were transformational. They

TABLE 12.1
Power Related to Transformation–Transactional Leadership

Reflected Status Differences	Transformational Leadership	Contingent Reward	Active Management-by-Exception	Passive Management-by-Exception
Legitimate power	.32**	.13**	.19**	−.22**
Reward power	.45**	.39**	.10	−.25**
Coercive power	−.03	.02	.14*	−.01

*$p < .05$; **$p < .01$.

Note. From *Power, Transformational, and Transactional Leadership* (Technical Report 7), by L. Atwater and F. J. Yammarino, 1989, Binghamton, NY: Center for Leadership Studies, State University of New York. Copyright 1989 by SUNY Binghamton. Reprinted with permission.

practiced active, but not passive, management-by-exception. They made use of their reward power but not their coercive power. Whereas legitimate power encouraged the leaders to more frequently display active management-by-exception, reward power energized them to display contingent rewarding more often.

Here then, we saw an effect of status accruing from one's supervisory position. Those with more legitimate and reward power from their positions as supervisors rolled out more transformational leadership and contingent reward and less passive leadership.

ORGANIZATIONAL LEVEL AND TRANSFORMATIONAL LEADERSHIP

Burns's (1978) seminal book, which introduced the notion of the transforming leader, was about leadership of organizations, political entities, and movements. When Bass began gathering interview and survey data in 1980, data from senior executives and U.S. Army colonels describing their leaders were sought. By 1985, it was clear that transformational leadership could be displayed by middle managers, U.S. Army noncommissioned officers and lieutenants, first-level supervisors, as well as team leaders with no formal rank in the organization. By 1992, it was clear from empirical evidence that transformational leadership could be exhibited by housewives active in a community (Avolio & Bass, 1994) as well as chief executive officers (CEOs) (Yokochi, 1989), U.S. Army colonels (Bass, 1985), world-class leaders of movements (Bass, 1985), and presidents of the United States (House et al., 1991). Also, the work shifted toward transformational teams (Avolio & Bass, 1993); it became clear that every member on a team could learn to be transformational. It is now routine to talk about transformational leadership at the shared, team level (Avolio, et al., 1996; Kozlowski, Gully, Salas, & Cannon-Bowers, 1996; Pearce & Conger, 2003).

Effects of Rank and Status in the Military

Perhaps the sector that is most concerned with issues of rank and status is the military. The military has long made a distinction between leadership and management (in our terms, whether to be transformational or transactional). Roberts (1980) declared that an army officer needed to be both a manager and a leader. Furthermore, Roberts felt that more leadership (transformational) was needed up to the level of the division commander (major general) where management skills become of equal importance. In the field, according to Roberts, the officer is part of a hierarchy "uncertain of its role (and) irresolute in supervision of established goals which themselves are suspect" (Boyd, 1988). Battles can be lost because of lack of management, but leadership is necessary if they are to be won (Bussey, 1980). In combat brigades, statistical-based efficiency can be dangerous (Sorely, 1979). General George S. Patton quipped that "leadership is the thing that wins battles" (Anon., 1985, p. 21). It may be that relatively more transformational leadership is required in combat by the platoon sergeant dealing with the terrain immediately in front than the general dealing with strategy and logistics.

Mixed findings were obtained about the effects of rank in the U.S. Army on the impact of transformational leadership. When it came to extra effort, no difference was found between a sample of 189 colonels and 72 lower level officers, each describing their superior. The impact on the officers' extra effort as a consequence of the transformational leadership they attributed to their superiors was the same for both samples, 37% and 36%, respectively. Nevertheless, leadership effectiveness was enhanced more (48%) by the transformational leadership observed in their superiors by the colonels than by officers at lower levels (27%) (Bass, 1985).

In a more recent study of U.S. Army officers, it was found that the positive effects of transformational army officers on subordinate reported levels of motivation and commitment increased as the rank of the officer increased (Kane & Tremble, 2000). Furthermore, higher ranking army officers were seen, as a group, as more transformational than the lower ranking officers.

In another study, a total of 372 American, Canadian, and German field grade officers serving in the North Atlantic Treaty Organization (NATO) completed the Multifactor Leadership Questionnaire (MLQ) about their immediate superior. Response rates from the 600 solicitations varied from the highest of 88% for Canadian majors to the lowest rate of 36% for German colonels. Whereas significant differences occurred according to nationality, the ranks of major, lieutenant colonel, and colonel did not show much difference in transformational leadership according to their subordinates. Charisma-inspiration means were for major, 2.5; for lieutenant colonel, 2.5; and for colonel, 2.6. For intellectual stimulation, they were, respectively, major, 2.4; lieutenant colonel, 2.5; and colonel, 2.6. For individualized consideration, they were likewise, respectively, for major, 2.4; lieutenant colonel, 2.5; and for colonel, 2.6 (Boyd, 1988).

The American officers' means tended to be the highest for each of the transformational factors (2.7, 2.6, & 2.8), the Canadians' means in the middle (2.6, 2.6, & 2.4), and the Germans' means, the lowest (2.2, 2.4, & 2.5). All three nationalities gave themselves significantly higher self-ratings than they gave their superiors. However, this difference was not attributed to the rank of the officer rated but to the general tendency of the officers to overvalue themselves—a phenomenon found in numerous other studies (Bass & Yammarino, 1991).

U.S. Navy Lieutenants and Captains. In the same way as Boyd (1988) and Yammarino and Bass (1990) found little difference in the mean MLQ profiles of their 186 junior-grade lieutenants, so did the U.S. Navy Surface Fleet rated by their subordinates and 318 naval captains' ratings of their immediate superiors (Deluga, 1990, 1991).

The mean results are shown in Table 12.2. As seen in Table 12.2, rank generally did not make as much difference as might have been expected and was the reverse of expectations. Deluga (1991, 1992) obtained the MLQ ratings of two independent samples of senior naval officers attending the Navy War College who were asked to describe their own immediate superiors. Yammarino and Bass (1990) provided the results on most of the same military form of the MLQ, for 186 U.S. Navy ensigns and junior-grade lieutenants, described by their immediate subordinates.

The junior naval officers were described as more charismatic (2.40) than the senior officers (1.97, 2.18). They were no different in inspirational leadership (2.26 vs. 2.30, 2.27) and a bit higher in intellectual stimulation (2.47 vs. 2.22, 2.37) and individualized consideration (2.50 vs. 2.30). Although there was no difference in laissez-faire leadership between the junior and senior officers (1.31 vs. 1.37), the junior officers were rated as more transactional by their subordinates. Contingent promises were greater for the junior officers than for the senior officers (1.61 vs. 1.34), contingent reward was greater for the junior officers than for the senior officers (2.38 vs. 2.17, 2.08), and active management-by-exception was greater (2.65 vs. 2.48, 2.48). However, passive management-by-exception appeared possibly a bit higher among the senior officers than for the junior officers (2.26 vs. 2.37, 2.45 for the senior officers).

TABLE 12.2
Ranks of Naval Officers Related to Their Subordinates

	Multifactor Leadership Questionnaire (MLQ) Ratings		
	186 Navy Ensigns and Junior-Grade Lieutenants	157 Senior Navy Officers	145 Senior Navy Officers
Transformational			
Charisma	2.40	1.97	2.18
Inspirational leadership	2.26	2.30	2.27
Intellectual stimulation	2.47	2.22	2.37
Individualized consideration	2.50	—	2.30
Transactional			
Contingent rewards (promises)	1.61	1.34	—
Contingent rewards (actual rewards)	2.38	2.17	2.08
Management-by-exception (active)	2.65	2.48	2.48
Management-by-exception (passive)	2.26	2.37	2.45
Nonleadership laissez-faire	1.31	—	1.37

Note. From "The Effects of Transformational, Transactional, and Laissez-Faire Leadership Characteristics on Subordinate Influencing Behavior," by F. J. Yammarino and B. M. Bass, 1990c, *Basic and Applied Psychology, 11*, pp. 191–203. Copyright 1990 by Lawrence Erlbaum Associates. Adapted with permission. Also from "The Relationship of Leader and Subordinate Influencing Activity in Naval Environments," by R. J. Deluga, 1990, *Military Psychology, 3*, pp. 25–39. Copyright 1990 by Lawrence Erlbaum Associates. Adapted with permission.

Impact of Rank and Status in Business and Education

New Zealand Administrators and Management Personnel. The earliest research on organizational rank and transformational leadership was reported in Bass (1985) for two samples from New Zealand. For a sample of 45 business professionals and managers describing their superiors with the MLQ (Form 4), the following nonsignificant correlations were obtained between the organizational level of the leader being rated and their MLQ scores: charisma, .23; intellectual stimulation, .15; individualized consideration, −.22; contingent reward, .14; and management-by-exception, −.21. A different pattern of results was obtained, again not statistically significant, for 23 educational ad-

TABLE 12.3
First- and Second-Level New Zealand
Supervisors and Managers Compared (*N* = 56)

	First-Level Supervisors	Second-Level Managers
Transformational		
Charismatic behavior	2.60	2.82
Intellectual stimulation	2.54	2.70
Individualized consideration	2.54	2.77
Transactional		
Contingent reward	1.91	2.32
Management-by-exception	2.02	1.95

Note. From "Transformational Leadership and the Falling Dominoes Effect," by B. M. Bass, D. A. Waldman, B. J. Avolio, and M. Bebb, 1987, *Group and Organization Studies, 12,* pp. 73–87. Copyright 1987 by Sage. Adapted by permission.

ministrators. The correlations with organizational level were charisma, –.18; intellectual stimulation, –.04; individualized consideration, –.16; contingent reward, –.04 and management-by-exception, –.26. It would seem if rank made any difference in the transformational–transactional leadership of administrators, the results depended on whether the leaders were in business or in educational administration.

MLQ (Form 4) data was collected about an additional 56 New Zealand first-level supervisors and their second-level management superiors by Bass et al. (1987). Table 12.3 shows the comparisons. Here the pattern obtained suggested that higher level leaders evidenced more transformational leadership and contingent reward and slightly less management-by-exception.

Japanese Executives and Managers. Yokochi (1989) was able to collect MLQ data on higher level executives and lower level managers, each described by their subordinates in 14 large Japanese corporations, and again found little difference in the levels of the focal executives and managers being rated. Table 12.4 displays the results.

Again, overall, no significance was attached to the rank of the two samples, except possibly in the use of contingent reward more frequently by the higher level executives (1.78) in comparison to the lower level managers (1.59)

It may appear reasonable to expect different patterns of transformational–transactional leadership from leaders of different rank and status at higher, compared to lower, organizational levels. Empirical

TABLE 12.4
Comparison of Managers and Senior Executives
in 14 Japanese Firms

	MLQ Scale	
	Managers (N = 60–66)	Executives (N = 62–66)
Transformational		
Charisma	2.34	2.30
Inspirational motivation	2.18	2.19
Intellectual stimulation	2.69	2.60
Individualized consideration	2.73	2.75
Transactional		
Contingent reward	1.59	1.78
Management-by-exception	1.71	1.71
Laissez-faire	1.18	1.29

Note. From *Leadership Styles of Japanese Business Executives and Managers: Transformational and Transactional,* by N. Yokochi, 1989, unpublished doctoral dissertation, United States International University, San Diego, CA. Copyright 1989, by United States International University. Adapted with permission.

results suggest that differences of consequence vary from one type of organizational setting to another. The envisioning, enabling, and empowering of the general may involve a broader and more abstract, complex array of issues than that of the sergeant, but the sergeant can show just as much transformational leadership in dealing with a more concrete and simpler array of tasks. The transformational–transactional model can be applied to each. The behaviors may differ, although the same concepts are relevant. Nonetheless, it is in a meta-analysis that some small, but significant, patterns may be discerned.

Meta-Analytic Results

The meta-analysis completed by Lowe et al. (1996) was partly described in chapter 1. The analysis compared leaders lower in their organizations with those higher in their same organizations. The analysts examined the differences in corrected correlations attained for lower and higher levels of rank and status between the MLQ components and rated effectiveness. For the 2,089 to 4,222 raters, little difference emerged in the correlations between levels. For the lower and higher levels of status in their organizations, the corrected correlations obtained by the leaders from their subordinates' ratings of MLQ scales and effectiveness for the lower and higher levels, respectively, were as follows: charisma, .70, .70; intellectual stimulation, .58, .61; individualized consideration, .60, .60; contingent reward, .36, .48; and management-by-exception, .10 and .12. Contingent reward did appear to contribute more to effectiveness among the higher level managers.

Some small but significant differences were found in mean MLQ scores between the upper and lower levels in rank. The means for the upper and lower levels are shown in Table 12.5. Although no mean differences in charisma and contingent reward appeared between leaders at the upper and lower organizational levels, it can be seen that leaders at the lower level were judged by their followers as somewhat more intellectually stimulating (2.5 vs. 2.41) and individually considerate (2.59 vs. 2.41) than their upper level counterparts. However, they were also seen as practicing considerably more management-by-exception (2.45 vs. 2.11).

For the broad array of organizations that were included in the many samples combined in the meta-analysis, it does not seem unreasonable to infer that management-by-exception, at least in New Zealand and U.S. civilian managers, is likely to be more frequently exhibited by lower levels of management. A study of power differences suggests that it is passive rather than active management-by-exception that is involved.

TABLE 12.5
Means MLQ Scores for Upper Level
and Lower Level Leaders

	Organizational Level of Leaders (N = 2,089 to 4,222 subordinate raters)	
MLQ Leadership Scale	Lower	Higher
Charisma	2.52	2.52
Intellectual stimulation	2.41	2.51
Individualized consideration	2.41	2.59
Contingent reward	1.85	1.82
Management-by-exception	2.11	2.45

Note. From "Effectiveness Correlates of Transformational and Transactional Leadership: A Meta-analytic Review of the MLQ Literature," by K. Lowe, K. G. Kroek, and N. Sivasubramanian, 1996, *Leadership Quarterly, 7,* pp. 385–425. Copyright 1996 JAI Press. Adapted with permission.

CONCLUSION

In sum, leaders are more likely to be transformational when they have legitimate and reward power; without it, they are more likely to practice passive management-by-exception. There is also some limited evidence (and there are certainly inconsistencies) that transformational leadership increases with the rank and status of the leader. But the rank of leader forms a complex pattern of results depending on the sector (e.g., military, business, education)—within the military the branch of service, the method of data collection, and nationality. The relationships are indeed complex. One factor that may have complicated these findings was the failure to differentiate the leader's individually considerate empowerment from laissez-faire leadership. This distinction will be discussed in the next chapter.

13

Empowerment and Transformational Leadership

In the past two decades, volumes have been written about the importance of empowerment. Empowerment is widely touted for its effectiveness, particularly where followers' commitment, loyalty, and involvement are sought. Empowering leadership means providing autonomy to one's followers. As much as possible, followers are allowed and encouraged to enable, direct, and control themselves in carrying out their responsibilities in aligning their goals with the goals of their leader and the larger organization. At the heart of transformational leadership is the development of followers, with much of this occurring through effective empowering of followers by leaders.

Empowerment is a product of individualized consideration, but it also involves elements of intellectual stimulation. Yet empowerment of followers by a leader involves delegating important tasks and responsibilities to them. To truly empower, the leader must at times take a hands-off approach. This passing of responsibility to followers, however, is also a characteristic of laissez-faire leadership. How is empowerment differentiated from laissez-faire leadership?

Laissez-faire leadership means that the autonomy of one's followers is obtained by default. The leader avoids providing direction and support, shows lack of caring for what the followers do, and abdicates responsibilities by burying himself or herself in busywork, deflecting requests for help, abdicating any responsibility for follower performance, and absenting himself or herself from the scene physically or mentally.

Sometimes, laissez-faire leadership can masquerade as empowerment. One of us knew a chair of an academic department who, when faced with a task, would delegate it to a department member or to a subcommittee. Under the guise of shared responsibility and development of junior faculty, this chairperson was able to delegate nearly all of his responsibilities, much of it to young, inexperienced faculty members. The department performed passably, but not well. Delegation was so complete that during a several week absence of the chairperson to deal with personal issues, no one even knew their leader was gone.

Laissez-faire leadership is negatively related to all of the components of transformational leadership and, ordinarily, is the epitome of ineptness and ineffectiveness. Truly empowered followers are more likely to have a transformational leader, and empowered followers typically perform better and have better personal development.

EMPOWERMENT

To illustrate what is meant by empowerment, consider the transformational leadership of two commanding generals, one in the U.S. Air Force and the other in the U.S. Army. Devilbiss and Siebold (1987) presented these two examples of transformational leadership by commanding generals and their empowering effects on an Air Command and an Army corps. When General W. L. Creech assumed command of the U.S. Air Force Tactical Air Command (TAC), he began with intellectual simulation. "He started by simply allowing himself to think in a different way" (Devilbiss & Siebold, 1987, p. 7). Creech saw the policies of centralization and consolidation were dehumanizing and focused on TAC's end-of-the-line product: TAC aircraft and the people responsible for them. He restructured the organization by moving authority and responsibility downward to meet clear and simple goals to instill pride, enthusiasm, a sense of ownership, and psychological investment in the product by those responsible. Individualized consideration was emphasized in treating people's needs and working conditions at all levels as important.

Smaller squadron multifunctional repair teams replaced the larger wings. Squadrons were assigned responsibility for specific aircraft. Squadron colors and crew chiefs' names were painted on the aircraft, along with the pilots' names. "Excellence became an obsession" (Finegan, 1987, p. 46). Dramatic improvements occurred in sortie rates and aircraft mission capability. In providing a professional environment, personnel developed pride of ownership and took more responsibility through their motivation to do so. Management control became less management-by-exception and more a matter of transformationally inspired and empowered worker motivation (Finegan, 1987).

The second example was General Walter F. Ulmer's enhancement of the readiness of III Corps at Ft. Hood, Texas. He restructured the corps through much delegation of authority, responsibility, and accountability. He created a "Greenbook," incorporating the new policies he set. Tips to leaders of all ranks included keeping "priorities, goals and objectives constantly in focus." An individually considerate climate of support and empowerment were to be fostered. Clear standards and trust were to be promoted by encouraging organizational consistency, professional education, and attention to the needs of the individual soldiers and their families.

The effects of the transformation at Ft. Hood were "greatly affected by each individual in the chain of leadership through whom information and power passed" (CATA, 1986, p. 17). Effects were noted in just a few months after the changeover. These effects included increased combat effectiveness of battalions, higher standards of discipline, stronger unit identity, more caring leadership, improved teamwork, and greater military professionalism. The leadership of the officers improved in information sharing, loyalty to the organization, intellectual stimulation of subordinates, setting of moral standards and good examples, and assuming of responsibilities (Malone, 1985). Objective improvements ranged from more effective use of soldiers to reduction in accidents. The fundamental mechanism underlying both the TAC and Ft. Hood transformations was empowerment.

Empowerment and Superleadership

Superleadership was seen as the ultimate vehicle for empowerment by Manz and Sims (1995, 2001). The empowering superleader educates the follower so that each learns how to act as a self-leader. Behavioral-focused and cognitive-focused strategies are employed to lead yourself.

The following list includes the behavior-focused and the cognitive-focused strategies. A behavioral strategy, for example, is selecting a specific behavior that you want to change. A cognitive-focused strategy is considering what is naturally rewarding about the work you do (Sims & Lorenzi, 1992).

Behavior-Focused Strategies

Self-Observation—observing and gathering information about specific behaviors that you have targeted for change.

Self-Set Goals—setting goals for your own work efforts.

Management of Cues—arranging and altering cues in the work environment to facilitate your desired personal behaviors.

Rehearsal—physical or mental practice of work activities before you actually perform them.

Self-Reward—providing yourself with personally valued rewards for completing desirable behaviors.

Self-Punishment/Criticism—administering punishments to yourself for behaving in undesirable ways.

Cognitive-Focused Strategies

Building Natural Rewards Into Tasks—self-redesign of where and how you do your work to increase the level of natural rewards in your job. Natural rewards that are part of, rather than separate from, the work (i.e., the work, like a hobby, becomes the reward) result from activities that cause you to feel the following:

- a sense of competence;
- a sense of self-control; and
- a sense of purpose.

Focusing Thinking on Natural Rewards—purposely focusing your thinking on the naturally rewarding features of your work.

Establishing Effective Thought Patterns—establishing constructive and effective habits or patterns in your thinking (e.g., a tendency to search for opportunities rather than obstacles embedded in challenges) by managing the following:

- beliefs and assumptions;
- mental imagery; and
- internal self-talk.

Evidence of the Value of Empowerment

Although not all empowerment of followers leads to effective outcomes, there is considerable evidence of payoff. Menon (2001) mentions that internalization of goals is an important component of successful empowerment of followers. Cohen and Ledford (1994) completed a quasi-experiment to assess the effectiveness of self-managing teams in a telecommunications firm. The teams were involved with customer service, technical and administrative support, and management. The study included 1,337 employees, supervisors, managers, and union presidents. Those in self-managing teams were more effective than those in traditionally managed units doing the same kind of work. Manz and Sims (1995) provide additional examples of improved outcomes from creating automonous work groups.

Masi (1994) collected MLQ (Form 5X) data on midlevel leaders from their subordinates and from the leaders themselves in the U. S. Army Recruting Command. He also gathered data from the same source on an "Empowerment for Quality" questionnaire (Masi & Cooke, 2000). The key 17 items included one scale of items that dealt with the alignment of employee and organization goals. A second set dealt with capabilities developed and resources provided. A third set dealt with trust, integrity, and cooperation. A fourth set dealt with discretionary authority and latitude. A response rate of 41.5% was obtained from the sample of 2,596 prospective respondents. Commitment to quality as well as motivation to achieve and to succeed were correlated with perceived cultural norms of empowerment.

Effects of Transformational Leadership. In a study of 47 teams of workers in four Korean organizations, Jung and Sosik (2002) explored the relationships between transformational leadership, follower empowerment, and perceived group effectiveness. They found not only that transformational leaders empowered followers but also that empowerment enhanced the team's collective sense of efficacy, which in turn led to enhanced perceptions of the work team's effectiveness. Although transformational leadership had direct effects on perceptions of group effectiveness, empowerment also played an important part. These results are similar to those found by Conger, Kanungo, and Menon (2000) with charismatic leaders.

Similar results were found by Brossoit (2000). In a study of more than 300 employees in a U.S. Fortune 100 company, transformational leadership, using the MLQ (Form 5X), had a direct effect on worker job satisfaction but did not correlate with worker performance based on supervisor ratings. However, it was found that the relationship between transformational leadership and job satisfaction was mediated by employee empowerment. Furthermore, transformational leadership did have a small impact on worker performance when mediated by employee empowerment. Fuller, Morrison, Jones, Bridger, & Brown (1999) also found that employee empowerment mediated the relationship between transformational leadership and follower job satisfaction. Jung et al. (2003) found that transformational leadership led to greater employee empowerment and a more creative/innovative organizational culture in Taiwanese companies.

When Empowerment Is Needed

Empowerment is not for every organization. Organizations have a life cycle: entrepreneurial beginnings, growth, maturity, and decline. If the organization survives in a renewal, the stages continue with restructuring, dismantling of the bureaucracy, employee involvement, continuous improvement, and cultural change. At each stage, leadership requirements may differ. The leader of renewal after the breakup of AT&T had to shift the thinking of the norms of its employees from concentrating on the organization as a service to an organization needing to meet the challenges of the marketplace and competition. Particularly important in accomplishing renewal is replacement of traditional control measures by empowerment of the workforce, which, with its commitment to renewal, brings on more self-planning, self-direction, and self-control—an approach first presented by Myers (1968) as "every employee, a manager."

Following the deregulation of utilities, one California energy provider conducted a detailed assessment of existing and potential managers' possession of skills relevant to the new environment focused on increased global competition and customer service. Emphasis was placed on selecting managers who felt a sense of personal empowerment, as well as those who possessed team skills and were able to challenge and empower followers (Bobrow & Leonards, 1997).

Spreitzer (1996) explored the conditions under which employees felt greater empowerment. She found that employees who have a sense of low role ambiguity, who have access to important organizational information, and who work in a participative environment felt more empowered.

The Dark Side of Empowerment

Leader empowerment of followers is ordinarily thought to be a good thing. However, empowerment can have negative consequences when the followers' goals are out of alignment with the organization's goals. Empowerment also can have negative consequences when the followers' goals oppose the organization's goals. Empowerment of followers may provide them with the opportunity to sabotage the organization. Empowerment may generate inflexible norms that are detrimental to the organization's and the individual follower's creativity.

Although the philosophically bright side of empowerment is to increase productivity and efficiency, overcome resistance to change, and increase the sense of ownership and responsibility, its dark side is also that it can be seen as paternalistic. According to a British scholar, "It's 'Thatcherism' clothed in the warmth of humanistic language." Leaders talk about empowering followers, but they actually are unwilling to share the power. The imbalance in power between leaders and followers is maintained. Empowerment of followers may mean that the followers become more responsible for failures. Moreover, leaders can take back the gift. Finally, in its encouragement of self-actualization in followers, empowerment can foster self-interest rather than goals that go beyond the individual follower (Alimo-Metcalfe, 1994).

As for empowering managers, those of lower ranks and status find more barriers to such empowerment, according to Howard and Wellins (1994). They surveyed 61 senior leaders and managers, 317 lower level leaders and managers, and 904 associates. The associates did not have anyone reporting directly to them. Although nominally a study of high involvement, the survey questioned how much the organization involved all levels of employees as true partners in achieving its objectives for "high involvement organizations empower their employees by pushing down decision-making responsibility. . . . They share information, knowledge, power to act, and rewards throughout the work force" (Howard & Wellins, 1994, p. 4).

Although transformational leaders can use intellectual stimulation and individualized consideration to empower followers, the charismatic elements, particularly idealized influence, can foster a potentially unhealthy dependence on the leader (Kark et al., 2003). This sort of follower dependence is noted in research on charismatic leaders (e.g., Conger & Kanungo, 1998; Kets de Vries, 1988).

Efforts of Level. First, Howard and Wellins (1994) found that the higher the organizational status of a respondent, the less frequently they found barriers to be highly involved in their work for the organization. The lower their status, the more they felt that the organization's and their leaders' motives were barriers. At the same time, the senior leaders/managers, as shown in Table 13.1, saw considerably more high involvement in their business unit than did those of lower ranks in their organizations.

As shown in Table 13.2, senior managers were seen to invest too little time and money to effect the changes necessary for empowerment.

Written comments about the dark side of empowerment in the Howard and Wellins (1994) survey included the following: "Consistent behavior should be a constant of someone in a leadership role. If this doesn't exist, then trust breaks down, and the whole ship begins

TABLE 13.1

Relation of Level in the Organization and the Perceived
Promotion and Implementation of High Involvement

	Extent High Involvement Promoted	Extent High Involvement Implemented
61 senior managers	4.3*	3.8
317 middle managers	3.9	3.6
904 associates	3.3	3.1

*1 = Not at all; 5 = To a very great extent.
Note. From *High-Involvement Leadership: Changing Roles for Changing Times,* by A. Howard and H. Wellins, 1994, Tenafly, NJ: Leadership Research Institute. Copyright 1994 by Leadership Research Institute. Adapted with permission.

TABLE 13.2

Barriers to Empowerment Due to Senior Management

	Senior Management as Barriers
Little time/money for change	3.35*
Directive leadership practices	3.22
Insufficient leadership	3.18
Reluctant to share information	3.16
Unclear vision and values	3.11
Not committed to change	3.11
No urgency for change	2.95

*1 = Not at all; 5 = To a very great extent. Respondents: All categories (N = 1,269).
Note. From *High-Involvement Leadership: Changing Roles for Changing Times,* by A. Howard and H. Wellins, 1994, Tenafly, NJ: Leadership Research Institute. Copyright 1994 by Leadership Research Institute. Adapted with permission.

to sink" (p. 5) and "Upper management often does not support high-involvement leadership practices when they have a negative short-term impact on performance" (p. 2).

In addition to an inadequate amount of trust building on the part of management and a lack of trust in them by their employees, leaders were seen too infrequently taking the roles of champion and supporter. Subordinates felt unencouraged in that leaders were only sometimes observed to get higher management to act on employees' suggestions or to reward employee performance with notes, public praise, or visible symbols. Employees were usually blamed for failures rather than circumstances. Rather than looking at process and system problems, leaders often assigned personal blame to individuals, a practice that discouraged justifiable risk taking.

As has been found repeatedly in MLQ research (see Bass & Yammarino, 1991), Howard and Wellins (1994) found that leaders inflated their self-reports. Leaders also were asked to describe how often they personally performed each of 22 empowering activities. Each leader's responses were matched to the average ratings of that leader's behavior by his or her subordinates. Such comparisons were made for 210 first-level and 56 midlevel leaders. The leaders inflated their ratings relative to those of their subordinates, especially in serving as models of trust, champions, change agents, and team builders.

The danger here is that if leaders believe they are better at empowering leadership than they really are, this could lessen their motivation to change. Furthermore, subordinates described themselves as less trustful when the leader's overevaluation was greater. Thus, leaders who are most out of touch with their subordinates' reports are likely to have difficulty in establishing trust between themselves and their followers.

There was disagreement between leaders and their subordinates about the leaders' empowering behavior, particularly in roles performed impersonally or behind the scenes. Agreement between 266 leaders and their matched subordinates on the frequency of leader behaviors was modest at best. Agreement between leaders and their subordinates was higher about performance such as envisioning, inspiring, and championing and lower about their relations with other departments and removal of obstacles that hinder employees in doing their jobs.

Delegation was seen to be problematic because some leaders had problems letting go. They were seen to delegate the responsibility but hold back resources. They asked for input on next year's budget at the last minute and then did not use the input. Empowerment turned to laissez-faire leadership when the leader's workload increased. "I have too much work to do"; "Don't bother me." Leaders were seen to fail to provide enough direction and coordination so that their subordinates remained comfortable with what supposedly they had been empowered to do.

THE EMPOWERING LEADER

Transformational Leadership and Empowerment

It is the transformational leader who fosters empowered followers. Thus, in a survey of two levels of leaders in the U. S. Army Recruiting Command, Masi (1994) found that the existence of a cultural norm of empowerment correlated .22 with the transformational style of the station commanders in 53 of the companies involved. Likewise, self-reported feelings of empowerment of 240 recruiters correlated .30 with reports of a cultural norm of empowerment at their stations. Individuals felt more empowered if their leaders were more transformational ($\beta = .19$) and less transactional ($\beta = -.05$).

Although Howard and Wellins used different labels, they were clearly describing transformational and transactional leadership and its effects. Their empowering leaders were transformational: visionary, inspirational, supportive, championing, facilitative, and individually considerate. They were not transactional "controllers, commanders, rulers, judges or guards." Instead of telling, they were now more likely to be asking.

Empowerment is assisted by the leader's attention to the attractiveness or cohesiveness of the followers or their attractiveness to each other. The empowering leader may highlight pending crises to energize followers into action. The leader will encourage feelings of warmth and acceptance among the followers.

The empowering leader displays inspirational motivation by striving to point out the importance of an assignment, the positive qualities of other followers, and the ways in which they can complement one another's strengths. The leader points to the challenge involved and the recognition that success will bring.

The importance of inspirational leadership is illustrated in a study by Seltzer and Miller (1990). They found a number of transformational

TABLE 13.3
Follower Reactions to Empowering
Leadership Behavior

Empowering Leader Behavior	Subordinate Reaction	
	Sense of Self-Efficacy	Intrinsic Motivation
Shared decision making	.13*	.15*
Cohesive team building	.16*	.18**
Encouragement of individual development	.13*	.10
Inspirational goal setting	.20**	.19**
Fostering of autonomy	.10	.14
Setting of high expectations	.16*	.18**

*p < .05; **p < .01.

Note. From Leader Behavior and Subordinate Empowerment in a Human Service Organization, by J. Seltzer and L. E. Miller, 1990, paper presented to the Academy of Management, San Francisco. Copyright 1990 by J. Seltzer & L. E. Miller. Reprinted with permission.

leader behaviors that contributed in a medium-sized human service organization to the organization's mission, which included creating an empowering environment for clients and staff. For a total of 194 respondents, followers' sense of self-efficacy and intrinsic motivation were positively correlated with the empowering leadership behaviors of their immediate superior. Correlations were as shown in Table 13.3. Note that the highest correlations were with inspirational goal setting and the setting of high expectations. Contingent rewards such as commendations and bonuses may provide tangible reinforcements making use of the empowerment.

Making Empowerment More Effective

As already noted in the dark side of empowerment, empowerment brings many problems. In particular, empowered followers may develop a set of norms that govern group members' behavior, and these norms may be inconsistent with or counter to the goals of the leader and the organization. These "empowered" follower cultures can impede group performance and inhibit critical decision-making processes. Two counterproductive group processes that can be linked to follower empowerment are groupthink and social loafing. Leaders need to be aware of these and be prepared to deal with them.

Countering Groupthink. Empowered followers may employ groupthink, in which they uncritically conform to each other's opinions to redefine their goals to perpetuate their own security and personal needs rather than as salutary changes to benefit the organization. They may avoid introducing disturbing information or disagreeing with each other so harmony will be preserved. This groupthink results in the loss of critical information and creative ideas (Janis & Mann, 1977). To help counter uncritical conformity and suppression of new or constructive ideas associated with the groupthink syndrome, the leader may intellectually stimulate followers by questioning the followers' thinking and assumptions, support followers who voice unusual or provocative ideas to reduce the conformity, and encourage more flexibility in the norms that may stem from empowerment. President John Kennedy demonstrated this form of transformational leadership when he challenged individual members of his cabinet to play a devil's advocate role in decision-making meetings (Janis, 1982).

Countering Social Loafing. A common complaint in group work is one or more members coasting along on the efforts of the other members, what has been termed social loafing (Latane, Williams, & Harkins, 1979). The loafers may take advantage of the fact that no single member is responsible for the group's performance. Shared responsibility may result in some members feeling no responsibility for the group's work. The empowering leader may need to use transactional and transformational leadership if empowerment results in social loafing by some of the followers. This can particularly occur when individual contributions are hard to identify.

Contingent reward, active management-by-exception, and transformational diagnosis and action may be needed to restore the loafers' commitments and involvements. If free-riding by a follower occurs as a consequence of empowerment, in which one follower shirks work because another is doing it, adjustments in workloads are needed.

Effectively Delegating. A very important component in making empowerment work is for the leader to delegate effectively. In any hierarchical organization, the most common approach to a leader empowering followers is by means of the delegation process. Avolio and Bass (1991) searched the literature on delegation and extracted 20 ways to make delegating more effective.

1. Share problems, offer suggestions and appropriate alternatives for completing an objective.
2. Give information necessary to do the task.
3. Maintain an appropriate level of personal responsibility.
4. Empower follower(s) with the authority to get the job done.
5. Give support and encouragement as needed.
6. Allocate necessary resources to complete the job.
7. Request progress reports.
8. Review effects of delegated performance.
9. Provide praise and rewards for successfully accomplishing objectives.
10. Avoid intervening, unless requested to do so by the follower(s).
11. Delegate the appropriate level of responsibility and authority to followers based on their needs and capabilities.
12. Assume that some mistakes may occur before the follower becomes proficient at the task.
13. Expect that it may initially take longer for the follower to complete the task than if you did it yourself.
14. Consider how the delegation of a task to one follower might affect another follower, a coworker, or a superior.
15. Make sure the task's objectives are clear, specific, and acceptable to the follower.
16. Try to use delegation to manage both performance and development.
17. Try to delegate tasks to followers that are meaningful and of interest to them.
18. Explain to your followers why you have chosen them to do the task.
19. Distinguish initially how much control you want to retain over the process and product of their efforts.
20. Try not to delegate tasks too often that you would not enjoy performing yourself.

Self-Defining Leadership. Kuhnert and Lewis (1987) noted that because self-defining leaders (i.e., transformational) are guided by their internal values rather than their personal needs or by purely external standards, they can and do base their delegation decisions in a broad context. They consider the long-term goals and interests of the organization, as well as of the follower, rather than being tied to immediate or short-range goals. The self-defining leader comfortably delegates autonomy to followers to develop them. Unlike self-oriented leaders who delegate to accomplish certain goals to enhance their own worth, or relations-oriented leaders, who delegate to feel appreciated by their colleagues and to maintain their own self-esteem, self-defining leaders are transformational in the confidence with which they delegate to accomplish tasks and higher order objectives. In the process, they help to move followers closer to becoming self-defining, transformational leaders themselves.

LAISSEZ-FAIRE LEADERSHIP

Early in the chapter, reference was made to the difference between a leader granting autonomy to followers in comparison to a leader displaying laissez-faire leadership (Bass, 1985). Laissez-faire leaders delay and appear indifferent to what is happening. They avoid taking stands on issues, do not emphasize results, refrain from intervening, and fail to perform follow-up. When interviewed, managers talked about laissez-faire leaders they had known. Some of the additional behaviors that came to the fore were that laissez-faire leaders avoid making decisions, abdicate responsibilities, divert attention from hard choices, refuse to take sides in a dispute, are disorganized in dealing with priorities and talk about getting down to work but never really do (Avolio & Bass, 1991).

A regional sales manager of a cosmetics manufacturer was a classic laissez-faire leader, yet he always looked the part of the successful manager. He regularly told his sales team that he was working on plans or about to make an important decision, but he provided little direction and was frequently absent from the office, networking. The sales staff took it upon themselves to develop strategies and make decisions, and the manager's clerical support staff covered for their leader by completing his paperwork. As a result, the team became empowered and successful in spite of the leader's abdication of his responsibilities. It was only after his promotion to national sales manager, based on the success of his sales team, that the manager's incompetency became apparent to company executives.

The problems associated with laissez-faire leadership can intensify when a follower does not have the capabilities to compensate. Such was the case with popular, but often laissez-faire, hands-off U.S. President Ronald Reagan. Things went well with policy-making if subordinates were competent but went poorly if they were incompetent. The problems multiplied if the subordinate cabinet member was also laissez-faire (Powell & Persico, 1995).

Laissez-faire leadership has been connected to low productivity, lack of innovation, more conflict, and lack of cohesion among subordinates. Unlike empowerment, correlations of laissez-faire leadership for samples of 1,006 respondents describing their leaders (Bass & Avolio, 1991a) with components of transformational leadership were all negative. The correlations with laissez-faire leadership were as follows: charisma, –.56; inspirational motivation, –.49; intellectual stimulation, –.47; and individualized consideration, –.55. Conversely, whereas empowerment correlated negatively with transactional leadership (Masi, 1994), laissez-faire leadership correlated positively (.25) with managing-by-exception but negatively with contingent reward (–.28).

Changing Laissez-Faire Into Empowering Leadership

Leaders are empowering rather than laissez-faire when they set the boundaries within which subordinates are given discretionary opportunities. Then, the empowering leaders follow up with resources, support, and caring. Thus, in a study of 21 research teams, when some of their leaders first consulted with the R&D teams who were empowered to make decisions, the teams were much more innovative subsequently than when there was no consultation beforehand (Farris, 1971).

In an analysis of why Operation Desert Storm (the first Iraqi War) was such a success, Ulmer (1992) pointed to the empowerment of the commander in the field, decisive Norman Schwarzkopf, by President George Bush and his head of the Joint Chiefs of Staff, Colin Powell. Equally important were the empowered and committed junior officers. This was in contrast to how President Lyndon Johnson micromanaged the Vietnam War or how Ronald Reagan articulated a goal for Nicaragua and then stood aloof in laissez-faire fashion.

In the case of Operation Desert Storm, President George Herbert Bush, Colin Powell, and headquarters staff focused on a basic strategy and the garnering of resources. Norman Schwarzkopf, the responsible commander in the field, executed the strategy empowered by the distant higher authority. It was neither the continued meddling of President Johnson and his staff nor was it the hands-off laissez-faire leadership of President Reagan:

> Most days in the Gulf War, Norm Schwarzkopf and his boss Colin Powell, the Chairman of the Joint Chiefs of Staff, had lengthy phone conversations. The commander in the field was probably given some guidance, had some questions answered, and made requests that were approved or denied or modified. The latitude given him notwithstanding, Norm Schwarzkopf operated routinely within two types of powerful guidelines: the value system of his profession (differentiating those actions that were proper from those that were improper); and the current macro political and resource realities as defined for him by his superiors. (Ulmer, 1992, p. 5)

Ulmer (1992) pointed out that Schwarzkopf himself benefited from 30 years of learning, practice, and development as well as the immediately preceding 30 months of planning, team building, and standard setting that strengthened the organization and its values, established systems, and developed the thousands of leaders at all levels collectively responsible for the operation's success:

> [H]igh-profile, decisive leadership is often appropriate but rarely by itself sufficient. Building the team and . . . culture over time is crucial. And although *empowered* and committed junior leaders are essential to organizational success, a *laissez-faire* style of leading can be as dysfunctional as can micro-management by higher authority. (p. 5)

Situations in Which Laissez-Faire Leadership May Be Appropriate. On occasion, laissez-faire leadership may be appropriate. An issue can truly make no difference to the leader and only to the parties concerned, such as when two coworkers schedule their individual flex times at work, but most problems call for more attention from leadership or substitutes for such leadership. And so, although it is possible to confuse empowerment with laissez-faire leadership, it is the transformational leaders who, with inspiration, delegation, and individualized consideration, make followers feel empowered. The leaders show they care. The laissez-faire leaders are not transformational, nor do they show they care about what their followers do with their autonomy. Empowerment heightens followers' sense of self-efficacy and reciprocal trust between the leaders and the followers. Laissez-faire leadership does the opposite. Yet can the need for leaders be eliminated completely by suitable task and organizational arrangements and competent, motivated, and professional followers? We look at substitutes for transformational leadership in the next chapter.

CONCLUSIONS

Empowerment of followers is a crucial process that both helps define transformational leadership and illustrates why it is effective in building follower commitment and inspiring better performance. Yet empowering followers is a delicate balance between sharing power and control and relinquishing it, as in the case of the laissez-faire leader. Drawing on social science research that tells us much about effective group decision-making processes can help us better understand the dynamics of effective empowerment.

14

Substitutes for Transformational Leadership and Teams as Substitutes

There are certainly groups and teams that function perfectly well without a designated leader. Professional groups of lawyers, health care providers, real estate agents, and providers of financial services may have members with differing levels of experience or expertise but no formal leader or manager. These groups often perform exceptionally well. They do so because the group of followers collectively possesses the characteristics that enable them to perform at high levels. In essence, we may be talking about the transformational qualities of the followers or the collective group.

Numerous subordinate characteristics, such as competence, task characteristics, such as unambiguity, and organizational characteristics, such as inflexibility, were suggested by Kerr (1977) and by Howell, Dorfman, and Kerr (1986) as possible substitutes, neutralizers, or enhancers that would moderate the effects of leadership. These substitutes for leadership were defined as follows:

Replacements. If an outcome such as the effective performance of a group is predicted by the members' ratings of the quality of the leadership of the group and if that prediction can be increased in accuracy by partially or fully replacing the measurement of the leadership with another measurement, such as the training of the members, then the training is a replacement for the ratings of the leadership.

Neutralizers. If the prediction of the outcome can be increased in accuracy by partially or fully subtracting another measurement, such as the rate of absenteeism of the members, then the rate of absenteeism is a neutralizer of the ratings of the leadership. *Enhancers.* If the prediction of the outcome can be increased in accuracy by partially or fully adding another measurement, such as the members' years of relevant experience, then years of relevant experience becomes an enhancer of the ratings of the leadership (Howell et al., 1986).

RESEARCH EVIDENCE

The notion of substitutes for leadership grew out of what we do to add several measurements together to make a prediction of some outcome. We find the best multipliers or weights to assign to each of the measures to find the most accurate prediction.

Subsequently, supportive anecdotal and survey evidence was found in a variety of organizational settings: military posts, manufacturing, computerized networks, book publishers, universities, banks, and police departments. However, when Podsakoff, Niehoff, et al. (1993) completed a systematic survey and analysis for a large sample of nonprofessionals, they found that although the substitute variables did make contributions to the participants' satisfaction and effectiveness, generally they failed to moderate the impact of leadership on the outcomes. Podsakoff, MacKenzie, et al. (1993) repeated the effort with 411 professional, managerial, and white-collar employees in 10 different organizations. Results were similar. The majority of expected substitutions, neutralizations, or enhancements failed to emerge. Table 14.1 shows the leadership surveyed and the proposed moderators employed by Podsakoff, Niehoff, et al. (1993) and Podsakoff, Mackenzie, et al. (1993).

Note that the leadership essentially involved interaction facilitation, initiation of structure, and contingent reinforcement. The leadership was mainly transactional, consistent with House's path-goal theory and Schriesheim's (1978) supportive and instrumental behavior scales. Supportive behavior focused on being friendly and considerate of subordinates' immediate needs. Instrumental leadership featured role clarification, work assignment, and specification of procedures. Contingent reinforcement included contingent reward and contingent

TABLE 14.1
Substitutes and Other Potential Moderators of Leader Behavior

Substitutes and Other Potential Moderators	Will Tend to Serve as Substitutes or Neutralizers for			
	Relationship-Oriented, Supportive, People-Centered Leadership	Task-Oriented, Instrumental, Job-Centered Leadership	Contingent Reward	Contingent Discipline
Subordinate Characteristics				
Ability, experience, training, and knowledge		X		
Need for independence	X	X	X	X
"Professional" orientation	X	X	X	X
Indifference toward organizational rewards	X	X	X	X
Task characteristics				
Unambiguous, routine, and methodologically invariant task		X		
Task-provided feedback concerning accomplishment		X	X	
Intrinsically satisfying task	X		X	
Organizational Characteristics				
Organizational formalization (explicit goals and areas of responsibility)		X		
Organizational inflexibility (rigid, unbending rules and procedures)		X		
Highly specified and active advisory and staff functions		X		
Closely knit, cohesive work groups	X	X	X	X
Organizational rewards not within the leader's control	X	X	X	X
Spatial distance between supervisor and subordinate	X	X	X	X

Note. From *New Dimensions in Leadership. A Special Report From Organizational Dynamics* (pp. 83–99), by J. P. Howell, D. E. Bowen, P. W. Dorfman, S. Kerr, and P. M. Podsakoff, 1993, New York: American Management Association. Copyright 1993 by American Management Association. Adapted with permission.

punishment, all conceived by Bass (1985) as transactional rather than transformational. Substitutes for leadership were surveyed with a 41-item scale refined from an original scale of 74 items of Podsakoff, Niehoff, et al. (1993). Table 14.2 shows the 41 items employed to assess the proposed moderators presented in Table 14.1.

TABLE 14.2
Revised Substitutes for Leadership Scale

Ability, Experience, Training, and Knowledge
  1. I have the ability, experience, training, or job knowledge to act independent of my immediate supervisor in performing my duties.
  2. I have all the required ability and experience to be my own boss on my job.
  3. I have enough training and job knowledge to handle most situations that I face in my job.

Professional Orientation
  4. I am a member of a professional group whose standards and values guide me in my work.
  5. I am a member of a professional organization with which I strongly identify.
  6. I am a member of a professional organization that has a code of ethics that I believe is important to follow.

Indifference Toward Organizational Rewards
  7. I cannot get very enthused about the rewards offered in this organization.
  8. This organization offers attractive opportunities to its employees. (R)
  9. I do not feel that the rewards I receive in this organization are worth very much.

Subordinate Need for Independence
  10. When I have a problem, I like to think it through myself without help from others.
  11. It is important for me to be able to feel that I can do my job without depending on others.
  12. I prefer to solve my work problems by myself.

Unambiguous, Routine, Methodologically Invariant Tasks
  13. My job does not change much from one day to the next.
  14. I perform the same types of activities every day in my job.
  15. Most of the work I do in my job is somewhat repetitive in nature.

Task-Provided Feedback Concerning Accomplishments
  16. My job provides me with feedback on how well I am doing.
  17. My job provides me with the feeling that I know whether I am performing well or poorly.
  18. My job provides me with the opportunity to find out how well I am performing.

Intrinsically Satisfying Tasks
  19. I get a great deal of personal satisfaction from the work I do.
  20. I like the tasks that I perform at work.
  21. My job is personally very rewarding.

(Continued)

TABLE 14.2 *(continued)*

Organizational Formalization
22. My job responsibilities are clearly specfied in writing.
23. Written schedules, programs, and work specifications are available to guide me in my work.
24. My duties, authority, and accountability are documented in policies, procedures, or job descriptions.
25. Written rules and guidelines do not exist to direct my work efforts. (R)

Organizational Inflexibility
26. In this organization, violations of rules and procedures are not tolerated.
27. In this organization, anytime there is a policy in writing that fits some situation, everybody has to follow that policy very strictly.
28. The policies and rules in this organization are followed to the letter.
29. This organization takes a relaxed approach to rules and policies. (R)

Advisory and Staff Support
30. In my job, I work closely with staff personnel who are based outside my work unit or department.
31. I often need to obtain information, data, and reports from staff members outside my department to complete my work.
32. Support from staff personnel outside my department is critical to success in my job.

Closely Knit, Cohesive, Interdependent Work Groups
33. The members of my work group are cooperative with each other.
34. My work group members know that they can depend on each other.
35. The members of my work group stand up for each other.

Organizational Rewards Not Within the Leader's Control
36. My chances for a pay raise depend on my immediate supervisor's recommendation. (R)
37. I am dependent on my immediate supervisor for important organizational rewards. (R)
38. My immediate supervisor's recommendation is necessary for me to be promoted. (R)

Spatial Distance Between Superior and Subordinate
39. On my job, my most important tasks take place away from where my immediate supervisor is located.
40. My immediate supervisor and I are seldom in actual contact or direct sight of one another.
41. My supervisor and I seldom work in the same area.

Note. (R) denotes reverse-coded items. From "Substitutes for Leadership and the Management of Professionals," by P. M. Podsakoff, S. B. MacKenzie, and R. Fetter, 1993, *Leadership Quarterly, 4,* pp. 1–44. Copyright 1993 by JAI Press. Reprinted with permission.

Prediction of Outcomes

The outcomes included followers' self-reported satisfaction, commitment, perceived role ambiguity, and role conflict. Additional outcomes were the superiors' ratings of the employees' performance, altruism, conscientiousness, courtesy, civic virtue, and sportsmanship.

As was expected, the constructive leadership behaviors contributed directly to follower outcomes. For instance, contingent reward of the superior correlated as follows with subordinate outcomes: .55, general satisfaction; .31, organizational commitment; –.36, role ambiguity; –.24, role conflict; and .27, conscientiousness. Likewise, contingent reward correlated with several potential substitutes as follows: indifference to rewards, –.35; task feedback, .39; organizational formalization, .23; and cohesive group, .24.

Neutralizers, Enhancers, or Replacements

Of 910 possible moderating effects on the seven leadership behavior scales studied, only 13, or 1.4%, had moderating effects that met Howell et al.'s (1986) criteria as neutralizers that weakened or subtracted from the impact of the leader's behavior on outcomes or acted as enhancers or replacements. Another 48, or 5.3%, revealed interacting effects between leadership and potential substitutes but could not be regarded as consistent replacement, neutralization, or enhancement. Although the authors concluded that few of the results of the Posdakoff, Niehoff, et al. (1993) and Podsakoff, MacKenzie, et al. (1993) analyses for nonprofessionals and professionals found consistent substitutes for the leadership they studied, they argued that their method might have been too conservative, and alternative methods were proposed. For instance, before they examined the moderation of each leadership style, they partialled out all the others.

For our purposes here, it still seems an open question as to whether there are substitutes for the components of transformational leadership. For instance, to what extent will the availability of computerized decision support systems replace, neutralize, or enhance intellectual stimulation? As we noted in earlier chapters, the components of transformational leadership are much more strongly predictive of outcomes in effectiveness, extra effort commitment, and satisfaction than is contingent reward. Contingent reward is more highly predictive of such outcomes than passive management-by-exception, and laissez-faire leadership is negatively correlated with outcomes. It would be an important contribution to efficiency if accurate substitutes for transformational leadership could be reliably demonstrated. Howell et al. (1993) argued that we may still find many effective alternatives to the necessity of leadership to achieve effective outcomes.

In a study of a variety of workplace leaders, it was found that job enrichment could substitute for transformational leadership, at least in terms of its effect on affective organizational commitment (Whittington, Goodwin, & Murray, 2004). In this same study, goal setting served to enhance the effect of transformational leadership on both affective commitment and on follower performance.

A test examining the direct and moderating effects of transformational leadership and substitutes for leadership demonstrated that each had independent effects on follower outcomes (satisfaction, organizational commitment, organizational citizenship behaviors) but that substitutes for leadership did not moderate the effects of transformational leadership (Podsakoff, MacKenzie, & Bommer, 1996). However, as the authors note, despite these results, the effects of substitutes for leadership are important to examine. There is a need for greater attention given to the role that followers play in the transformational process of groups and organizations.

SUGGESTED SUBSTITUTES FOR TRANSFORMATIONAL LEADERSHIP

In crisis conditions, overtraining, training for adaptive and critical thinking, and competence of followers can substitute for the direction provided by the leader (Kozlowski, 1998). In dealing with the aftermath of the 2001 terrorist attacks on the World Trade Center, competent but obscure city employees, such as New York Port Authority engineer Peter Rinaldi, were able to develop their own plans for conducting searches for victims and containing the damage wrought by the Twin Towers' collapse, without oversight from designated leaders and with little or no contact with official leaders (Langewiesche, 2002). Rinaldi called on his vast knowledge of the intricate underground systems at the World Trade Center site, and his experience in the earlier 1993 Twin Towers bombing, to lead rescue attempts and efforts to contain dangerous gases and other potential hazards caused by the devastation.

Indeed, the initiative of followers may best be seen when the group is challenged by the tasks confronting it. For example, in a camping equipment firm, consultation disclosed the intrinsic satisfaction that employees derived from their work in producing a high-quality product. This substituted for the need for strong leadership. When the employees had to work on low-quality products, closer supervision was required (Howell et al., 1993).

The authors note that feedback, coaching, and guidance (which we see as important elements in individualized consideration) could be provided by a computerized intelligent system instead of by a supervisor. Indeed, research by Sosik, Avolio, et al. (1997, 1998) demonstrated that elements of effective transformational leadership could occur via computer. This would make it possible to flatten organizations and to increase span of control. This might also help to foster empowerment. For professional employees such as accountants, engineers, or nurses, professional education and socialization processes may substitute for transformational leadership in promoting autonomy and empowerment.

Extensive subordinate education was found to substitute for direction and supportive leadership in a book publishing house, a branch bank, and a Midwestern university. Again, high-ability, experienced workers appear to require little direct supervision at Cummins Engine, General Motors, or Procter & Gamble (Howell et al., 1993; Howell & Dorfman, 1986).

Teams as Substitutes for Transformational Leadership

It has been suggested that transformational teams can function in ways to generate the extra effort, performance, and satisfaction expected from transformational leadership. In another sense, transformational leadership could be shared among the team members. As noted in chapter 10, research is beginning to explore transformational team leadership.

We might see a small military team whose esprit had been built by a previous history of success, gallantry, and mutual support of members for each other. Its formally appointed officer might find the membership on the team provided sufficient member self-esteem without any effort on the part of the officer. The attractiveness of the team to each member resulting in the team's cohesiveness would only require of the formal appointed leader that the team's and the organization's goals be in alignment.

Instead of motivation being supplied by identification of members with an idealized, charismatic leader, similar motivation would be supplied by identification with the team or the ideal team member. There would be the desire to emulate the other team members rather than the formally appointed team leader. Respect and admiration of all other members would substitute for the direction of such feelings toward the leader. Inspiration would come from a sharing of mutually articulated goals, simplified wording in each other's language, and clarification of the mission by and for each other. Norms for the team would support efforts for members to intellectually stimulate one another. Member competence and experience might replace or enhance leadership in achievement of goals and creative completion of tasks.

Transformational leaders focus a great deal of their energy on the alignment of goals among constituents. Research on team leadership suggests that teams can be more effective if members have a shared mental model of the team's appropriate processes, goals, and expectations (Burke, Fiore, & Salas, 2003; Zaccaro, Rittman, & Marks, 2001). Presumably, if team members have such shared cognitions, this can serve as a substitute for certain aspects of formal leadership.

In addition, the individual consideration provided by the formally appointed leader can be provided by the members for each other, particularly if team members are trained to discern the individual differences among them and the importance of mutual coaching depending on the differences in their initial experience and knowledge.

Empowered, self-managed work teams ideally epitomize substitution for much of what was done before by the formal hierarchical leader (Kirkman & Rosen, 1999). Each team is assigned closely related production or service tasks. The teams are set off from each other by physical space and work in progress. Each team is responsible for assigning tasks to its members, inspecting its own work, and tracking its quality of performance and the hours each member works. Absenteeism and discipline are handled by the team. The members are trained in maintaining effective meetings and group problem solving. A supervisor is responsible for each team but only supplies guidance and support in the early stages of the team's development. Self-observation, self-evaluation, and self-reinforcement are encouraged by the supervisor. Supervisors of effective teams act like consultants. They spend time obtaining resources for the team, representing the team to a higher authority, training new members, and coaching the team members in providing feedback to each other.

Cox, Pearce, and Perry (2003) give the example of new product development teams as an example of self-managed, shared team leadership. They suggest that shared leadership emerges because these teams are highly empowered and consist of members who are highly knowledgeable and skilled, working on a complex, interdependent task.

Self-managed teams also display transactional leadership behavior. For instance, the members may provide each other with contingent reward in the form of resource allocations based on achievements. Or the team or its members may practice managing-by-exception in maintaining discipline and controlling social loafing (Manz & Sims, 1995; Sims & Lorenzi, 1992).

In one study of undergraduate students working in project teams, groups high on transformational team leadership (using the Team Multi-Factor Leadership Questionnaire) had higher levels of group potency and better team performance than those with low transformational team leadership (Sivasubramaniam et al., 2002). In addition, teams high on team laissez-faire leadership had lower levels of group potency and performance.

Work Rules, Policies, and Procedures

Work rules, policies, and procedures may be replacements for or enhancers of transactional leadership, particularly managing-by-exception. Failure to comply with safety rules may be automatically called to an employee's attention by a signal. Howell et al. (1993) suggest that this type of leadership substitute can be particularly important when consistent behavior is imperative.

The military may introduce special procedures, symbols, codes, uniforms, badges, and difficult entrance requirements to promote identification with a unit with a special mission. All of these may substitute to some degree for the transformational identification with the charismatic-inspired leadership. They are likely to serve as enhancers of the leader's efforts to inspire the unit about its mission.

The organization can also enhance an already effective leader's transformational or transactional performance by providing additional resources, more discretion in allocating resources, and more access to important information and key people at higher levels.

Other Possible Substitutes

The following list contains other potential enhancers or replacements of a transformational leader's effectiveness:

- Peer appraisals to increase acceptability of feedback
- Controls over quality by employees
- Peer support networks
- Automatic gain-sharing reward systems
- Mission statements and codes of conduct
- Redesigned jobs to have ideological importance and performance feedback from the task
- A visible organizational champion of the leader
- Assignment of the leader to important organizational responsibilities
- In-house publicity of the leader's image
- "Small" success experiences to increase the subordinates' confidence in the leader
- Ceremony and myth to promote a transformational organizational culture
- Superordinate goals from a higher authority to encourage high-performance norms

Other substitutes or enhancements of the effects of transformational leadership might include crisis reduction through in-place effective and rapid communication systems, ideologically committed followers, organizational cultures with transformational characteristics that give members a sense of empowerment, acceptance of innovation, the importance of learning, and the value of doing the right thing instead of just doing things right. Conversely, organizations that avoided bureaucratic entanglements and that fostered cooperation rather than competition among its members (members competed against their own previous records rather than the records of others) provided substitutes for transformational leadership. Introducing gain-sharing reward systems might substitute for transactional leadership.

Additionally, Sergiovanni (1990a, 1990b) suggested that leadership can be replaced or enhanced by the professionalization of followers. The ideals of the profession can provide the moral authority for action without the intervention of leadership. For instance, in teaching, professional ideals include a commitment to caring toward the profession itself and practice toward valued social ends in an exemplary way. Organizational norms can also substitute for leadership. Followers are committed to pursue certain paths because of their desire to conform to the organizational norms rather than because of leadership. One may speculate, for example, that more substitution for leadership takes place if a military is professionalized with ideals of exemplary performance, patriotism, duty, and service to the country and to the profession itself.

Neutralizers of Transformational and Transactional Leadership

Leadership neutralizers are characteristics of subordinates, tasks, and organizations that interfere with a leader's performance. Neutralizers offset the leader's impact and reduce the leader's influence and effectiveness. The same rules that are supposed to substitute for transactional leadership can work to neutralize transformational leadership. The military leader who tries to be intellectually stimulating might generate the soldier's reaction of "Yes, but we are not supposed to do things that way." The corporate leader who tries to inspire a sense of mission might be greeted with "Yes, but that's not what we get paid to do." The leader who tries to rejuvenate a follower who reached a plateau in effort might hear the response, "Yes, but next year I will be forced to retire."

The physical distance between leader and subordinate may be a neutralizer. When subordinates must work at a physical distance from the leader as in the case of U.S. Army station heads and the company commanders above them, the leadership may be neutralized. Physical distances may be too great for much personal interaction and serve to neutralize much of the commander's transformational influence as well as his ability to manage-by-exception.

Regional managers at Kinko's, which provides professional copying services at widely dispersed locations nationwide, have voiced frustration in their inability to provide guidance and personal support for new store managers because physical distance prevents personal interaction. In international organizations, leaders and followers may live and work in different time zones and be unable to share the same workday. Again, physical distance has become a potential neutralizer as more employees work at home or at client sites (Howell et al., 1993).

Physical distance may be eliminated as a neutralizer of leadership by the increasing availability of telecommunication, teleconferencing, and other forms of electronic communication. More leader–follower relationships are maintained primarily by electronic communication (Avolio & Kahai, 2003a, 2003b).

Systems that provide rewards primarily for seniority, such as in civil services, where promotion is based on examination, may neutralize the possibilities for a leader to engage in contingent reward. (On the other hand, supervisors may be more transformational in encouraging employees to prepare for the examination.) Again, leaders may be unable to practice management-by-exception because union contracts mandate employees with a given job classification be paid the same wages. Neutralization may occur because rewards may be controlled by higher management in ways that prevent the immediate supervisor from exerting influence, such as when organizations require numerous higher level approvals before a salary recommendation can take effect. Timing can be a neutralizer. Reward may be constrained by fiscal periods or employee anniversary dates (Howell et al., 1993).

The leaders' influence may be neutralized if they are bypassed by subordinates going above them in the hierarchy for a decision or, conversely, by superiors going directly to the leaders' subordinates with decisions. Yet the aggregate effect might be salutary on the subordinates' performance if the leaders were laissez-faire or incompetent. Substitutes for leadership should be sought or created where the leadership is too costly, where it is incompetent and cannot be trained, or where the leaders themselves cannot be replaced.

CONCLUSIONS

We are only now beginning to see evidence that team and shared leadership can serve as replacements, neutralizers, and enhancers of transformational leadership. If team leadership takes hold, the team, as a whole, and its individual members may prove to be one of the more successful examples for the replacing of the single individual leader with shared leadership—that is, where any member of the team, alone or together with other members, exerts needed leadership based on the member's particular competencies and perceptions of the need for the leadership. At the same time, we should look to transformational team and organization as ways of enhancing the performance of the transformational leadership of appointed, elected, or emergent individual leaders. Yet these and other aspects of transformational leadership remain in need of further investigation.

15

Transformational Leadership: Future Challenges and Applications

In his book, *Transforming Leadership*, James MacGregor Burns (2003) asserts that transformational leadership is needed to solve the world's most critical problems, such as global poverty. This needed leadership is not top-down, Burns argues, but must occur at the grassroots level, by thousands of leaders who are close to the poor, who will listen to and be responsive to their needs, who will empower them and help develop impoverished communities into self-sustaining ones. Burns clearly set a grand future challenge for leadership in general and for transformational leadership in particular.

Transformational leadership has become a very popular model generating a great deal of discussion and research. Perhaps the reason that the model of transformational leadership has received so much attention from scholars and practitioners is that it represents the changing nature of effective leadership as we now see it and know it in businesses, government, and social movements. Early on, critics of transformational leadership suggested that it might simply represent good or effective managerial/leadership practices (Tracey & Hinkin, 1998). We don't necessarily disagree with that assertion. We would argue, however, that transformational leadership is the best-fitting model for effective leadership in today's world. The mounting research evidence seems to back this up, suggesting that transformational leaders are more effective than transactional or nontransformational leaders. Why?

Much of the reason is because the nature of leadership has changed drastically in recent years. The world has gotten increasingly complex and fast paced. This requires individuals, groups, and organizations to continually change and adapt. Transformational leadership is, at its core, about issues around the processes of transformation and change.

The role of the leader has changed. Autocratic and authoritarian leaders, although they still exist, are no longer the norm. Leaders are expected to listen to followers and be responsive to their needs and concerns and include them in decision making. Mentoring, coaching, empowering, developing, supporting, and caring are not only expected leader behaviors but also necessary for today's effective leader.

Transformational leaders are individually considerate, but they intellectually stimulate and challenge followers. They are attentive and supportive, but they also inspire and serve as leadership exemplars. On occasion, and when necessary, transformational leaders may, however, have to stand their ground, making unpopular decisions and asserting their authority. For example, in an emergency, when consultation is not possible, the transformational leader must be willing and able to take firm, directive charge.

Importantly, followers have also changed. Often, they are knowledge workers—informed, enlightened, and often knowing more than the leader about how to get the task done. However, they are also an increasingly diverse group, and one leadership style cannot work with them all. They are empowered, have varied and more numerous needs, and want to be able to see how following the leader is consistent with their own personal goals. Moreover, they are the future leaders, so if a unit or organization is going to succeed over time, followers' leadership potential must be developed and realized. Transformational leaders develop followers into leaders. For today's followers, an adaptive type of leader is needed—one who can be individually considerate of each specific follower's needs and concerns and also be stimulating and inspirational. Transformational leaders are adaptive leaders.

The intent of this book was to provide a better understanding of transformational leadership and to review the sizable body of research that the model has stimulated in a relatively short period of time.

After discussing transformational leadership and the Full Range Leadership (FRL) model in chapter 1, and exploring measurement of the constructs in chapter 2, we turned to logical explanation and the results of experimental findings and field studies to try to better understand the dynamics and outcomes of transformational leadership.

Chapter 3 examined some of the ways transformational leadership enhances the commitment, loyalty, involvement, and satisfaction of followers. Chapter 4 focused on how transformational leadership affects leader, follower, and group performance.

Chapter 5 looked at how transformational leaders operate under crisis or stress. It shows that transformational leaders help followers cope with stress. Transactional leaders, by contrast, may induce more stress.

The topic of chapter 6 deals with how contingencies in the environment, organization, task, goals, and relationships might affect the use of transformational leadership.

Chapter 7 explored how organizational culture interacts with transformational leadership, and chapter 8 reviewed gender effects in transformational leadership. Chapter 9 discussed the implications of transformational leadership for organizations and organizational policies.

Chapter 10 asked how transformational leadership could be taught and learned and provided detailed examples of development programs. Research on the predictors and correlates of transformational leadership were reviewed in chapter 11 and suggestions of promising predictors were made. Chapter 12 asked whether rank and status were of consequence to exhibiting transformational leadership or whether it is as present as much among first-line supervisors and platoon sergeants as among chief executive officers (CEOs) and brigade commanders.

Chapter 13 looked at the role of empowerment in transformational leadership and differentiated notions of empowerment, a successful leadership strategy, with laissez-faire behavior, an unsuccessful strategy. Chapter 14 discussed possible substitutes for transformational leadership and looked at how transformational leadership can be shared by team members.

In this final chapter, we attempt to do two things: First, we discuss some of the issues that are important for a better understanding of transformational leadership: the issue of self-interests of the leader (and self-interests of the followers) versus the interests of the group, the organization, and society; issues involving the model of transformational leadership and related measurement concerns; and the relationship of transformational leadership to other leadership theories and concepts.

Second, we suggest areas where additional research is needed as well as try to chart a course for future research on transformational leadership and research to better understand the FRL model.

TRANSCENDING SELF-INTERESTS: GOING BEYOND SELF-ACTUALIZATION

The importance of going beyond one's self-interests is something forgotten by those who press hard on the developmental function of the transformational leader. It needs to be remembered that Handy (1994) was 16 years behind Burns (1978) in his suggestion that Maslow's (1954) hierarchy of needs should be extended upward to go beyond one's self-oriented concerns:

> Maslow . . . postulated that there was a hierarchy of needs, that when you had enough material goods you moved your sights to social prestige and then to self-realization. . . . his hierarchy did not reach far enough. There could be a stage beyond self-realization, a stage we might call idealization, the pursuit of an ideal or a cause that is more than oneself. It is this extra stage that would redeem the self-centered tone of Maslow's thesis, which for all that it rings true of much of our experience, has a rather bitter aftertaste. (Handy, 1994, p. 275)

Burns, of course, 16 years earlier had handled this possible bitter aftertaste by describing the transforming leader as one who not only moved followers up on Maslow's hierarchy but also moved them to transcend their own self-interests.

One paradox for us may be that as we push the transformational process, particularly focusing on development of followers, we may shortchange the transcending of followers' self-interests. The transformational leader needs to do both by aligning the followers' self-interests in development with the interests of the group, organization, or society. Williams's (1994) work, and subsequent research, showed that transformational leaders, as measured by the Multifactor Leadership Questionnaire (MLQ), display more citizenship behaviors, such as altruism, conscientiousness, sportsmanship, courtesy, and civic virtue, and imbue such ideas in their subordinates. This is one reason why Avolio and Bass (1991) chose to substitute for charisma, in training and elsewhere, the term idealized influence, that is, being influential about ideals. At the highest level of morality are selfless ideal causes to which leaders and followers may dedicate themselves. For example, serving one's country to the best of one's abilities can be a powerful motivator in the military or in government. It is not a new idea; it is found in Homer's *Iliad*, that "he serves me most who serves his country best."

Needed is research that deals with the potential conflict of the would-be transformational leaders striving for achievement and self-actualization and their pursuit of the greater good for group, organization, or society. The resolution may lie in the alignment of their own personal principles with those of the group, organization, and society. Yet other seemingly unresolvable conflicts may exist, particularly regarding issues of loyalty to the group or organization if it is reaching its goals but doing it by engaging in questionable or obviously unethical behavior. This was particularly true in many of the recent ethical scandals in businesses but is also a problem for military officers and cadets who are faced with threats to the achievement of their goals if, as expected in the honor code, they notify authorities of unethical behavior they observe in fellow officers. Reporting others' unethical behavior may impair the quality of relationships that are expected to be maintained with fellow members.

A 2004 summit of the University of Nebraska's Gallup Leadership Institute focused specifically on authentic leadership, with a great deal of the research and discussion on authentic and inauthentic transformational leadership. Clearly, the issue of authentic, socialized transformational leaders is an important one for greater understanding of the dynamics of effective leadership and for fostering better leadership in government, business, military, education, and the nonprofit sectors.

CONCEPTUALIZATION AND MEASUREMENT OF TRANSFORMATIONAL LEADERSHIP

The model of transformational leadership, consisting of four factors—Idealized Influence, Inspirational Motivation, Individualized Consideration, and Intellectual Stimulation—does a good job of representing the elements of the transformational leader. In early research, the first two factors were combined to form a charisma factor. Clearly, Idealized Influence and Inspirational Motivation are correlated factors that have been combined in previous research. We believe, however, that it makes good sense to conceptualize them separately, for both greater understanding of the charismatic elements of transformational leadership and for leader development purposes. For example, a leader can be inspirational—move followers toward common goals, provide meaning, and generate acceptance of missions—without necessarily being charismatic. Likewise, a leader can be a paragon of exceptional leadership, highly admired and imitated, but still lack the ability to inspire followers. In short, we believe that the four factors are each important in understanding transformational leadership.

A large part of the findings that were presented earlier were based on using the Multifactor Leadership Questionnaire (MLQ) as the measure of transformational leadership and the FRL model. Also reviewed were studies that used other measures of transformational leadership or charismatic leadership measures. As mentioned in chapter 2, there have been criticisms of both the dimensional structure of the FRL model and the MLQ (e.g., Bycio et al., 1995; Tejeda et al., 2001). However, the most recent psychometric investigations support the factor structure of the MLQ (Antonakis et al., 2003).

An important contribution of the MLQ is that it allows for the collection of similar types of data using the same instruments, constructs, and model across all levels of leadership (Sosik, et al., 2004; Yammarino & Bass, 1991): leadership of the small group (microleadership), leadership of the large organization (macroleadership), and leadership of movements and societies (metaleadership) (Nicholls, 1987, 1990). Thus, we see applications at the microlevel (Hater & Bass, 1988; Whittington et al., 2004), at the macrolevel (Pritzker, 2002; Yokochi, 1989), and at the meta-level (Bass, Avolio, et al., 1987) of the same model of transformational leadership. It also has been shown to generalize in concept across nationalities and language (e.g., Bass, 1997; Den Hartog et al., 1999; Francois, 1990).

Despite the popularity and widespread use of the MLQ as a measure of transformational leadership, it is important to develop other methods of assessing transformational leadership. The use of observational methods to objectively code transformational (and other) leadership behaviors, or behavioral diaries, will provide a different perspective, without relying on follower reports/ratings of leader behavior. In addition, focusing on shared, team leadership behaviors offers another approach to measuring and understanding transformational leadership.

We also need to appreciate what the nonquantitative scholars in psychohistory, sociology, and political science have to say about charisma and transformational leadership. Instructive are works such as Caro's (1974, 1982) biographies of Lyndon Johnson and Robert Moses and Kets de Vries's (1984) psychoanalytic views of defects in charismatic leadership. Jacobsen and House (2001) used an interesting simulation model to study the impact of charismatic leaders such as John F. Kennedy, Chrysler's CEO Lee Iacocca, and Christian Science Church founder Mary Baker Eddy. Mumford and Strange (2002) used a psychohistorical approach to study a number of charismatic world leaders, distinguishing between those who were personalized (inauthentic) and socialized (authentic) in their orientations. Berson (1999) talks about a triangulation of qualitative and quantitative methods in assessing transformational leadership.

TRANSFORMATIONAL LEADERSHIP
AND RELATED CONCEPTS
AND THEORIES

Charismatic Leadership

Clearly, transformational leadership is most closely related to theories of charismatic leadership. In fact, the two are often viewed as interchangeable, even though we would argue that transformational leadership is broader, with charisma an important component of the transformational model, but also encompassing individualized consideration and intellectual stimulation. Nevertheless, there are similarities between transformational leadership and charismatic leadership theories as articulated by House (1977) and Conger and Kanungo (1988, 1998).

Directive and Participative Leadership

The now-classic dichotomy of leadership categories or styles focuses on the distinction between leaders who are directive, authoritarian, and task focused versus leaders who are participative, democratic, and focused on followers. Transformational leaders can be directive or participative, authoritarian or democratic. Nelson Mandela was directive and transformational when he declared "Forget the past." He was participative and transformational when he actively supported and involved himself in open, multiracial consultations. He was directive and transactional when he promised Blacks better housing in exchange for their votes and was participative and transactional when he reached mutual agreements about sharing power with the White minority. The same leaders display both transformational and transactional behavior as well as a mix of providing direction and encouraging participation.

Leader–Member Exchange (LMX)

LMX concentrates on the perceived quality of the dyadic relationship between a subordinate and their immediate supervisor (Graen & Scandura, 1987). Tejeda and Scandura (1994) examined the relationship between supervisors and subordinates in a health care organization in terms of both transformational leadership and LMX. This was preceded by attempts by Yukl (1989) to deal with LMX as transactional leadership because of LMX's reliance on exchange of rewards. However, subsequent examination of the development process in LMX by Graen and Uhl-Bien (1991) was able to reframe LMX as a transactional and a transformational leadership process. LMX unfolds in several stages in which trust, loyalty, and respect develop. In the first stage, LMX is transactional. If the last stage is reached, it is transformational. These notions are supported by research by Gerstner and Day (1997).

Howell and Hall-Merenda (1999) found a positive relationship between the quality of leader–member relations and both transformational and transactional leadership. Subsequent research highlighted the role of trust in the LMX relationship (Brower, Schoorman, & Tan, 2000; Gomez & Rosen, 2001). Follower trust in the leader has also been shown to be an important element in transformational leadership.

TRANSFORMATIONAL LEADERSHIP: FUTURE RESEARCH AND DIRECTIONS

There has been a great deal of research on transformational leadership since the first edition of this book. Importantly, research on transformational leadership continues to grow at a rapid rate and will likely continue into the future. In this final section, we highlight areas that need to be addressed in future research with the intent of providing some direction for the better understanding of transformational leadership.

The Development of Transformational Leadership

We still need to learn a lot more about the roots of leadership, generally, and of transformational leadership in particular. As noted in chapter 10, parents and early life experience likely set the stage for the development of transformational leadership (e.g., Popper & Mayseless, 2003). For example, parents' values and moral standards and their role modeling of leadership behaviors are likely important precursors of children's interest in leadership and influence the type of leaders they become. Likewise, leadership experiences in school and extracurricular activities forecast subsequent tendencies to be more transformational as adult leaders (Avolio, 1994). Avolio and Gibbons (1988) reported that industrial executives who were rated by their immediate subordinates as highly transformational reported in retrospective interviews that their parents provided them with difficult challenges but also supported the nascent leaders' efforts whether or not they resulted in success (Gibbons, 1986). Similarly, transformational community leaders described childhood and adolescent experiences with caring but challenging parents who held high standards. Schools also made a difference (Avolio & Bass, 1994). Yet much of this is speculative. Needed is research that examines the developmental foundations of leadership. It would be fruitful to involve developmental psychologists in this effort.

Continued use of retrospective studies, asking young and more established leaders about the early influences on their leadership development, along with analyses of biographical and autobiographical information, will expand our understanding. Comparisons of parents' patterns of leadership and that of their children might shed some light on how leadership is transmitted between generations. Research comparing siblings might help us understand the specific family and environmental influences that are important in leadership development. At least one study focused on studying personality and MLQ ratings of twins, comparing fraternal and identical twins in an effort to gain some insight into the "born versus made" question of leadership (Johnson, Vernon, Harris, & Jang, 2004). These results suggest that personality correlates (e.g., extraversion) of transformational leadership show, not surprisingly, some genetic origin, and there may be some carryover into transformational leadership. However, more research is needed. Most valuable, however, will be longitudinal studies following young people as they develop into leaders and studies that follow established leaders throughout their careers.

Authentic Transformational Leadership

It is quite clear that the concept of the authentic transformational leader is inextricably bound to the notion of the "good" leader—the ethical leader who is driven by sound values and good judgment and is focused not on personal gains but on what benefits the followers, the organization, and society. The inaugural summit of the Gallup Leadership Institute at the University of Nebraska, Lincoln in June, 2004, focused on authentic leadership. It was clear from the program and from the discussion of participants that authentic leadership, in general, and authentic transformational leadership, in particular, are important topics but ones that are difficult to investigate. A number of books have been published on the topic of authentic leadership (e.g., Begley, 2004; George, 2004; Terry, 1993), yet this is an area that has received relatively little research attention (although see Gardner & Schermerhorn, 2004; May, Chan, Hodges, & Avolio, 2003).

Much more needs to be learned about the ethical and moral factors that distinguish the truly transformational leader from the pseudo-transformational leader. This will require research from multiple disciplinary perspectives, bringing together what is known in philosophy, psychology, management, political science, and other areas to gain an understanding of the construct of authenticity and how it manifests itself in transformational leadership.

Predictors and Contingencies

Although a great deal of recent research has investigated both predictors of transformational leadership and the circumstances under which transformational leadership may be more or less effective, additional research is still called for. Promising new predictors of leadership, such as multiple intelligences, are being investigated and applied to leadership (Gardner, 1999; Riggio et al., 2002). Other promising predictors were discussed in chapter 11.

As the world becomes increasingly global and our workforces become more cross-culturally diverse, the challenges for leaders become more demanding. We need to better understand how transformational leadership translates across cultures and across different groups. It is encouraging to see studies of transformational leadership in countries outside of the United States, but much more work is needed. Although some elements of transformational leadership seem to transcend culture, it is quite clear that culture can mediate and moderate the effects of transformational leadership. The same can be said for the leadership of men and women and of different ethnic groups within a country or region. Finally, as life expectancies increase, the range of age of the workforce will increase, with employees working side-by-side with colleagues who differ in age by 60 years or more (see Bass, 2002b).

Leadership today and in the future relies much more on communication technology. Work organizations and work teams can be distributed across the country or across the globe, and many leaders and followers communicate more electronically than face-to-face. The dynamics of this e-leadership has begun to be studied (Avolio, Kahai, & Dodge, 2000; Cascio & Shurygailo, 2003; Zaccaro & Bader, 2003), but certainly more work needs to be done to fully understand e-leading from a distance, across time zones and nations, as well as across the floors of an office building.

Transformational Leadership Training

Although significant work has been done in transformational leadership training (e.g., Avolio & Bass, 1994; see chapter 10), much more is needed. Avolio (2005) provides a good guidebook to help in individual leader development following the transformational and FRL model. As transformational leadership development programs continue to expand, we hope that evaluation research, particularly longitudinal investigations of leadership development, will also increase to help inform continuous program development.

Clearly, we also need to better understand the roots of transformational leadership development, to help in early training interventions. In the past decade, the number of youth leadership development programs has exploded. As has been mentioned, the roots of leadership begin early, so it can be argued that involving youth in leadership development—even as young as 8 years of age (Church, 2001)—could be an important step toward developing future transformational leaders. However, to be as effective as possible in youth leadership development requires good research with young leaders.

As we gain a greater understanding of authentic transformational leadership, attention must focus on authenticity in leadership development. How can we develop leaders who are both transformational and authentic? This is indeed a critical leadership challenge.

The Broader Picture

Future research on transformational leadership needs to take a broader and more varied perspective. Although a great deal of research has focused on the outcomes of transformational leadership, less attention has been given to the process. Moreover, the focus, like much of leadership research, is on the transformational leader—the leader-centric perspective. More attention needs to be given to the followers of transformational leadership and to the leader–follower transformational relationship (see Hollander, 1992; Vecchio, 1997). Indeed, combining the emphasis both on followers and developmental issues, it would be interesting to examine longitudinally the leadership development of followers of transformational leaders. Put simply, do transformational leaders help create more transformational leaders?

The popularity of transformational leadership has led many researchers to ignore the broader, FRL elements measured by the MLQ. It is important to emphasize that it is important to look at transformational leadership in the larger context of the full range. In addition, because the best leaders tend to be both transactional and transformational, it is critical to not overlook the impact of transactional leadership.

Popper and Mayseless (2002) wrote a chapter called the "Internal World of Transformational Leaders" that focuses on who the transformational leaders are and their motivations, with a particular emphasis on developmental issues, some of which are discussed in chapter 10. It would indeed be informative to better understand the inner workings of the transformational leader, their psychological makeup, and their motivations.

Finally, the theory of transformational leadership has been criticized for being too positive a portrayal of leadership (Beyer, 1999; Yukl, 1999). Although we believe that transformational leadership does indeed represent the positive end of the continuum of leadership, it is important to explore the negative aspects of transformational leadership. We believe, however, that the negative aspects to transformational and charismatic leadership largely occur when the leadership is inauthentic and personalized, rather than socialized. Yet there may be circumstances when transformational leadership is less effective than other forms of leadership, and these need to be studied. In addition, there may be negative side-effects to transformational leadership. For example, transformational leadership, with its emphasis on developing followers, challenging and intellectually stimulating them, while motivating and providing individualized consideration, requires a great deal of energy and input from the leader. Being transformational and fostering effective working and mentoring relationships with followers requires more work than being transactional, for instance. This may lead to leader burnout or may cause work–family conflicts and imbalances. These potential negative side-effects of being transformational have not been researched.

Each year, our understanding of transformational leadership grows in significant ways and in an ever-increasing amount. Yet leadership is perhaps the most complex of human constructs, and we still have a long way to go.

References

Alban-Metcalfe, R. J., & Alimo-Metcalfe, B. (2000). An analysis of the convergent and discriminant validity of the Transformational Leadership Questionnaire. *International Journal of Selection and Assessment, 8,* 158–175.

Alimo-Metcalfe, B. (1994, July). *An investigation of female and male constructs of leadership and empowerment.* Paper presented at the International Congress of Applied Psychology, Madrid, Spain.

Alimo-Metcalfe, B., & Alban-Metcalfe, R. J. (2001). The development of a new Transformational Leadership Questionnaire. *Journal of Occupational and Organizational Psychology, 74,* 1–27.

Allen, N. J., & Meyer, J. P. (1990). The measurement and antecedents of affective, continuance, and normative commitment to the organization. *Journal of Occupational Psychology, 63*(1), 1–18.

Anon. (1985). *Leadership: Statements and quotes.* Washington, DC: Department of the Army.

Ansoff, H. I., & Sullivan, P. A. (1991). Strategic responses to environmental turbulence. In R. H. Kilmann & I. Kilmann (Eds.), *Making organizations competitive: Enhancing networks and relationships across traditional boundaries* (pp. 21–50). San Francisco: Jossey-Bass.

Antonakis, J., Avolio, B. J., & Sivasubramaniam, N. (2003). Context and leadership: An examination of the nine-factor full-range leadership theory using the Multifactor Leadership Questionnaire. *The Leadership Quarterly, 14*(3), 261–295.

Antonakis, J., & House, R. J. (2002). The full-range leadership theory: The way forward. In B. J. Avolio & F. J. Yammarino (Eds.), *Transformational and charismatic leadership: The road ahead* (pp. 3–33). Boston: JAI.

Argenti, P. (2002). Crisis communication lessons from 9/11. *Harvard Business Review, 80*(2), 103–109.

Ashforth, B. E., & Humphrey, R. H. (1995). Emotion in the workplace: A reappraisal. *Human Relations, 48*(2), 97–125.

Atwater, D. C., & Bass, B. M. (1994). Transformational leadership in teams. In B. M. Bass & B. J. Avolio (Eds.), *Improving organizational effectiveness through transformational leadership* (pp. 48–83). Thousand Oaks, CA: Sage.

Atwater, L. E., Avolio, B. J., & Bass, B. M. (1991). *A retrospective/prospective view of leadership development, emergence, and performance.* Alexandria, VA: U.S. Army Research Institute for the Behavioral and Social Sciences.

Atwater, L. E., Camobreco, J. F., Dionne, S. D., Avolio, B. J., & Lau, A. N. (1997). Effects of rewards and punishments on leader charisma, leader effectiveness and follower reactions. *The Leadership Quarterly, 8*(2), 133–152.

Atwater, L. E., Lau, A. W., Bass, B. M., Avolio, B. J., Camobreco, J., & Whitmore, N. (1994). *The content, construct and criterion-related validity of leader behavior measures* (ARI Research Note 95–01). Alexandria, VA: U.S. Army Research Institute for the Behavioral and Social Sciences.

Atwater, L. E., & Yammarino, F. J. (1989). *Power, transformational, and transactional leadership* (ONR Tech. Rep. 7). Binghamton, NY: State University of New York, Center for Leadership Studies.

Atwater, L. E., & Yammarino, F. J. (1993). Personal attributes as predictors of superiors' and subordinates' perceptions of military academy leadership. *Human Relations, 46,* 645–668.

Austin, J. E. (2000). *The collaboration challenge: How nonprofits and businesses succeed through strategic alliances.* San Francisco: Jossey-Bass.

Avolio, B. J. (1994). The "natural": Some antecedents to transformational leadership. *International Journal of Public Administration, 17,* 1559–1581.

Avolio, B. J. (1999). *Full leadership development: Building the vital forces in organizations.* Thousand Oaks, CA: Sage.

Avolio, B. J. (2005). *Leadership development in balance: Made/born.* Mahwah, NJ: Lawrence Erlbaum Associates.

Avolio, B. J., & Bass, B. M. (1991). *The full range of leadership development: Basic and advanced manuals.* Binghamton, NY: Bass, Avolio, & Associates.

Avolio, B. J., & Bass, B. M. (1993). *Cross generations: A full range leadership development program.* Binghamton, NY: Center for Leadership Studies, Binghamton University.

Avolio, B. J., & Bass, B. M. (1994). *Evaluate the impact of transformational leadership training at individual, group, organizational, and community levels* (Final report to the W. K. Kellogg Foundation). Binghamton, NY: Binghamton University.

Avolio, B. J., & Bass, B. M. (1999). You can drag a horse to water but you can't make it drink unless it is thirsty. *Journal of Leadership Studies, 5,* 4–17.

Avolio, B. J., & Bass, B. M. (Eds.). (2002). *Developing potential across a full range of leadership: Cases on transactional and transformational leadership.* Mahwah, NJ: Lawrence Erlbaum Associates.

Avolio, B. J., Bass, B. M., Atwater, L. E., Lau, A. W., Dionne, S., Camembreco, J., & Whitmore, N. (1994). *Antecedent predictors of the "full range" of leadership and management styles* (Contract MDA-903-91–0131). Binghamton, NY: Center for Leadership Studies, Binghamton University.

Avolio, B. J., Bass, B. M., & Jung, D. I. (1997). *Replicated confirmatory factor analyses of the Multifactor Leadership Questionnaire.* Binghamton, NY: Center for Leadership Studies, Binghamton University.

Avolio, B. J., Bass, B. M., & Jung, D. I. (1999). Re-examining the components of transformational and transactional leadership using the Multifactor Leadership Questionnaire. *Journal of Occupational and Organizational Psychology, 72,* 441–462.

Avolio, B. J., & Gibbons, T. C. (1988). Developing transformational leaders: A lifespan approach. In J. A. Conger & R. N. Kanungo (Eds.), *Charismatic leadership: The elusive factor in organizational effectiveness* (pp. 276–308). San Francisco: Jossey-Bass.

Avolio, B. J., & Howell, J. M. (1992). The impact of leader behavior and leader-follower personality match on satisfaction and unit performance. In K. E. Clark, M. B. Clark, & D. R. Campbell (Eds.), *Impact of leadership* (pp. 225–247. Greensboro, NC: The Center for Creative Leadership.

Avolio, B. J., Jung, D. I., Murry, W. D., & Sivasubramaniam, N. (1996). Building highly developed teams: Focusing on shared leadership process, efficacy, trust, and performance. In M. M. Beyerlein, D. A. Johnson, & S. T. Beyerlein (Eds.), *Advances in inter-disciplinary studies of work teams* (pp. 173–209). Greenwich, CT: JAI Press.

Avolio, B. J., & Kahai, S. (2003a). Placing the "E" in e-leadership: Minor tweak or fundamental change. In S. M. Murphy & R. E. Riggio (Eds.), *The future of leadership development* (pp. 49–70). Mahwah, NJ: Lawrence Erlbaum Associates.

Avolio, B. J., & Kahai, S. (2003b). Adding the "E" to e-leadership: How it may impact your leadership. *Organizational Dynamics, 31,* 325–338.

Avolio, B. J., Kahai, S., & Dodge, G. E. (2000). E-leadership: Implications for theory, research, and practice. *The Leadership Quarterly, 11,* 615–668.

Avolio, B. J., Waldman, D. A., & Einstein, W. O. (1988). Transformational leadership in a management game simulation: Impacting the bottomline. *Group and Organization Studies, 13,* 59–80.

Avolio, B. J., & Yammarino, F. J. (Eds.). (2002). *Transformational and charismatic leadership: The road ahead.* Boston: JAI.

Ayman, R., Adams, S., Fisher, B., & Hartman, E. (2003). Leadership development in higher education institutions: A present and future perspective. In S. E. Murphy & R. E. Riggio (Eds.), *The future of leadership development* (pp. 201–222). Mahwah, NJ: Lawrence Erlbaum Associates.

Bachman, S., & Gregory, K. I. (1993). *Mentor and prodigy gender: Effects on mentoring roles and outcomes.* Oakland, CA: Kaiser Medical Care Program.

Bandura, A. (1997). *Self-efficacy: The exercise of control.* New York: W. H. Freeman.

Banerji, P., & Krishnan, V. R. (2000). Ethical preferences for transformational leaders: An empirical investigation. *Leadership and Organization Development Journal, 21,* 405–413.

Barbuto, J. E., Fritz, S. M., & Matkin, G. S. (2001). Leaders' bases of social power and anticipation of targets' resistance as predictors of transactional and transformational leadership. *Psychological Reports, 89,* 661–666.

Barling, J., Loughlin, C., & Kelloway, E. K. (2002). Development and test of a model linking safety-specific transformational leadership and occupational safety. *Journal of Applied Psychology, 87,* 488–496.

Barling, J., Weber, T., & Kelloway, E. K. (1996). Effects of transformational leadership training on attitudinal and financial outcomes: A field experiment. *Journal of Applied Psychology, 81,* 827–832.

Barnlund, D. C. (1962). Consistency of emergent leadership in groups with changing tasks and members. *Speech Monographs, 29,* 45–52.

Bass, B. M. (1954). The leaderless group discussion. *Psychological Bulletin, 51,* 465–492.

Bass, B. M. (1960). *Leadership, psychology, and organizational behavior.* New York: Harper & Row.

Bass, B. M. (1967). Social behavior and the orientation inventory: A review. *Psychological Bulletin, 68,* 260–292.

Bass, B. M. (1983). *Organizational decision making.* Homewood, IL: Irwin.

Bass, B. M. (1985). *Leadership and performance beyond expectations.* New York: Free Press.

Bass, B. M. (1990a). *Bass and Stogdill's handbook of leadership: Theory, research, and managerial applications* (3rd ed.). New York: Free Press.

Bass, B. M. (1990b). From transactional to transformational leadership: Learning to share the vision. *Organizational Dynamics, 18,* 19–36.

Bass, B. M. (1992). *VMI's high contrast culture: A setting for the development of civilian and military leaders* (Tech. Rep. No. 1). Binghamton, NY: Center for Leadership Studies.

Bass, B. M. (1997). Does the transactional/transformational leadership paradigm transcend organizational and national boundaries? *American Psychologist, 52,* 130–139.

Bass, B. M. (1998a). *Transformational leadership: Industrial, military, and educational inmpact.* Mahwah, NJ: Lawrence Erlbaum Associates.

Bass, B. M. (1998b). The ethics of transformational leadership. In J. Ciulla (Ed.), *Ethics: The heart of leadership* (pp. 169–192). Westport, CT: Praeger.

Bass, B. M. (1999). Two decades of research and development in transformational leadership. *European Journal of Work and Organizational Psychology, 8,* 9–32.

Bass, B. M. (2002a). Cognitive, social, and emotional intelligence of transformational leaders. In R. E. Riggio, S. E. Murphy, & F. J. Pirozzolo (Eds.), *Multiple intelligences and leadership* (pp. 105–118). Mahwah, NJ: Lawrence Erlbaum Associates.

Bass, B. M. (2002b). Forecasting organizational leadership: From back (1967) to the future (2034). In B. J. Avolio & F. J. Yammarino (Eds.), *Transformational and charismatic leadership: The road ahead* (pp. 375–384). Oxford, UK: JAI/Elsevier.

Bass, B. M., & Avolio, B. J. (1989). Potential biases in leadership measures: How prototypes, leniency, and general satisfaction relate to ratings and rankings of transformational and transactional leadership constructs. *Educational and Psychological Measurement, 49,* 509–527.

Bass, B. M., & Avolio, B. J. (1990a). The implications of transactional and transformational leadership for individual, team and organizational development. In R. W. Woodman & W. A. Passmore (Eds.), *Research in organizational change and development* (pp. 231–272). Greenwich, CT: JAI.

Bass, B. M., & Avolio, B. J. (1990b). Training and development of transformational leadership: Looking to 1992 and beyond. *European Journal of Industrial Training, 14,* 21–27.

Bass, B. M., & Avolio, B. J. (1990c). *Transformational leadership development: Manual for the Multifactor Leadership Questionnaire.* Palo Alto, CA: Consulting Psychologists Press.

Bass, B. M., & Avolio, B. J. (1991a). *The transformational and transactional leadership behavior of women and men as described by the men and women who directly report to them* (CLS Report No. 91–3). Binghamton: Center for Leadership Studies, State University of New York at Binghamton.

Bass, B. M., & Avolio, B. J. (1991b). *The diffusion of transformational leadership in organizational settings.* Turin, Italy: ISVOR-Fiat.

Bass, B. M., & Avolio, B. J. (1992). *Manual for the Organizational Description Questionnaire (ODQ).* Palo Alto, CA: Consulting Psychologists Press.

Bass, B. M., & Avolio, B. J. (1993a). Transformational leadership: A response to critiques. In M. M. Chemers & R. Ayman (Eds.), *Leadership theory and research: Perspectives and directions* (pp. 49–80). New York: Academic Press.

Bass, B. M., & Avolio, B. J. (1993b). Transformational leadership and organizational culture. *Public Administration Quarterly, 17,* 112–122.

Bass, B. M., & Avolio, B. J. (1994). *Improving organizational effectiveness through transformational leadership.* Thousand Oaks, CA: Sage.

Bass, B. M., & Avolio, B. J. (1996). *MLQ Multifactor Leadership Questionnaire for Teams.* Redwood City, CA: Mind Garden.

Bass, B. M., & Avolio, B. J. (1997). *Revised manual for the Multifactor Leadership Questionnaire.* Palo Alto, CA: Mind Garden.

Bass, B. M., & Avolio, B. J. (2000). *MLQ: Multifactor Leadership Questionnaire* (2nd ed.). Redwood City, CA: Mind Garden.

Bass, B. M., & Avolio, B. J. (n.d.). *Intuitive-empirical approach to biodata analysis.* Unpublished manuscript.

Bass, B. M., Avolio, B. J., & Atwater, L. (1996). The transformational and transactional leadership of men and women. *International Review of Applied Psychology, 45,* 5–34.

Bass, B. M., Avolio, B. J., & Goodheim, L. (1987). Biography and the assessment of transformational leadership at the world-class level. *Journal of Management, 13,* 7–19.

Bass, B. M., Avolio, B. J., Jung, D. I., & Berson, Y. (2003). Predicting unit performance by assessing transformational and transactional leadership. *Journal of Applied Psychology, 88,* 207–218.

Bass, B. M., & Steidlmeier, P. (1999). Ethics, character, and authentic transformational leadership. *The Leadership Quarterly, 10,* 181–217.

Bass, B. M., Waldman, D. A., Avolio, B. J., & Bebb, M. (1987). Transformational leadership and the falling dominoes effect. *Group and Organization Studies, 12,* 73–87.

Bass, B. M., & Yammarino, F. J. (1991). Congruence of self and others' leadership ratings of naval officers for understanding successful performance. *Applied Psychology: An International Review, 40,* 437–454.

Becker, T. E., & Billings, R. S. (1993). Profiles of commitment: An empirical test. *Journal of Organizational Behavior, 14,* 177–190.

Begley, P. (2004). *Authentic leadership.* Thousand Oaks, CA: Sage.

Behling, O., & McFillen, J. M. (1996). A syncretical model of charismatic/transformational leadership. *Group and Organizational Management, 21,* 163–191.

Bennis, W. G., & Nanus, B. (1985). *Leaders: The strategies for taking charge.* New York: Harper & Row.

Ben-Yoav, O., Hollander, E. P., & Carnevale, P. J. (1983). Leader legitimacy, leader-follower interactions, and followers' ratings of the leader. *Journal of Social Psychology, 121,* 111–115.

Berkowitz, L. (1953). Sharing in small, decision-making groups. *Journal of Abnormal and Social Psychology, 48,* 231–238.

Bersoff, D. N., Borgida, E., & Fiske, S. T. (1991). Social science research on trial: Use of sex stereotyping research in Price Waterhouse vs. Hopkins. *American Psychologist, 46,* 1049–1070.

Berson, Y. (1999). *A comprehensive assessment of leadership using triangulation of qualitative and quantitative methods.* Unpublished doctoral dissertation, State University of New York at Binghamton.

Berson, Y., & Avolio, B. J. (2004). Transformational leadership and the dissemination of organizational goals: A case study of a telecommunication firm. *The Leadership Quarterly, 15,* 625–646.

Berson, Y., Shamir, B., Avolio, B. J., & Popper, M. (2001). The relationship between vision strength, leadership style, and context. *The Leadership Quarterly, 12,* 53–73.

Bettin, P. J., & Kennedy, J. K. (1990). Leadership experience and leader performance: Some empirical support at last. *The Leadership Quarterly, 1,* 219–228.

Beyer, J. M. (1999). Taming and promoting charisma to change organizations. *The Leadership Quarterly, 10,* 307–330.

Blake, R. R., & Mouton, J. S. (1964). *The managerial grid.* Houston, TX: Gulf Publishing.

Blake, R. R., & Mouton, J. S. (1982). A comparative analysis of situationalism and 9, 9 management by principle. *Organizational Dynamics, 10*(4), 20–43.

Blanchard, K., Zigarmi P., & Zigarmi, D. (1985). *Leadership and the one minute manager: Increasing effectiveness through situational leadership.* New York: Morrow.

Boal, K. B., & Bryson, J. M. (1988). Charismatic leadership: A phenomonological and structural approach. In J. G. Hunt, B. R. Baliga, H. P. Dachler, & C. A. Schriesheim (Eds.), *Emerging leadership vistas* (pp. 11–28). Lexington, MA: Heath.

Bobrow, W., & Leonards, J. S. (1997). Development and validation of an assessment center during organizational change. *Journal of Social Behavior and Personality, 12,* 217–236.

Bommer, W. H., Rubin, R. S., & Baldwin, T. T. (2004). Setting the stage for effective leadership: Antecedents of transformational leadership behavior. *The Leadership Quarterly, 15,* 195–210.

Bono, J. E., & Judge, T. A. (2004). Personality and transformational and transactional leadership: A meta-analysis. *Journal of Applied Psychology, 89,* 901–910.

Boorstin, J. (2004). 1 J. M. Smucker. *Fortune, 149*(1), 58–59.

Boyce, L. A., & Herd, A. M. (2003). The relationship between gender role stereotypes and requisite military leadership characteristics. *Sex Roles, 49,* 365–378.

Boyd, J. T., Jr. (1988). *Leadership extraordinary: A cross-national military perspective on transactional versus transformational leadership.* Unpublished doctoral dissertation, Nova University, Boca Raton, FL.

Bradley, R. T. (1987). *Charisma and social structure: A study of love and power, wholeness and transformation.* New York: Paragon House.

Brenner, O. C., & Bromer, J. A. (1981). Sex stereotypes and leaders' behavior as measured by the Agreement Scale for Leadership Behavior. *Psychological Reports, 48,* 960–962.

Brossoit, K. B. (2000). *Understanding employee empowerment in the workplace: Exploring the relationships between transformational leadership, employee perceptions of empowerment, and key work outcomes.* Unpublished doctoral dissertation. Claremont Graduate university, Claremont, CA.

Brower, H. H., Schoorman, F. D., & Tan, H. H. (2000). A model of relational leadership: The integration of trust and leader-member exchange. *The Leadership Quarterly, 11,* 227–250.

Brown, F. W., & Moshavi, D. (2002). Herding academic cats: Faculty reactions to transformational and contingent reward leadership by department chairs. *Journal of Leadership Studies, 8,* 79–94.

Brown, M. E., & Trevino, L. K. (2003, August). *The influence of leadership styles on unethical conduct in work groups: An empirical test.* Paper presented at the meeting of the Academy of Management, Seattle, WA.

Bryman, A. (1992). *Charisma and leadership in organizations.* London: Sage.

Burgess, K. A., Salas, E., Cannon-Bowers, J. A., & Hall, J. K. (1992). *Training guidelines for team leaders under stress.* Paper presented at the meeting of the Human Factors Society, Atlanta, GA.

Burke, C. S., Fiore, S. M., & Salas, E. (2003). The role of shared cognition in enabling shared leadership and team adaptability. In C. L. Pearce & J. A. Conger (Eds.), *Shared leadership: Reframing the hows and whys of leadership* (pp. 103–122). Thousand Oaks, CA: Sage.

Burke, W. W. (1994). *Leadership Assessment Inventory* (rev. ed.). Pelham, NY: W. Warner Burke and Associates.

Burns, J. M. (1956). *Roosevelt: The lion and the fox.* New York: Harcourt Brace.

Burns, J. M. (1978). *Leadership.* New York: Harper & Row.

Burns, J. M. (2003). *Transforming leadership.* New York: Grove Press.

Burns, T. (1961). *Management of innovation.* London: Tavistock.

Bussey, C. D. (1980, July). Leadership for the Army. *Military Review, 1,* 69–76.

Bycio, P., Hackett, R. D., & Allen, J. S. (1995). Further assessments of Bass's (1985) conceptualization of transactional and transformational leadership. *Journal of Applied Psychology, 80,* 468–478.

Camara, W. J., & Schneider, D. L. (1994). Integrity tests: Facts and unresolved issues. *American Psychologist, 49*(2), 112–114.

Cannella, A. A., & Monroe, M. J. (1997). Contrasting perspectives on strategic leaders: Toward a more realistic view of top managers. *Journal of Management, 23,* 213–237.

Carless, S. A., Wearing, A. J., & Mann, L. (2000). A short measure of transformational leadership. *Journal of Business and Psychology, 14,* 389–405.

Carli, L. L., & Eagly, A. H. (2001). Gender, hierarchy, and leadership: An introduction. *Journal of Social Issues, 57,* 629–636.

Caro, R. A. (1974). *The power broker: Robert Moses and the fall of New York.* New York: Knopf.

Caro, R. A. (1982). *The years of Lyndon Johnson: The path to power.* New York: Knopf.

Cascio, W. F. (1995). Whither industrial and organizational psychology in a changing world of work? *American Psychologist, 50*, 928–939.

Cascio, W. F., & Shurygailo, S. (2003). E-leadership and virtual teams. *Organizational Dynamics, 31*, 362–376.

CATA (Combined Arms Training Activity). (1986). *Fort Hood leadership study: Leadership lessons learned.* Fort Leavenworth, KS: Author.

Cattell, R. (1950). *Personality: A systematic, theoretical, and factual study.* New York: Mc-Graw-Hill.

Charbonneau, D., Barling, J., & Kelloway, E. K. (2001). Transformational leadership and sports performance: The mediating role of intrinsic motivation. *Journal of Applied Social Psychology, 31*, 1521–1534.

Chemers, M. M. (1997). *An integrative theory of leadership.* Mahwah, NJ: Lawrence Erlbaum Associates.

Chemers, M. M. (2002). Efficacy and effectiveness: Integrating models of leadership and intelligence. In R. E. Riggio, S. E. Murphy, & F. J. Pirozzolo (Eds.), *Multiple intelligences and leadership* (pp. 139–160). Mahwah, NJ: Lawrence Erlbaum Associates.

Chemers, M. M., Watson, C. B., & May, S. T. (2000). Dispositional affect and leadership effectiveness: A comparison of self-esteem, optimism and efficacy. *Personality and Social Psychology Bulletin, 26*, 267–277.

Chen, X., Hui, C., & Sego, D. J. (1998). The role of organizational citizenship behavior in turnover: Conceptualization and preliminary tests of key hypotheses. *Journal of Applied Psychology, 83*, 922–931.

Choi, Y., & Mai-Dalton, R. R. (1999). The model of followers' responses to self-sacrificial leadership: An empirical test. *The Leadership Quarterly, 10*, 397–421.

Chrislip, D. D., & Larson, C. E. (1994). *Collaborative leadership: How citizens and civic leaders can make a difference.* San Francisco: Jossey-Bass.

Church, A. H., & Waclawski, J. (1998). The relationships between individual personality orientation and executive leadership behaviour. *Journal of Occupational and Organizational Psychology, 71*, 99–125.

Church, T. (2001). Where the leaders are: The promise of youth leadership. In W. Bennis, G. M. Spreitzer, & T. G. Cummings (Eds.), *The future of leadership* (pp. 211–225). San Francisco: Jossey-Bass.

Cohen, S. G., & Ledford, G. E. (1994). The effectiveness of self-managing teams: A quasi-experiment. *Human Relations, 47*, 13–43.

Collins, J. C., & Porras, J. I. (1994). *Built to last: Successful habits of visionary companies.* New York: HarperCollins.

Conger, J. A. (1990). The dark side of leadership. *Organizational Dynamics, 19*, 44–55.

Conger, J. A., & Benjamin, B. (1999). *Building leaders: How successful companies develop the next generation.* San Francisco: Jossey-Bass.

Conger, J. A., & Kanungo, R. N. (1988). *Charismatic leadership: The elusive factor in organization effectiveness.* San Francisco: Jossey-Bass.

Conger, J. A., & Kanungo, R. N. (1998). *Charismatic leadership in organizations.* Thousand Oaks, CA: Sage.

Conger, J. A., Kanungo, R. N., & Menon, S. T. (2000). Charismatic leadership and follower effects. *Journal of Organizational Behavior, 21*, 747–767.

Conger, J. A., & Toegel, G. (2003). Action learning and multirater feedback: Pathways to leadership development? In S. E. Murphy & R. E. Riggio (Eds.), *The future of leadership development* (pp. 107–125). Mahwah, NJ: Lawrence Erlbaum Associates.

Connolly, J. J., & Viswesvaran, C. (2000). The role of affectivity in job satisfaction: A meta-analysis. *Personality and Individual Differences, 29*, 265–281.

Cox, C. M. (1926). *The early mental traits of three hundred genius.* Stanford, CA: Stanford University Press.

Cox, J. F., Pearce, C. L., & Perry, M. L. (2003). Toward a model of shared leadership and distributed influence in the innovation process. In C. L. Pearce & J. A. Conger (Eds.), *Shared leadership: Reframing the hows and whys of leadership* (pp. 48–76). Thousand Oaks, CA: Sage.

Crant, J. M., & Bateman, T. S. (2000). Charismatic leadership viewed from above: The impact of proactive personality. *Journal of Organizational Behavior, 21*, 63–75.

Crookall, P. (1989). *Management of inmate workers: A field test of transformational and situational leadership.* Unpublished doctoral dissertation, University of Western Ontario, London, Ontario.

Curphy, G. J. (1990). *An empirical study of Bass's (1985) theory of transformational and transactional leadership.* Unpublished doctoral dissertation, The University of Minnesota, Minneapolis.

Curphy, G. J. (1992). An empirical investigation of the effects of transformational and transactional leadership on organizational climate, attrition and performance. In K. E. Clark, M. B. Clark, & D. R. Campbell (Eds.), *Impact of leadership* (pp. 177–187). Greensboro, NC: The Center for Creative Leadership.

Dahle, T. L. (1954). Transmitting information to employees: A study of five methods. *Journal of Business Personnel, 29*, 243–246.

Dasborough, M. T., & Ashkanasy, N. M. (2002). Emotion and attribution of intentionality in leader-member relationships. *The Leadership Quarterly, 13*, 615–634,

Davis, D. D., Guaw, P., Luo, J., & Maahs, C. J. (1994, April). *Need for continuous improvement, organization citizenship, transformational leadership, and service climate in a Chinese state enterprise.* Paper presented at the Society for Organizational and Industrial Psychology, St. Louis, MO.

Day, D. V. (2000). Leadership development: A review in context. *The Leadership Quarterly, 11*, 581–613.

Day, D. V., & O'Connor, P. M. G. (2003). Leadership development: Understanding the process. In S. E. Murphy & R. E. Riggio (Eds.), *The future of leadership development* (pp. 11–28). Mahwah, NJ: Lawrence Erlbaum Associates.

Deal, T. E., & Kennedy, A. A. (1982). *Corporate cultures: The rites and rituals of corporate life.* Reading, MA: Addison-Wesley.

DeGroot, T., Kiker, D. S., & Cross, T. C. (2000). A meta-analysis to review organizational outcomes related to charismatic leadership. *Canadian Journal of Administrative Sciences, 17*, 356–371.

Deluga, R. J. (1990). The effects of transformational, transactional, and laissez-faire leadership characteristics on subordinate influencing behavior. *Basic and Applied Social Psychology, 11*, 191–203.

Deluga, R. J. (1991). The relationship of leader and subordinate influencing activity in naval environments. *Military Psychology, 3*, 25–39.

Deluga, R. J. (1995). The relation between trust in the supervisor and subordinate organizational citizenship behavior. *Military Psychology, 7*, 1–16.

Deluga, R. J. (1997). Relationship among American presidential charismatic leadership, narcissism, and rated performance. *The Leadership Quarterly, 8*, 49–65.

Deluga, R. J. (1998). American presidential proactivity, charismatic leadership, and rated performance. *The Leadership Quarterly, 9*, 265–291.

Deluga, R. J. (2001). American presidential Machiavellianism: Implications for charismatic leadership and rated performance. *The Leadership Quarterly, 12*, 339–363.

Den Hartog, D. N., House, R. J., Hanges, P. J., Ruiz-Quintanilla, S. A., & Dorfman, P. W. (1999). Culture specific and cross-cultural generalizable implicit leadership theories: Are attributes of charismatic/transformational leadership universally endorsed? *The Leadership Quarterly, 10*, 219–256.

Den Hartog, D. N., Van Muijen, J. J., & Koopman, P. L. (1997). Transactional vs. transformational leadership: An analysis of the MLQ. *Journal of Occupational and Organizational Psychology, 70*(1), 19–34.

Denmark, F. L. (1977). Styles of leadership. *Psychology of Women Quarterly, 2*, 99–113.

DePaulo, B. M., & Friedman, H. S. (1998). Nonverbal communication. In D. T. Gilbert, S. T. Fiske, & G. Lindzey, Eds.), *The handbook of social psychology* (Vol. 2, 4th ed., pp. 3–40). New York: McGraw-Hill.

Dettmann, J. R., & Beehr, T. (2004). Training transformational leadership: A field experiment in the non-profit sector. Paper presented at the meeting of the Society for Industrial and Organizational Psychology, Chicago.

Devilbiss, M. C., & Siebold, G. L. (1987). *Values and commitment in U.S. Army combat units.* Paper presented at the meeting of the Southern Sociological Society, Atlanta, GA.

De Vries, R. E., Roe, R. A., & Taillieu, T. C. B. (2002). Need for leadership as a moderator of the relationships between leadership and individual outcomes. *The Leadership Quarterly, 13*, 121–137.

Dorfman, P. W., Hanges, P. J., & Brodbeck, F. C. (2004). Leadership and cultural variation: The identification of culturally endorsed leadership profiles. In R. J. House, P. J. Hanges, M. Javidan, P. W. Dorfman, & V. Gupta (Eds.), *Culture, leadership, and organizations: The GLOBE study of 62 societies* (pp. 669–719). Thousand Oaks, CA: Sage.

Downton, J. V. (1973). *Rebel leadership: Commitment and charisma in the revolutionary process.* New York: Free Press.

Druskat, V. U. (1994). Gender and leadership style: Transformational and transactional leadership in the Roman Catholic Church. *The Leadership Quarterly, 5*, 99–119.

Dubinsky, A. J., Yammarino, F. J., & Jolson, M. A. (1995). An examination of linkages between personal characteristics and dimensions of transformational leadership. *Journal of Business and Psychology, 9*, 315–335.

Dumdum, U. R., Lowe, K. B., & Avolio, B. J. (2002). A meta-analysis of transformational and transactional leadership correlates of effectiveness and satisfaction: An update and extension. In B. J. Avolio & F. J. Yammarino (Eds.), *Transformational and charismatic leadership: The road ahead* (pp. 35–66). Oxford, UK: JAI/Elsevier

Dvir, T., Eden, D., Avolio, B. J., & Shamir, B. (2002). Impact of transformational leadership on follower development and performance: A field experiment. *Academy of Management Journal, 45*, 735–744.

Eagly, A. H. (1991). *Gender and leadership.* Paper presented at the meeting of the American Psychological Association, San Francisco.

Eagly, A. H., & Carli, L. L. (2003). The female leadership advantage: An evaluation of the evidence. *The Leadership Quarterly, 14*, 807–834.

Eagly, A. H., & Crowley, M. (1986). Gender and helping behavior: A meta-analytic review of the social psychological literature. *Psychological Bulletin, 100*, 283–308.

Eagly, A. H., & Johannesen-Schmidt, M. C. (2001). The leadership styles of women and men. *Journal of Social Issues, 57*, 781–797.

Eagly, A. H., Johannesen-Schmidt, M. C., & van Engen, M. L. (2003). Transformational, transactional, and laissez-faire leadership styles: A meta-analysis comparing men and women. *Psychological Bulletin, 129*, 569–591.

Eagly, A. H., & Johnson, B. T. (1990). Gender and leadership styles: A meta-analysis. *Psychological Bulletin, 108*, 233–256.

Eagly, A. H., & Karau, S. J. (2002). Role congruity theory of prejudice toward female leaders. *Psychological Review, 109*, 573–598.

Eagly, A. H., Makhijani, M. G., & Klonsky, K. B. G. (1992). Gender and the evaluation of leaders: A meta-analysis. *Psychological Bulletin, 111*, 3–22.

Eagly, A. H., Mladinic, A., & Otto, S. (1991). Are women evaluated more favorably than men? *Psychology of Women Quarterly, 15*, 203–216.

Eden, D., & Ravid, G. (1982). Pygmalion vs. self-expectency: Effects of instrutor and self-expectancy on trainee performance. *Organizational Behavior and Human Performance, 30*, 351–364.

Eden, D., & Sulimani, R. (2002). Pygmalion training made effective: Greater mastery through augmentation of self-efficacy and means efficacy. In B. J. Avolio & F. J. Yammarino (Eds.), *Transformational and charismatic leadership: The road ahead* (pp. 287–308). Oxford, UK: JAI/Elsevier.

Egri, C. P., & Herman, S. (2000). Leadership in the North American environmental sector: Values, leadership styles, and contexts of environmental leaders and their organizations. *Academy of Management Journal, 43*, 571–604.

Elenkov, D. S. (2002). Effects of leadership on organizational performance in Russian companies. *Journal of Business Research, 55*, 467–480.

Elkins, T., & Keller, R. T. (2003). Leadership in research and development organizations: A literature review and conceptual framework. *The Leadership Quarterly, 14*, 587–606.

Epstein, S., & Meier, P. (1989). *Constructive thinking: A broad coping variable with specific components.* Working paper, University of Massachusetts at Amherst.

Farris, G. F. (1971). *Colleagues' roles and innovation in scientific teams* (Working paper No. 552–71). Cambridge, MA: Alfred P. Sloan School of Management, MIT.

Fiedler, F. E. (1967). *A theory of leadership effectiveness.* New York: McGraw-Hill.

Fiedler, F. E. (1986). The contribution of cognitive resources and leader behavior to organizational performance. *Journal of Applied Social Psychology, 16*, 532–548.

Fiedler, F. E. (1995). Cognitive resources and leadership performance. *Applied Psychology—An International Review, 44*, 5–28.

Fiedler, F. E. (2002). The curious role of cognitive resources in leadership. In R. E. Riggio, S. E. Murphy, & F. J. Pirozzolo (Eds.), *Multiple intelligences and leadership* (pp. 91–104). Mahwah, NJ: Lawrence Erlbaum Associates.

Fiedler, F. E. & Garcia, J. E. (1987). *New approaches to effective leadership: Cognitive resources and organizational performance.* New York: Wiley.

Finegan, J. (1987). Four-star management. *Inc. 9*(1), 42–44, 46.

Francois, P. H. (1990). Être un leader, avoir du charisme [To be a leader, have some charisma]. *Journal de Psychologues, 81*, 54–60.

Frank, H. H., & Katcher, A. H. (1977). The qualities of leadership: How male medical students evaluate their female peers. *Human Relations, 30*, 403–416.

French, J. R. P., & Raven, B. (1959). The bases of social power. In D. Cartwright (Ed.), *Studies in social power* (pp. 15–167). Ann Arbor: University of Michigan, Institute for Social Research.

Fullager, C., McCoy, D., & Shull, C. (1992). The socialization of union loyaly. *Journal of Organizational Behavior, 13*, 13–26.

Fuller, J. B., Morrison, R., Jones, L., Bridger, D., & Brown, V. (1999). The effects of psychological empowerment on transformational leadership and job satisfaction. *Journal of Social Psychology, 139*, 389–391.

Gal, R. (1985). Commitment and obedience in the military: An Israeli case study. *Armed Forces and Society, 11*, 553–564.

Gal, R. (1987). *Yesterday's conventional warfare—Tomorrow's nuclear warfare? Lessons from the Israel experience.* Paper presented at the Conference on Military Leadership, U.S. Naval Academy, Annapolis, MD.

Gal, R., & Jones, F. D. (1985). *Psychological aspects of combat stress: A model derived from Israeli and other combat experiences.* Unpublished manuscript, Zikron Ya'acov, Israel.

Gallup Leadership Institute. (2004). *100 year review of leadership intervention research* (Briefings report 2004–01). Lincoln: University of Nebraska

Ganster, D. C., Fusilier, M. R., & Mayes, B. T. (1986). Role of social support in the experience of stress at work. *Journal of Applied Psychology, 71*, 102–110.

Gardner, H. (1999). *Intelligence reframed: Multiple intelligences for the 21st century*. New York: Basic Books.

Gardner, J. (1987). *Attributes and context* (Leadership Papers, No. 6). Washington, DC: Leadership Studies Program, Independent Sector.

Gardner, L., & Stough, C. (2002). Examining the relationship between leadership and emotional intelligence in senior level managers. *Leadership and Organization Development Journal, 23*, 68–78.

Gardner, W. L., & Schermerhorn, J. R. (2004). Performance gains through positive organizational behavior and authentic leadership. *Organizational Dynamics, 33*, 270–281.

Gasper, J. M. (1992). *Transformational leadership: An integrative review of the literature.* Unpublished doctoral dissertation, Western Michigan University, Kalamazoo.

Gellis, Z. D. (2001). Social work perceptions of transformational and transactional leadership in health care. *Social Work Research, 25*, 17–25.

George, B. (2004). *Authentic leadership: Rediscovering the secrets to creating lasting value.* San Francisco: Jossey-Bass.

George, J. M. (2000). Emotions and leadership: The role of emotional intelligence. *Human Relations, 53*, 1027–1055.

Gerstner, C. R., & Day, D. V. (1997). Meta-analytic review of leader-member exchange theory: Correlates and construct issues. *Journal of Applied Psychology, 82*, 827–844.

Ghiselli, E. E. (1963). Intelligence and managerial success. *Psychological Reports, 12*, 898.

Gibbons, T. C. (1986). *Revisiting: The question of born vs. made: Toward a theory of development of transformational leaders.* Unpublished doctoral dissertation, Fielding Institute, Santa Barbara, CA.

Gibson, F. W., Fiedler, F. E., & Barrett, K. M. (1993). Stress, babble and the utilization of the leader's intellectual abilities. *The Leadership Quarterly, 4*, 189–208.

Giuliani, R. W., & Kurson, K. (2002). *Leadership.* New York: Miramax.

Goleman, D. (1995). *Emotional intelligence.* New York: Bantam.

Goleman, D., McKee, A., & Boyatzis, R. E. (2002). *Primal leadership: Realizing the power of emotional intelligence.* Boston: Harvard Business School Press.

Gomez, C., & Rosen, B. (2001). The leader-member exchange as a link between managerial trust and employee empowerment. *Group and Organization Management, 26*, 53–69.

Goodstein, L. D., & Lanyon, R. I. (1999). Applications of personality assessment to the workplace: A review. *Journal of Business and Psychology, 13*, 291–322.

Goodwin, V. L., Wofford, J. C., & Boyd, N. (2000). A laboratory experiment testing the antecedents of leader cognitions. *Journal of Organizational Behavior, 21*, 769–788.

Gough, H. G. & Heilbrun, A. B. (1983). *The Adjective Checklist manual.* Palo Alto, CA: Consulting Psychologists Press.

Graen, G., & Scandura, R. A. (1987). Toward a psychology of dyadic organizing. *Research in Organizational Behavior, 9*, 175–208.

Graen, G., & Uhl-Bien, M. (1991). The transformation of professionals into self-managing and partially self-designing contributors: Toward a theory of leadership making. *Journal of Systems Management, 42*, 25–39.

Groves, K. S. (2005). Linking leader skills, follower attitudes, and contextual variable via an integrated model of charismatic leadership. *Journal of Management, 31*, 255–277.

Hackett, J. W. (1979). Today and tomorrow. In M. Wakin (Ed.), *War, morality and the military profession* (pp. 91–106). Boudler, CO: Westview.

Hackman, J. R., & Oldham, G. R. (1976). Motivation through the design of work: Test of a theory. *Organizational Behavior and Human Performance, 16*, 250–279.

Hackman, J. R., & Oldham, G. R. (1980). *Word redesign.* Reading, MA: Addison-Wesley.

Hackman, M. Z., Furniss, A. H., Hills, M. J., & Paterson, R. J. (1992). Perceptions of gender–role characteristics and transformational and transactional leadership behaviours. *Perceptual and Motor Skills, 75,* 311–319.

Hall, D. T., & Mansfield, R. (1971). Organizational and individual response to external stress. *Administrative Science Quarterly, 16,* 533–547.

Hall, J. A. (1976). To achieve or not: The manager's choice. *California Management Review, 18,* 5–18.

Hall, J. A. (1984). *Nonverbal sex differences: Accuracy of communication and expressive style.* Baltimore: Johns Hopkins University Press.

Hamblin, R. L. (1958). Group integration during a crisis. *Human Relations, 11,* 67–76.

Handy, C. (1994). *Age of paradox.* Cambridge, MA: Harvard University Press.

Harland, L. K., Harrison, W., Jones, J. R., & Reiter-Palmon, R. (2005). Leadership behaviors and subordinate resilience. *Journal of Leadership and Organizational Studies, 11,* 1–14.

Harman, D. (1984). Lessons learned about emergency preparedness. *Public Management, 66*(3), 5–8.

Hart, S. L., & Quinn, R. E. (1993). Roles executives play: CEOs, behavioral complexity, and firm performance. *Human Relations, 46,* 543–574.

Harvey, S., Royal, M., & Stout, D. (2003). Instructor's transformational leadership: University student attitudes and ratings. *Psychological Reports, 92,* 395–402.

Hater, J. J., & Bass, B. M. (1988). Superiors' evaluations and subordinates' perceptions of transformational and transactional leadership. *Journal of Applied Psychology, 73*(4), 695–702.

Hawn, C., & Overholt, A. (2004, January). If he's so smart . . . Steve Jobs, Apple, and the limits of innovation. *Fast Company,* 68–74.

Heilman, M. E. (2001). Description and prescription: How gender stereotypes prevent women's ascent up the organizational ladder. *Journal of Social Issues, 57,* 657–674.

Helgesen, S. (1990). *The female advantage: Woman's ways of leadership.* Garden City, NY: Doubleday.

Hennig, N., & Jardim, A. (1977). *The managerial women.* Garden City, NY: Doubleday.

Hersey, P., & Blanchard, K. H. (1969). *Management of organizational behavior.* Englewood Cliffs, NJ: Prentice-Hall.

Herzberg, F. I. (1966). *Work and the nature of man.* New York: Crowell.

Hickman, G. R. (2004). Organizations of hope: Leading the way to transformation, social action, and profitability. In R. E. Riggio & S. S. Orr (Eds.), *Improving leadership in nonprofit organizations* (pp. 151–162). San Francisco: Jossey-Bass.

Hofstede, G. (1991). *Cultures and organizations: Software of the mind.* New York: McGraw-Hill.

Hofstede, G., & Bond, M. H. (1988). The Confucius connection: From cultural roots to economic growth. *Organizational Dynamics, 16,* 4–24.

Hollander, E. P. (1992). Leadership, followership, self and others. *Leadership Quarterly, 3,* 43–54.

Homans, G. C. (1950). *The human group.* New York: Harcourt, Brace.

Hoover, N. R. (1987). *Transformational and transactional leadership: A test of the model.* Unpublished doctoral dissertation, University of Louisville, Louisville, KY.

Hoover, N. R., Petrosko, J. M., & Schulz, R. R. (1991). *Transformational and transactional leadership: An empirical test of a theory.* Paper presented at meeting of the American Educational Research Association, Chicago, IL.

House, R. J. (1971). A path goal theory of leader effectiveness. *Administrative Science Quarterly, 16,* 321–338.

House, R. J. (1977). A 1976 theory of charismatic leadership. In J. G. Hunt & L. L. Larson (Eds.), *Leadership: The cutting edge* (pp. 189–207). Carbondale: Southern Illinois University Press.

House, R. J. (1992). The distribution and exercise of power in mechanistic and organic organizations. In H. L. Tosi (Ed.), *The environment/organization/person contingency model: A meso approach to the study of organizations* (pp. 119–144). Greenwich, CT: JAI.

House, R. J. (1995). Leadership in the twenty-first century: A speculative inquiry. In A. Howard (Ed.), *The changing nature of work.* San Francisco: Jossey-Bass.

House, R. J. (1998). Appendix: Measures and assessments for the charismatic leadership approach: Scales, latent constructs, loadings, Cronbach alphas, interclass correlations. In F. Dansereau & F. J. Yammarino (Ed.), *Leadership: The multiple-level approaches contemporary and alternative* (24, Part B, pp. 223–230). London: JAI Press.

House, R. J., Hanges, P. J., Javidan, M., Dorfman, P. W., & Gupta, V. (Eds.). (2004). *Culture, leadership, and organization: The GLOBE study of 62 societies.* Thousand Oaks, CA: Sage.

House, R. J., & Howell, J. M. (1992). Personality and charismatic leadership. *The Leadership Quarterly, 3,* 81–108.

House, R. J., & Rizzo, J. R. (1972). Role conflict and ambiguity as critical variables in a model of organizational behavior. *Organizational Behavior and Human Performance, 7,* 467–505.

House, R. J., & Shamir, B. (1993). Toward the integration of transformational, charismatic and visionary theories. In M. M. Chemers & R. Ayman (Eds.), *Leadership theory and research: Perspective and directions* (pp. 81–107). New York: Academic Press.

House, R. J., Spangler, W., & Woycke, J. (1991). Personality and charisma in the U.S. Presidency: A psychological theory of leader effectiveness. *Administrative Science Quarterly, 36,* 364–396.

Howard, A., & Wellins, H. (1994). *High-involvement leadership: Changing roles for changing times.* Tenafly, NJ: Leadership Research Institute, Developmental Dimensions International.

Howell, J. M. (1992). Organization contexts, charismatic and exchange leadership. In H. L. Tosi (Ed.), *The environment/organization/person contingency model: A meso approach to the study of organizations.* Greenwich, CT: JAI.

Howell, J. M., & Avolio, B. J. (1993). Transformational leadership, transactional leadership, locus of control, and support for innovation: Key predictors of consolidated business-unit performance. *Journal of Applied Psychology, 78,* 891–902.

Howell, J. M., & Hall-Merenda, K. E. (1999). The ties that bind: The impact of leader-member exchange, transformational and transactional leadership, and distance on predicting follower performance. *Journal of Applied Psychology, 84,* 680–694.

Howell, J. M., & Higgins, C. A. (1990). Champions of technological innovations. *Administrative Science Quarterly, 35,* 317–341.

Howell, J. M., & House, R. J. (1992). *Socialized and personalized charisma: An essay on the bright and dark sides of leadership.* Unpublished manuscript, Western Business School, The University of Western Ontario, London, Ontario, Canada.

Howell, J. M., & Shamir, B. (2005). The role of followers in the charismatic leadership process: Relationships and their consequences. *Academy of Management Review, 30,* 96–112.

Howell, J. P., Bowen, D. E., Dorfman, P. W., Kerr, S., & Podsakoff, P. M. (1993). New dimensions in leadership. A special report from organizational dynamics. *American Management Association,* pp. 83–99.

Howell, J. P., & Dorfman, P. W. (1986). Leadership and substitutes for leadership among professional and non-professional workers. *Journal of Applied Behavioral Science, 22,* 29–46.

Howell, J. P., Dorfman, P. W., & Kerr, S. (1986). Moderator variables in leadership research. *Academy of Management Review, 11,* 88–102.

Hoyt, C. L., & Blascovich, J. (2003). Transformational and transactional leadership in virtual and physical environments. *Small Group Research, 34,* 678–715.

Hoyt, C. L., Murphy, S. E., Halverson, S. K., & Watson, C. B. (2003). Group leadership: Efficacy and effectiveness. *Group Dynamics: Theory, Research, and Practice, 7,* 259–274.

Hummel, R. P. (1973). *Charisma in politics: Psychosocial causes of revolution as preconditions of charismatic outbreaks within the framework of Weber's epistemology.* Master's thesis, New York University.

Hunt, J. G. (1991). *Leadership: A new synthesis.* Newbury Park, CA: Sage.

Jacobsen, C., & House, R. J. (2001). Dynamics of charismatic leadership: A process theory, simulation model, and tests. *The Leadership Quarterly, 12,* 75–112.

Janis, I. L. (1982). *Groupthink: Psychological studies of policy decisions and fiascoes* (2nd ed.). New York: Houghton Mifflin.

Janis, I. L., & Mann, L. (1977). *Decision making: A psychological analysis of conflict, choice, and commitment.* New York: Free Press.

Johnson, A. M., Vernon, P. A., Harris, J. A., & Jang, K. L. (2004). A behavior genetic investigation of the relationship between leadership and personality. *Twin Research, 7,* 27–32.

Jolson, M. A., Dubinsky, A. J., Yammaraino, F. J., & Comer, L. B. (1993). Transforming the salesforce with leadership. *Sloan Management Review, 34,* 95–106.

Judge, T. A., & Bono, J. E. (2000). Five-factor model of personality and transformational leadership. *Journal of Applied Psychology, 85,* 751–765.

Judge, T. A., & Piccolo, R. G. (2004). Transformational and transactional leadership: A meta-analytic test of their relative validity. *Journal of Applied Psychology, 89,* 755–768.

Jung, D. I. (2001). Transformational and transactional leadership and their effects on creativity in groups. *Creativity Research Journal, 13,* 185–195.

Jung, D. I., & Avolio, B. J. (2000). Opening the black box: An experimental investigation of the mediating effects of trust and value congruence on transformational and transactional leadership. *Journal of Organizational Behaviour, 21,* 949–964.

Jung, D. I., Chow, C., & Wu, A. (2003). The role of transformational leadership in enhancing organizational innovation: Hypotheses and some preliminary findings. *The Leadership Quarterly, 14,* 525–544.

Jung, D. I., & Sosik, J. J. (2002). Transformational leadership in work groups: The role of empowerment, cohesiveness, and collective-efficacy on perceived group performance. *Small Group Research, 33,* 313–336.

Jung, D. I., Sosik, J. J., & Bass, B. M. (1995). Bridging leadership and cultures: A theoretical consideration of transformational leadership and collectivistic cultures. *Journal of Management Inquiry, 2,* 3–18.

Kahai, S. S., Sosik, J. J., & Avolio, B. J. (2003). Effects of leadership style, anonymity, and rewards on creativity-relevant processes and outcomes in an electronic meeting system context. *The Leadership Quarterly, 14,* 499–524.

Kalay, E. (1983). *The commander in stress situations in IDF combat units during the "Peace for Galilee" campaign.* Paper presented at the Third International Conference on Psychological Stress and Adjustment in Time of War and Peace, Tel Aviv, Israel.

Kane, T. D., & Tremble, T. R. (2000). Transformational leadership effects at different levels of the army. *Military Psychology, 12,* 137–160.

Kark, R., & Shamir, B. (2002). The dual effect of transformational leadership: Priming relational and collective selves and further effects on followers. In B. J. Avolio & F. J. Yammarino (Eds.), *Transformational and charismatic leadership: The road ahead* (pp. 67–91). Oxford, UK: JAI/Elsevier

Kark, R., Shamir, B., & Chen, G. (2003). The two faces of transformational leadership: Empowerment and dependency. *Journal of Applied Psychology, 88,* 246–255.

Kartez, J. D. (1984). Crisis response planning. *Journal of the American Planning Association, 50,* 9–21.

Katz, D. (1951). Survey research center: An overview of the human relations programme. In H. Guetzkow (Ed.), *Groups, leadership and men* (pp. 68–85). Pittsburgh, PA: Carnegie Press.

Katz, R. (1977). The influence of group conflict on leadership effectiveness. *Organizational Behavior and Human Performance, 20,* 265–286.

Katz, R., Phillips, E., & Cheston, R. (1976). *Methods of conflict resolution: A re-examination.* Unpublished manuscript.

Keegan, J. (1976). *The face of battle.* New York: Viking.

Keller, R. T. (1992). Transformational leader and the performance of research and design project groups. *Journal of Management, 18,* 489–501.

Kelloway, E. K., & Barling, J. (1993). Members' participation in local union activities: Measurement, prediction, and replication. *Journal of Applied Psychology, 78,* 262–279.

Kelloway, E. K., Barling, J., & Helleur, J. (2000). Enhancing transformational leadership: The role of training and feedback. *Leadership and Organization Development Journal, 21,* 145–149.

Kelman, H. C. (1958). Compliance, identification, and internalization: Three processes of attitude change. *Journal of Conflict Resolution, 2,* 51–60.

Kenny, D. A. & Zaccaro, S. J. (1983). An estimate of variance due to traits in leadership. *Journal of Applied Psychology, 68,* 678–685.

Kerr, S. (1977). Substitutes for leadership: Some implications for organizational design. *Organization and Administrative Science, 8,* 135–146.

Kets de Vries, M. F. R. (1984). Managers can drive their subordinates mad. In M. F. R. Kets de Vries (Ed.), *The irrational executive: Psychoanalytic explorations in management.* New York: International Universities Press.

Kets de Vries, M. F. R. (1988). Origins of charisma: Ties that bind the leader and the led. In J. A. Conger & R. N. Kanungo (Eds.), *Charismatic leadership* (pp. 237–252). San Francisco: Jossey-Bass.

Kets de Vries, M. F. R. (1994). The leadership mystique. *Academy of Management Executive, 8,* 73–92.

Kierein, N. M., & Gold, M. A. (2000). Pygmalion in work organizations: A meta-analysis. *Journal of Organizational Behavior, 21,* 913–928.

Kirby, P. C., Paradise, L. V., & King, M. I. (1992). Extraordinary leaders in education: Understanding transformational leadership. *Journal of Educational research, 85,* 303–311.

Kirkman, B. L., & Rosen, B. (1999). Beyond self-management: Antecedents and consequences of team empowerment. *Academy of Management Journal, 42,* 58–74.

Kirkpatrick, S. A., & Locke, E. A. (1996). Direct and indirect effects of three core charismatic leadership components on performance and attitudes. *Journal of Applied Psychology, 81,* 36–51.

Klein, A. L. (1976). Changes in leadership appraisal as a function of the stress of a simulated panic situation. *Journal of Personality and Social Psychology, 34,* 1143–1154.

Kline, T. J. B. (2003). *Teams that lead: A matter of market strategy, leadership skills, and executive strength.* Mahwah, NJ: Lawrence Erlbaum Associates.

Kobasa, S. C., Maddi, S. R., & Kahn, S. (1982). Hardiness and health: A prospective study. *Journal of Personality and Social Psychology, 43,* 168–177.

Koh, W. L. (1990). *An empirical validation of the theory of transformational leadership in secondary schools in Singapore.* Unpublished doctoral dissertation, University of Oregon, Eugene.

Koh, W. L., Steers, R. M., & Terborg, J. R. (1995). The effects of transformational leadership on teacher attitudes and student performance in Singapore. *Journal of Organizational Behavior, 16,* 319–333.

Komives, S. R. (1991). The relationship of hall directors' transformational and transactional leadership to select resident assistant outcomes. *Journal of College Student Development, 32,* 509–515.

Korten, D. C. (1962). Situational determinants of leadership structure. *Journal of Conflict Resolution, 6,* 222–235.

Kotter, J. P. (1982). *The general manager.* New York: Free Press.

Kotter, J. P., & Heskett, J. L. (1992). *Corporate culture and performance.* New York: Free Press.

Kouzes, J. M., & Posner, B. Z. (1987). *The leadership challenge: How to get extraordinary things done in organizations.* San Francisco: Jossey-Bass.

Kouzes, J. M., & Posner, B. Z. (1988). *The Leadership Practices Inventory.* San Diego, CA: Pfeiffer.

Kouzes, J. M., & Posner, B. Z. (2003). *The leadership challenge workbook.* San Francisco: Jossey-Bass.

Kozlowski, S. W. J. (1998). Training and developing adaptive teams: Theory, principles, and research. In J. A. Cannon-Bowers & E. Salas (Eds.), *Making decisions under stress: Implications for individual and team training* (pp. 115–153). Washington, DC: American Psychological Association.

Kozlowski, S. W. J., Gully, S. M., Salas, E., & Cannon-Bowers, J. A. (1996). Team leadership and development: Theories, principles, and guidelines for training leaders and teams. In M. M. Beyerlein, D. A. Johnson, & S. T. Beyerlein (Eds.), *Advances in interdisciplinary studies of work teams* (pp. 253–291). Greenwich, CT: JAI Press.

Krackhardt, D., & Stern, R. N. (1988). Informal networks and organizational crises: An experimental simulation. *Social Psychology Quarterly, 51,* 123–140.

Krishnan, V. R. (2002). Transformational leadership and value system congruence. *International Journal of Value-Based Management, 15,* 19–33.

Kristof, N. D. (1996, September). North Koreans slip into south in submarines. *The New York Times,* pp. A1, A11.

Kruse, L., & Wintermantel, M. (1986). Leadership ms-qualified: The gender bias in everyday and scientific thinking. In C. F. Graumann & S. Moscovic (Eds.), *Changing conceptions of leadership* (pp. 171–197). New York: Springer-Verlag.

Kugihara, N., & Misumi, J. (1984). An experimental study of the effect of leadership types on followers' escaping behavior in a fearful emergency maze-situation. *Japanese Journal of Psychology, 55,* 214–220.

Kuhnert, K. W., & Lewis, P. (1987). Transactional and transformational leadership: A constructive/developmental analysis. *Academy of Management Review, 12,* 648–657.

Lafferty, C. L. (1998). Transformational leadership and the hospice R. N. case manager: A new critical pathway. *Hospice Journal, 13,* 35–48.

Langewiesche, W. (2002). *American ground: Unbuilding the world trade center.* New York: North Point Press.

Lanzetta, J. T. (1953). *An investigation of group behavior under stress. Office of Naval Task Order V.* Rochester, NY: University of Rochester.

Lashinsky, A. (2002). CEOs under fire: Now for the hard part. *Fortune, 148* (November, 18).

Latane, B., Williams, K., & Harkins, S. (1979). Many hands make light the work: The causes and consequences of social loafing. *Journal of Personality and Social Psychology, 37,* 822–832.

Law, K. S., Wong, C., & Song, L. J. (2004). The construct and criterion validity of emotional intelligence and its potential utility for management studies. *Journal of Applied Psychology, 89,* 483–496.

LeBrasseur, R., Whissell, R., & Ojha, A. (2002). Organisational learning, transformational leadership and implementation of continuous quality improvement in Canadian hospitals. *Australian Journal of Management, 27,* 141–162.

Lee, S. M., Yoo, S. J., & Lee, T. M. (1991). Korean chaebols: Corporate values and strategies. *Organizational Dynamics, 19,* 36–50.

Leung, S. L., & Bozionelos, N. (2004). Five-factor model traits and the prototypical image of the effective leader in the Confucian culture. *Employee Relations, 26,* 62–71.

Levinson, H. (1980). Power, leadership, and the management of stress. *Professional Psychology, 11,* 497–508.

Levy, P. E., Cober, R. T., & Miller, T. (2002). The effect of transformational and transactional leadership perceptions on feedback-seeking intentions. *Journal of Applied Social Psychology, 32,* 1703–1720.

Lipman-Blumen, J. (1996). *The connective edge: Leading in an interdependent world.* San Francisco: Jossey-Bass.

Loden, M., & Rosener, J. B. (1991). *Workforce America: Managing employee diversity as a vital resource.* Homewood, IL: Irwin.

Longshore, J. M. (1988). *The associative relationship between transformational and transactional leadership styles and group productivity.* Unpublished doctoral dissertation, Nova University, Boca Raton, FL.

Lord, R. G., Foti, R. J., & DeVader, C. L. (1984). A test of leadership categorization theory: Internal structure, information processing, and leadership perceptions. *Organizational Behavior and Human Performance, 34,* 343–378.

Lord, R. G., & Maher, K. J. (1993). *Leadership and information processing: Linking perceptions and performance.* New York: Routledge.

Lowe, K. B., Kroeck, K. G., & Sivasubramaniam, N. (1996). Effectiveness correlates of transformational and transactional leadership: A meta-analytic review of the MLQ literature. *The Leadership Quarterly, 7*(3), 385–425.

MacKenzie, S. B., Podsakoff, P. M., & Rich, G. A. (2001). Transformational and transactional leadership and salesperson performance. *Journal of the Academy of Marketing Science, 29,* 115–134.

Malone, D. M. (1985). Implementation of the leadership goal: A summary. *Army Organizational Effectiveness Journal, 9,* 9–15.

Mann, R. D. (1959). A review of the relationships between personality and performance in small groups. *Psychological Bulletin, 56,* 241–270.

Manz, C. C., & Sims, H. P. (1995). *Business without bosses: How self-managing teams are building high performing companies.* New York: Wiley.

Manz, C. C., & Sims, H. P. (2001). *The new Superleadership: Leading others to lead themselves.* San Francisco: Berrett-Koehler.

March, J. G., & Olsen, J. P. (Eds.). (1976). *Ambiguity and choice in organizations.* Bergen, Norway: Universitetsforlaget.

Marks, M. L., & Mirvis, P. H. (1998). *Joining forces: Making one plus one equal three in mergers, acquisitions, and alliances.* San Francisco: Jossey-Bass.

Markus, H. R., & Kitayama, S. (1991). Culture and the self: Implications for cognition, emotion, and motivation. *Psychological Review, 98,* 224–253.

Martin, R., & Epitropaki, O. (2001). Role of organizational identification on implicit leadership theories (ILTs), transformational leadership and work attitudes. *Group Processes and Intergroup Relations, 4,* 247–262.

Masi, R. J. (1994). *Transformational leadership and its roles in empowerment, productivity, and commitment to quality.* Unpublished doctoral dissertation, University of Illinois, Chicago.

Masi, R. J., & Cooke, R. A. (2000). Effects of transformational leadership on subordinate motivation, empowering norms, and organizational productivity. *International Journal of Organizational Analysis, 8,* 16–47.

Maslow, A. H. (1954). *Motivation and personality.* New York: Harper.

May, D. R., Chan, A. Y. L., Hodges, T. D., & Avolio, B. J. (2003). Developing the moral component of authentic leadership. *Organizational Dynamics, 32,* 247–260.

Mayer, J. D., & Salovey, P. (1997). What is emotional intelligence? In P. Salovey & D. Sluyter (Eds.), *Emotional development and emotional intelligence: Education implications* (pp. 3–34). New York: Basic Books.

McCauley, C. D. (1987). Stress and the eye of the beholder. *Issues and Observations, 7,* 1–16.

McClelland, D. C. (1975). *Power: The inner experience.* New York: Irvington.

McColl-Kennedy, J. R., & Anderson, R. D. (2002). Impact of leadership style and emotions on subordinate performance. *The Leadership Quarterly, 13,* 545–559.

McNatt, D. B. (2000). Ancient Pygmalion joins contemporary management: A meta-analysis of the result. *Journal of Applied Psychology, 85,* 314–322.

Megerian, L. E., & Sosik, J. J. (1996). An affair of the heart: Emotional intelligence and transformational leadership. *Journal of Leadership Studies, 3,* 31–48.

Menon, S. T. (2001). Employee empowerment: An integrative psychological approach. *Applied Psychology, 50,* 153–180.

Messick, D. M., & Bazerman, M. H. (2001). Ethical leadership and the psychology of decision making. In J. Dienhart, D. Moberg, & R. Duska (Eds.), *The next phase of business ethics: Integrating psychology and ethics: Research in ethical issues in organizations.* (Vol. 3, pp. 213–238). Greenwich, CT: Elsevier Science/JAI Press.

Mileti, D. S., Drabek, T. E., & Haas, J. E. (1975). *Human systems in extreme environments: A sociological perspective.* Boulder, CO: Institute of Behavioral Science.

Mills, J. (1979). *Six years with god: Life inside Rev. Jim Jones's Peoples Temple.* New York: A & W Publishers.

Misumi, J. (1985). *The behavioral science of leadership. An interdisciplinary Japanese research program.* Ann Arbor: University of Michigan Press.

Misumi, J., & Sako, H. (1982). An experimental study of the effect of leadership behaviors on followers' behavior of following after the leader in a simulated emergency situation. *Japanese Journal of Experimental Social Psychology, 21,* 49–59.

Mitroff, I. A., Shrivastava, P., & Udwadia, F. E. (1987). Effective crisis management. *Academy of Management Executive, 1,* 283–92.

Monroe, M. J. (1997). *Leadership of organizational change: Antecedents and implications.* Unpublished doctoral dissertation, Texas A & M University.

Morrison, A. M., White, R. P., Van Velsor, E., & The Center of Creative Leadership. (1987). *Breaking the glass ceiling: Can women make it to the top in America's largest corporations?* Reading, MA: Addison-Wesley.

Moss, A. T. (1992). *Some how's and why's of leadership: An exploratory study of situational variance and power motive patterns in transformational and transactional leadership practices.* Master's thesis, Auckland University, Auckland, New Zealand.

Mulder, M., deJong, R. D., Koppelaar, L., & Verhage, J. (1986). Power, situation, and leader's effectiveness: An organizational field study. *Journal of Applied Psychology, 71,* 566–570.

Mulder, M., van Eck, J. R., & deJong, R. D. (1971). An organization in crisis and noncrisis situations. *Human Relations, 24,* 19–41.

Mumford, M. D., Connelly, S., & Gaddis, B. (2003). How creative leaders think: Experimental findings and cases. *The Leadership Quarterly, 14,* 411–432.

Mumford, M. D., Scott, G. M., Gaddis, B., & Strange, J. M. (2002). Leading creative people: Orchestrating expertise and relationships. *The Leadership Quarterly, 13,* 705–750.

Mumford, M. D., & Strange, J. M. (2002). Vision and mental models: The case of charismatic and ideological leadership. In B. J. Avolio & F. J. Yammarino (Eds.), *Transfor-*

national and charismatic leadership: The road ahead (pp. 109–142). Oxford, UK: JAI/ Elsevier.

Murphy, S. E. (1992). *The contribution of leader experience and self-efficacy to group performance under evaluation apprehension.* Unpublished doctoral dissertation, University of Washington.

Murphy, S. E. (2002). Leader self-regulation: The role of self-efficacy and multiple intelligences. In R. E. Riggio, S. E. Murphy, & F. J. Pirozzolo (Eds.), *Multiple intelligences and leadership* (pp. 163–186). Mahwah, NJ: Lawrence Erlbaum Associates.

Murphy, S. E., Chemers, M. M., Kohles, J. C., & Macaulay, J. L. (2005). *The contribution of leadership self-efficacy to performance under stress: An extension of cognitive resources theory.* Working Paper. Kravis Leadership Institute, Claremont McKenna College.

Myers, I. B., & McCauley, M. H. (1985). *Manual: A guide to the development and use of the Myers-Briggs type indicator.* Palo Alto, CA: Consulting Psychologists Press.

Myers, M. S. (1968). Every employee a manager. *California Management Review, 10,* 9–20.

Nelson, J. E. (1978). Child care crises and the role of the supervisor. *Child Care Quarterly, 7,* 318–326.

Neumann, A. (1992). Colleges under pressure: Budgeting, presidential competence, and faculty uncertainty. *The Leadership Quarterly, 3,* 191–215.

Nicholls, J. (1987). Leadership in organizations: Meta, macro, and micro. *European Management Journal, 6,* 16–25.

Nicholls, J. (1990). Rescuing leadership from Humpty Dumpty. *Journal of General Management, 16,* 76–90.

Niehoff, B. P., Enz, C. A., & Grover, R. A. (1990). The impact of top management actions on employee attitudes and perceptions. *Group and Organization Studies, 15,* 337–352.

Numerof, R. E., Cramer, K. D., & Shachar-Hendin, S. A. (1984). Stress in health administrators: Sources, symptoms, and coping strategies. *Nursing Economics, 2,* 270–279.

Numerof, R. E., & Gillespie, D. F. (1984, August). *Predicting burnout among health service providers.* Paper presented at the Academy of Management, Boston.

Nystrom, P. C., & Starbuck, W. H. (1984). To avoid organizational crises, unlearn. *Organizational Dynamics, 12,* 53–65.

O'Connor, J., Mumford, M. D., Clifton, T. C., Gessner, T. L., & Connelly, M. S. (1995). Charismatic leadership and destructiveness: A historiometric study. *The Leadership Quarterly, 6,* 529–555.

Offerman, L. R, & Gowing, M. K. (1990). Organizations of the future: Changes and challenges. *American Psychologist, 45,* 95–108.

Offerman, L. R., & Phan, L. U. (2002). Culturally intelligent leadership for a diverse world. In R. E. Riggio, S. E. Murphy, & F. J. Pirozzolo (Eds.), *Multiple intelligences and leadership* (pp. 187–214). Mahwah, NJ: Lawrence Erlbaum Associates.

O'Keeffe, M. J. (1989). *The effects of leadership style on the perceived effectiveness and satisfaction of selected Army officers.* Unpublished doctoral dissertation, Temple University, Philadelphia.

Onnen, M. K. (1987). *The relationship of clergy and leadership characteristics to growing or declining churches.* Unpublished doctoral dissertation, University of Louisville, Louisville, KY.

Organ, D. W. (1988). *Organizational citizenship behavior: The good soldier syndrome.* Lexington, MA: Lexington.

Osborn, R. N., & Vicars, W. M. (1976). Sex stereotypes: An artifact in leader behavior and subordinate satisfaction analysis? *Academy of Management Journal, 19,* 439–449.

Owens, W. A., & Schoenfeldt, L. (1979). Towards a classification of persons. *Journal of Applied Psychology, 63,* 569–607.

Palmer, B., Walls, M., Burgess, Z., & Stough, C. (2001). Emotional intelligence and effective leadership. *Leadership and Organization Development Journal, 22,* 5–10.

Parry, K. W. (1999). Enhancing adaptability: Leadership strategies to accommodate change in local government settings. *Journal of Organizational Change Management, 12,* 134–156.

Parry, K. W. (2002). Four phenomenologically determined social processes of organizational leadership: Further support for the construct of transformational leadership. In B. J. Avolio & F. J. Yammarino (Eds.), *Transformational and charismatic leadership: The road ahead* (pp. 339–372). Oxford, UK: JAI/Elsevier.

Parry, K. W., & Proctor-Thomson, S. B. (2002). Perceived integrity of transformational leaders in organisational settings. *Journal of Business Ethics, 35,* 75–96.

Patterson, C., Fuller, J. B., Kester, K., & Stringer, D. Y. (1995). *A meta-analytic examination of leadership style and selected compliance outcomes.* Paper presented at the Society for Industrial and Organizational Psychology, Orlando, FL.

Paul, J., Costley, D. L., Howell, J. P., Dorfman, P. W., & Trafimow, D. (2001). The effects of charismatic leadership on followers' self-concept accessibility. *Journal of Applied Social Psychology, 31,* 1821–1844.

Pawar, B. S., & Eastman, K. K. (1997). The nature and implications of contextual influences on transformational leadership: A conceptual examination. *Academy of Management Review, 22,* 80–109.

Pearce, C. L., & Conger, J. A. (Eds.). (2003). *Shared leadership: Reframing the hows and whys of leadership.* Thousand Oaks, CA: Sage.

Pearce, C. L., & Sims, H. P. (2002). Vertical versus shared leadership as predictors of the effectiveness of change management teams: An examination of aversive, directive, transactional, transformational, and empowering leader behaviors. *Group Dynamics: Theory, Research, and Practice, 6,* 172–197.

Penley, L. E., & Gould, S. (1988). Etzioni's model of organizational involvement: A perspective for understanding commitment to organizations. *Journal of Organizational Behavior, 9,* 43–59.

Pile, S. (1988). *Visionary leadership: Creating a generative internal map.* Unpublished master's thesis, Pepperdine University, Los Angeles.

Pillai, R., Schriesheim, C. A., & Williams, E. S. (1999). Fairness perceptions and trust as mediators for transformational and transactional leadership: A two-sample study. *Journal of Management, 25,* 897–933.

Pines, M. (1980). Psychological hardiness. *Psychology Today, 14,* 38–39.

Pirola-Merlo, A., Hartel, C., Mann, L., & Hirst, G. (2002). How leaders influence the impact of affective events on team climate and performance in R&D teams. *The Leadership Quarterly, 13,* 561–581.

Pitman, B. (1993). *The relationship between charismatic leadership behaviors and organizational commitment among white-collar workers.* Unpublished doctoral dissertation, Georgia State University, Atlanta.

Ployhart, R. E., Lim, B. C., & Chan, K. Y. (2001). Exploring relations between typical and maximum performance ratings and the five factor model of personality. *Personnel Psychology, 54,* 809–843.

Podsakoff, P. M., MacKenzie, S. B., & Bommer, W. H. (1996). Transformational leader behaviors and substitutes for leadership as determinants of employee satisfaction, commitment, trust, and organizational citizenship behaviors. *Journal of Management, 22,* 259–298.

Podsakoff, P. M., MacKenzie, S. B., & Fetter R. (1993). Substitutes for leadership and the management of professionals. *The Leadership Quarterly, 4,* 1–44.

Podsakoff, P. M., MacKenzie, S. B., Moorman, R. H., & Fetter, R. (1990). Transformational leader behaviors and their effects on followers' trust in leader, satisfaction, and organizational citizenship behaviors. *The Leadership Quarterly, 1,* 107–142.

Podsakoff, P. M., Niehoff, B. P., MacKenzie, S. B., & Williams, M. L. (1993). Do substitutes for leadership really substitute for leadership? An empirical examination of Kerr and Jermier's situational leadership model. *Organizational Behavior and Human Decision Processes, 54*, 1–44.

Podsakoff, P. M., & Schriescheim, C. A. (1985). Leader reward and punishment behavior: A methodological and substantive review. In B. Staw & L. L. Cummings (Eds.), *Research in organizational behavior.* San Francisco: Jossey-Bass.

Popper, M. (2002). Narcissism and attachment patterns of personalized and socialized charismatic leaders. *Journal of Social and Personal Relationships, 19*, 797–809.

Popper, M., Landau, O., & Gluskinos, U. (1992). The Isaeli defense forces: An example of transformational leadership. *Leadership and Organizational Development Journal, 13*(1), 3–8.

Popper, M., & Mayseless, O. (2002). Internal world of transformational leaders. In B. J. Avolio & F. J. Yammarino (Eds.), *Transformational and charismatic leadership: The road ahead* (pp. 203–229). Oxford, UK: Elsevier

Popper, M., & Mayseless, O. (2003). Back to basics: Applying a parenting perspective to transformational leadership. *The Leadership Quarterly, 14*, 41–65.

Popper, M., Mayseless, O., & Castelnovo, O. (2000). Transformational leadership and attachment. *The Leadership Quarterly, 11*, 267–289.

Porter, L. W., & McKibbin, L. E. (1988). *Management education and development: Drift or thrust into the 21st century.* New York: McGraw-Hill.

Porter, N., Geis, F. L., Cooper, E., & Newman, E. (1985). Androgyny and leadership in mixed-sex groups. *Journal of Personality and Social Psychology, 49*, 808–823.

Pounder, J. S. (2003). Employing transformational leadership to enhance the quality of management development instruction. *Journal of Management Development, 22*, 6–13.

Powell, C. L., & Persico, J. E. (1995). *My American journey.* New York: Ballantine.

Pritzker, M. A. (2002). *The relationship among CEO dispositional attributes, transformational leadership behaviors and performance effectiveness.* Unpublished doctoral dissertation, Illinois Institute of Technology, Chicago.

Raelin, J. A. (1993). The Persean ethic: Consistency of belief and action in managerial practice. *Human Relations, 46*, 575–621.

Rafferty, A. E., & Griffin, M. A. (2004). Dimensions of transformational leadership: Conceptual and empirical extensions. *The Leadership Quarterly, 15*, 329–354.

Rai, S., & Sinha, A. K. (2000). Transformational leadership, organizational commitment, and facilitating climate. *Psychological Studies, 45*, 33–42.

Ridgeway, C. L. (2001). Gender, status, and leadership. *Journal of Social Issues, 57*, 637–655.

Riggio, R. E. (1987). *The charisma quotient.* New York: Dodd-Mead.

Riggio, R. E. (1989). *Manual for the Social Skills Inventory.* Palo Alto, CA: Consulting Psychologists Press.

Riggio, R. E. (1992). Social interaction skills and nonverbal behavior. In R. S. Feldman (Ed.), *Applications of nonverbal behavioral theories and research* (pp. 3–30). Hillsdale, NJ: Lawrence Erlbaum Associates.

Riggio, R. E., Bass, B. M., & Orr, S. S. (2004). Transformational leadership in nonprofit organizations. In R. E. Riggio & S. S. Orr (Eds.), *Improving leadership in nonprofit organizations* (pp. 49–62). San Francisco: Jossey-Bass.

Riggio, R. E., & Carney, D. C. (2003). *Manual for the Social Skills Inventory* (2nd ed.). Redwood City, CA: Mind Garden.

Riggio, R. E., Ciulla, J. B., & Sorenson, G. J. (2003). Leadership education at the undergraduate level: A liberal arts approach to leadership development. In S. E. Murphy & R. E. Riggio (Eds.), *The future of leadership development* (pp. 223–236). Mahwah, NJ: Lawrence Erlbaum Associates.

Riggio, R. E., Murphy, S. E., & Pirozzolo, F. J. (2002). *Multiple intelligences and leadership.* Mahwah, NJ: Lawrence Erlbaum Associates.

Roberts, J. E. L. (1980, July). Managing soldiers: A personal philosophy of management. *Military Review, 2,* 44–50.

Rose, M. R. (1998). *An integrative investigation of job stress, situational moderators, and group-level patterns within the leader-member exchange model of leadership.* Unpublished doctoral dissertation, University of South Florida, St. Petersburg.

Rosener, J. B. (1990). Ways women lead. *Harvard Business Review, 68,* 119–225.

Rosener, J. B. (1995). *America's competitive secret: Utilizing women as a management strategy.* New York: Oxford University Press.

Ross, R. B. (1982). Emergency planning paid off. *Security Management, 26,* 62–65.

Ross, S. M. (1990). *Transformational leadership: Measurement of personality attributes and performance effects on work groups.* Unpublished doctoral dissertation, George Washington University, Washington, DC.

Ross, S. M., & Offerman, L. R. (1997). Transformational leaders: Measurement of personality attributes and work group performance. *Personality and Social Psychology Bulletin, 23,* 1078–1086.

Rotter, J. (1966). Generalized expectancies for internal versus external control of reinforcement. *Psychological Monographs, 80,* 1–28.

Rubin, R. S., Munz, D. C., & Bommer, W. H. (2004). *Leading from within: A note on the effects of emotional intelligence and personality on transformational leadership behavior.* Manuscript submitted for publication.

Salovey, P., & Mayer, J. D. (1990). Emotional intelligence. *Imagination, Cognition, and Personality, 9,* 185–211.

Salter, D. J. (1989). *Leadership styles in United States Marine Corps transport helicopter squadrons.* Master's thesis, Naval Postgraduate School, Monterey, CA.

Sanders, G. S., & Malkis, F. S. (1982). Type A behavior, need for control, and reactions to group participation. *Organizational Behavior and Human Performance, 30,* 71–86.

Sarkesian, S. C. (1981). Moral and ethical foundations of military professionalism. In J. Brown & M. Collins (Eds.), *Military ethics and professionalism: A collection of essays* (pp. 1–22). Washington, DC: National Defense University Press.

Sashkin, M. (1996). *The visionary leader: Leadership Behavior Questionnaire trainer's guide.* Amherst, MA: HRD Press.

Schein, E. H. (1992). *Organizational culture and leadership* (2nd ed.). San Francisco: Jossey-Bass.

Schiffer, I. (1973). *Charisma: A psychoanalytical look at mass society.* Toronto, Canada: University of Toronto Press.

Schriesheim, C. A. (1978). *Development, validation, and application of new leader behavior and expectancy research instruments.* Unpublished doctoral dissertation, Ohio State University, Columbus.

Schwarzwald, J., Koslowsky, M., & Agassi, V. (2001). Captain's leadership type and police officers' compliance to power bases. *European Journal of Work and Organizational Psychology, 10,* 273–290.

Schweiger, D. M., Ivancevich, J. M., & Power, F. R. (1987). Executive actions for managing human resources before and after acquisition. *Academy of Management Executive, 1,* 127–138.

Seltzer, J., & Bass, B. M. (1990). Transformational leadership: Beyond initiation and consideration. *Journal of Management, 16,* 693–703.

Seltzer, J., & Miller, L. E. (1990). *Leader behavior and subordinate empowerment in a human service organization.* Paper presented at the Academy of Management, San Francisco.

Seltzer, J., Numerof, R. E., & Bass, B. M. (1989). Transformational leadership: Is it a source of more or less burnout or stress? *Journal of Health and Human Resources Administration, 12,* 174–185.

Sergiovanni, T. J. (1990a). Adding value to leadership gets extraordinary results. *Educational Leadership, 47,* 23–27.

Sergiovanni, T. J. (1990b). *Value-added leadership: How to get extraordinary performance in schools.* San Diego, CA: Harcourt Brace Jovanovich.

Shamir, B. (1995). Social distance and charisma: Theoretical notes and an exploratory study. *The Leadership Quarterly, 6,* 19–47.

Shamir, B., House, R. J., & Arthur, M. B. (1993). The motivational effects of charismatic leadership: A self-concept based theory. *Organization Science, 4,* 577–594.

Shapira, Z. (1976). A facet analysis of leadership styles. *Journal of Applied Psychology, 61,* 136–139.

Shaw, M. E. (1981). *Group dynamics: The psychology of small group behavior* (3rd ed.). New York: McGraw Hill.

Shin, S. J., & Zhou, J. (2003). Transformational leadership, conservation, and creativity: Evidence from Korea. *Academy of Management Journal, 46,* 703–714.

Shostrom, E. L. (1974). *POI Manual: An inventory for the measurement of self actualization.* San Diego, CA: Educational and Industrial Testing.

Shrivastava, P., & Nachman, S. A. (1989). Strategic leadership patterns. *Strategic Management Journal, 10,* 51–66.

Simons, T. L. (1999). Behavioral integrity as a critical ingredient for transformational leadership. *Journal of Organizational Change Management, 12,* 89–104.

Simonton, D. K. (1988). Presidential style: Personality, biography, and performance. *Journal of Personality and Social Psychology, 55,* 928–936.

Sims, H. P., Jr., & Lorenzi, P. (1992). *The new leadership paradigm: Social learning and cognition in organizations.* Newbury Park, CA: Sage.

Singer, M. S. (1985). Transformational vs. transactional leadership: A study of New Zealand company managers. *Psychological Reports, 57,* 143–146.

Sivanathan, N., & Fekken, G. C. (2002). Emotional intelligence, moral reasoning and transformational leadership. *Leadership and Organization Development Journal, 23,* 198–204.

Sivasubramaniam, N., Murry, W. D., Avolio, B. J., & Jung, D. I. (2002). A longitudinal model of the effects of team leadership and group potency on group performance. *Group and Organization Management, 27,* 66–96.

Smith, P. B., Misumi, J., Tayeb, M., Peterson, M. F., & Bond, M. (1989). On the generality of leadership style measure across cultures. *Journal of Occupational Psychology, 62,* 97–109.

Snyder, L., & Foster, L. G. (1983). An anniversary review and critique: The Tylenol crisis/reply. *Public Relations Review, 9,* 24–34.

Sorely, L. (1979, October). Professional evaluation and combat readiness. *Military Review, 42.*

Sosik, J. J. (1997). Effects of transformational leadership and anonymity on idea generation in computer-mediated groups. *Change and Organization Management, 22,* 460–487.

Sosik, J. J., Avolio, B. J., & Kahai, S. S. (1997). Effects of leadership style and anonymity and group potency and effectiveness in a group decision support system environment. *Journal of Applied Psychology, 82,* 89–103.

Sosik, J. J., Avolio, B. J., Kahai, S. S, & Jung, D. I. (1998). Computer-supported work group potency and effectiveness: The role of transformational leadership, anonymity, and task interdependence. *Computers in Human Behavior, 14,* 491–511.

Sosik, J. J., & Dworakivsky, A. C. (1998). Self-concept based aspects of the charismatic leader: More than meets the eye. *The Leadership Quarterly, 9,* 503–526.

Sosik, J. J., & Godshalk, V. M. (2000). Leadership styles, mentoring functions received, and job-related stress: A conceptual model and preliminary study. *Journal of Organizational Behavior, 21*, 365–390.

Sosik, J. J., Godshalk, V. M., & Yammarino, F. J. (2004). Transformational leadership, learning goal orientation, and expectations for career success in mentor-protégé relationships: A multiple levels of analysis perspective. *The Leadership Quarterly, 15*, 241–261.

Sosik, J. J., Kahai, S. S., & Avolio, B. J. (1998). Transformational leadership and dimensions of creativity: Motivating idea generation in computer-mediated groups. *Creativity Research Journal, 11*, 111–122.

Sosik, J. J., Kahai, S. S., & Avolio, B. J. (1999). Leadership style, anonymity, and creativity in group decision support systems: The mediating role of optimal flow. *Journal of Creative Behavior, 33*, 227–257.

Sosik, J. J., & Megerian, L. E. (1999). Understanding leader emotional intelligence and performance: The role of self-other agreement on transformational leadership perceptions. *Group and Organization Management, 24*, 367–390.

Southwick, R. B. (1998). *Antecedents of transformational, transactional, and laissez-faire leadership.* Unpublished doctoral dissertation, University of Georgia, Athens.

Sparks, J. R., & Schenck, J. A. (2001). Explaining the effects of transformational leadership: An investigation of the effects of higher-order motives in multilevel marketing organizations. *Journal of Organizational Behavior, 22*, 849–869.

Spreitzer, G. M. (1996). Social structural characteristics of psychological empowerment. *Academy of Management Journal, 39*, 483–504.

Spreitzer, G. M., McCall, M. W., & Mahoney, J. D. (1997). Early identification of international executive potential. *Journal of Applied Psychology, 82*, 6–29.

Stajkovic, A. D., & Luthans, F. (1998). Self-efficacy and work-related performance: A meta-analysis. *Psychological Bulletin, 124*, 240–261.

Steers, R. M., Shin, Y. R., Ungson, G. R., & Nam, S. (1990). Korean corporate culture: A comparative analysis. In B. B. Shaw & J. E. Beck (Eds.), *Research in personnel and human resource management* (pp. 247–262). Greenwich, CT: JAI.

Steiner, M., & Neuman, M. (1978). Traumatic neurosis and social support in the Yom Kippur War returnees. *Military Medicine, 143*, 866–868.

Sternberg, R. J. (2002). Successful intelligence: A new approach to leadership. In R. E. Riggio, S. E. Murphy, & F. J. Pirozzolo (Eds.), *Multiple intelligences and leadership* (pp. 9–28). Mahwah, NJ: Lawrence Erlbaum Associates.

Sternberg, R. J., Forsythe, G. B., Hedlund, J., Horvath, J., Snook, S., Williams, W. M., Wagner, R. K., & Grigorenko, E. L. (2000). *Practical intelligence in everyday life.* New York: Cambridge University Press.

Sternberg, R. J., & Wagner, R. K. (Eds.). (1986). *Practical intelligence: Nature and origins of competence in the everyday world.* New York: Cambridge University Press.

Stogdill, R. M. (1948). Personal factors associated with leadership: A survey of the literature. *Journal of Psychology, 25*, 35–71.

Stouffer, S. A., Suchman, E. A., DeVinney, L. C., Star, S. A., & Williams, R. M., Jr. (1949). *The American soldier: Adjustment during Army life (Studies in Social Psychology in World War II, Vol. 2).* Oxford, UK: Princeton University Press.

Tannenbaum, S. I., Mathieu, J. E., Salas, E., & Cannon-Bowers, J. A. (1991). Meeting trainees' expectations: The influence of training fulfillment on the development of commitment, self-efficacy, and motivation. *Journal of Applied Psychology, 76*, 759–769.

Tejeda, M. J., & Scandura, T. A. (1994). *Leader-member exhange: Exchange or charisma?* Paper presented at the Southern Management Association, New Orleans, LA.

Tejeda, M. J., Scandura, T. A., & Pillai, R. (2001). The MLQ revisited: Psychometric properties and recommendations. *The Leadership Quarterly, 12*, 31–52.

Terry, R. W. (1993). *Authentic leadership: Courage in action.* San Francisco: Jossey-Bass.

Thiagarajan, K. M. (2004). Missionary leadership: Harnessing the power of the mission. In R. E. Riggio & S. S. Orr (Eds.), *Improving leadership in nonprofit organizations* (pp. 39–48). San Francisco: Jossey-Bass.

Thomas, K. W. (1976). Conflict and conflict management. In M. D. Dunnette (Ed.), *Handbook of industrial and organizational psychology* (pp. 889–936). Chicago: Rand McNally.

Thorndike, E. L. (1920). Intelligence and its uses. *Harper's Magazine, 140,* 227–235.

Tichy, N., & Devanna, M. A. (1986). *The transformational leadership.* New York: Wiley.

Tjosvold, D. (1984). Effects of crises orientation on managers' approach to controversy in decision making. *Academy of Management Journal, 27,* 130–138.

Torrance, E. P. (1957). Group decision making and disagreement. *Social Forces, 35,* 314–318.

Tracey, J. B., & Hinkin, T. R. (1998). Transformational leadership or effective managerial practices? *Group and Organization Management, 23,* 220–236.

Trevino, L. K., Brown, M., & Hartman, L. P. (2003). A qualitative investigation of perceived executive ethical leadership: Perceptions from inside and outside the executive suite. *Human Relations, 56,* 5–37.

Triandis, H. C. (1993). The contingency model in cross-cultural perspective. In M. M. Chemers & R. Ayman (Eds.), *Leadership theory and research perspectives and directions* (pp. 167–188). San Diego, CA: Academic Press.

Tucker, M. L., Bass, B. M., & Daniel, L. G. (1990). Transformational leadership's impact on higher education: Satisfaction, effectiveness, and extra effort. In K. E. Clark & M. R. Clark (Eds.), *Measures of leadership* (pp. 169–176). Greensboro, NC: Center for Creative Leadership.

Turner, N., Barling, J., Epitropaki, O., Butcher, V., & Milner, C. (2002). Transformational leadership and moral reasoning. *Journal of Applied Psychology, 87,* 304–311.

Ulmer, W. F., Jr. (1992). Inside view. *Issues and Observations, 12,* 5.

U.S. Bureau of Labor Statistics. (2003). Labor force statistics from the current population survey. http://data.bls.gov.

Vandenberghe, C., Stordeur, S., & D'hoore, W. (2002). Transactional and transformational leadership in nursing: Structural validity and substantive relationships. *European Journal of Psychological Assessment, 18,* 16–29.

Vecchio, R. P. (1997). Effective followership: Leadership turned upside down. In R. P. Vecchio (Ed.), *Leadership: Understanding the dynamics of power and influence in organizations* (pp. 114–123). Notre Dame, IN: University of Notre Dame Press.

Vecchio, R. P. (2002). Leadership and gender advantage. *The Leadership Quarterly, 13,* 643–671.

Vicino, F., & Bass, B. M. (1978). Lifespace variables and managerial success. *Journal of Applied Psychology, 63,* 81–88.

Vroom, V. H., & Yetton, P. N. (1973). *Leadership and decision making.* Pittsburgh, PA: University of Pittsburgh Press.

Wagner, R. K., & Sternberg, R. J. (1991). *Tacit knowledge inventory for managers.* San Antonio, TX: Psychological Corporation.

Waldman, D. A., Bass, B. M., & Einstein, W. O. (1985). *Effort, performance, and transformational leadership in industrial and military service* (Working Paper 85-80). Binghamton: State University of New York at Binghamton.

Waldman, D. A., Bass, B. M., & Einstein, W. O. (1987). Leadership and outcomes of performance appraisal process. *Journal of Occupational Psychology, 60,* 177–186.

Waldman, D. A., Bass, B. M., & Yammarino, F. J. (1990). Adding to contingent-reward behavior: The augmenting effect of charismatic leadership. *Group and Organizational Studies, 15,* 381–394.

Waldman, D. A., & Javidan, M. (2002). Charismatic leadership at the strategic level.: Taking a new look at upper echelons theory. In B. J. Avolio & F. J. Yammarino (Eds.), *Transformational and charismatic leadership: The road ahead* (pp. 173–199). Oxford, UK: JAI/Elsevier.

Waldman, D. A., Javidan, M., & Varella, P. (2004). Charismatic leadership at the strategic level: A new application of upper echelons theory. *The Leadership Quarterly, 15*, 355–380.

Waldman, D. A., Ramirez, G. G., House, R. J., & Puranam, P. (2001). Does leadership matter? CEO leadership attributes under conditions of perceived environmental uncertainty. *Academy of Management Journal, 44*, 134–143.

Walters, C. L. (1998). *Leadership in maximum/close custody prison settings.* Unpublished doctoral dissertation, Gonzaga University, Spokane, WA.

Walumbwa, F. O., & Lawler, J. J. (2003). Building effective organizations: Transformational leadership, collectivist orientation, work-related attitudes and withdrawal behaviours in three emerging economies. *International Journal of Human Resource Management, 14*, 1083–1101.

Walumbwa, F. O., Wang, P., Lawler, J. J., & Shi, K. (2004). The role of collective efficacy in the relations between transformational leadership and work outcomes. *Journal of Occupational and Organizational Psychology, 77*, 515–530.

Watson, B. M., Jr. (1984). Lawrence, Kansas—Before and after "The Day After." *Public Management, 66*, 13–15.

Watson, C. B., Chemers, M. M., & Preiser, N. (2001). Collective efficacy: A multilevel analysis. *Personality and Social Psychology Bulletin, 27*, 1057–1068.

Weber, M. (1947). *The theory of social and economic organizations* (T. Parsons, Trans.). New York: Free Press. (Original work published in 1924)

Weinberg, S. B. (1978). A predictive model of group panic behavior. *Journal of Applied Communication Research, 6*, 1–9.

Welch, J. F., Jr. (1989). *Background to work-out!* Crotonville, NY: Organization Effectiveness Centre.

Whittington, J. L., Goodwin, V. L., & Murray, B. (2004). Transformational leadership, goal difficulty, and job design: Independent and interactive effects on employee outcomes. *The Leadership Quarterly, 15*, 593–606.

Williams, E. S. (1994). *Tying up loose ends: The role of transformational leadership in OCBs, commitment, trust and fairness perceptions.* Paper presented at the meeting of the Southern Management Association, New Orleans, LA.

Williams, W. M., Horvath, J. A., Bullis, R. C., Forsythe, G. B., & Sternberg, R. J. (1996). *Tacit knowledge for military leadership inventories: Platoon leader, company commander, and battalion commander levels.* Alexandria, VA: U.S. Army Institute for the Behavioral and Social Sciences.

Willner, A. R. (1968). *Charismatic political leadership: A theory* [Research Monograph No. 32]. Princeton, NJ: Center for International Studies, Princeton University.

Willner, A. R. (1984). *The spellbinders: Charismatic political leadership.* New Haven, CT: Yale University Press.

Wilson-Evered, E., Hartel, C. E. J., & Neale, M. (2001). A longitudinal study of work group innovation: The importance of transformational leadership and morale. *Advances in Health Care Manaagement, 2*, 315–340.

Wofford, J. C., Goodwin, V. L., & Whittington, J. L. (1998). A field study of a cognitive approach to understanding transformational and transactional leadership. *The Leadership Quarterly, 9*, 55–84.

Wofford, J. C., Whittington, J. L., & Goodwin, V. L. (2001). Follower motive patterns as situational moderators for transformational leadership effectiveness. *Journal of Managerial Issues, 13*, 196–211.

Wong, C., & Law, K. S. (2002). The effects of leader and follower emotional intelligence on performance and attitude: An exploratory study. *The Leadership Quarterly, 13,* 243–274.

Yammarino, F. J., & Bass, B. M. (1990a). Long-term forecasting of transformational leadership and its effects among naval officers: Some preliminary findings. In K. E. Clark & M. R. Clark (Eds.), *Measures of leadership* (pp. 151–169). Greensboro, NC: Center for Creative Leadership.

Yammarino, F. J., & Bass, B. M. (1990b). The effects of transformational, transactional, and laissez-faire leadership characteristics on subordinate influencing behavior. *Basic and Applied Social Psychology, 11,* 191–203.

Yammarino, F. J., & Bass, B. M. (1991). Person and situation views of leadership: A multiple levels of analysis approach. *The Leadership Quarterly, 2,* 121–139.

Yammarino, F. J., & Dubinsky, A. J. (1994). Transformational leadership theory: Using levels of analysis to determine boundary conditions. *Personnel Psychology, 47,* 787–811.

Yammarino, F. J., Dubinsky, A. J., Comer, L. B., & Jolson, M. A. (1997). Women and transformational and contingent reward leadership: A multiple-levels-of-analysis perspective. *Academy of Management Journal, 40,* 205–222.

Yammarino, F. J., Spangler, W. D., & Bass, B. M. (1993). Transformational leadership and performance: A longitudinal investigation. *The Leadership Quarterly, 4,* 81–102.

Yammarino, F. J., Spangler, W. D., & Dubinsky, A. J. (1998). Transformational and contingent reward leadership: Individual, dyad, and group levels of analysis. *The Leadership Quarterly, 9,* 27–54.

Yarmolinsky, A. (1987). *Leadership in crisis situations.* Paper presented at the First Annual Conference on Leadership, Wingfoot, Racine, WI.

Yokochi, N. (1989). *Leadership styles of Japanese business executives and managers: Transformational and transactional.* Unpublished doctoral dissertation, United States International University, San Diego, CA.

Yukl, G. (1989). Managerial leadership: A review of theory and research. *Journal of Management, 15,* 251–289.

Yukl, G. (1998). *Leadership in organizations.* Upper Saddle River, NJ: Prentice-Hall.

Yukl, G. (1999). An evaluation of conceptual weaknesses in transformational and charismatic leadership theories. *The Leadership Quarterly, 10,* 285–305.

Zaccaro, S. J. (1995). Leader resources and the nature of organizational problems. *Applied Psychology: An International Review, 44,* 32–36.

Zaccaro, S. J. (2002). Organizational leadership and social intelligence. In R. E. Riggio, S. E. Murphy, & F. J. Pirozzolo (Eds.), *Multiple intelligences and leadership* (pp. 29–54). Mahwah, NJ: Lawrence Erlbaum Associates.

Zaccaro, S. J., & Bader, P. (2003). E-leadership and the challenges of leading E-teams: Minimizing the bad and maximizing the good. *Organizational Dynamics, 31,* 377–387.

Zaccaro, S. J., Rittman, A. L., & Marks, M. A. (2001). Team leadership. *The Leadership Quarterly, 12,* 451–483.

Zacharatos, A., Barling, J., & Kelloway, E. K. (2000). Development and effects of transformational leadership in adolescents. *The Leadership Quarterly, 11,* 211–226.

Zohar, D. (2002). The effects of leadership dimensions, safety climate, and assigned priorities on minor injuries in work groups. *Journal of Organizational Behavior, 23,* 75–92.

Author Index

Subject Index